Ineke Phaf-Rheinberger/Tiago de Oliveira Pinto (eds.)
**AfricAmericas:**
**Itineraries, Dialogues, and Sounds**

# BIBLIOTHECA IBERO-AMERICANA

Publicaciones del Instituto Ibero-Americano
Fundación Patrimonio Cultural Prusiano
Vol. 119

BIBLIOTHECA IBERO-AMERICANA

Ineke Phaf-Rheinberger/Tiago de Oliveira Pinto (eds.)

# AfricAmericas:

## Itineraries, Dialogues, and Sounds

Iberoamericana · Vervuert

2008

**Bibliografic information published by Die Deutsche Nationalbibliothek**
Die Deutsche Nationalbibliothek lists this publication in the Deutsche
Nationalbibliografie; detailed bibliografic data are available on the Internet
at http://dnb.ddb.de

© Iberoamericana 2008
Amor de Dios, 1
E-28014 Madrid
info@iberoamericanalibros.com
www.ibero-americana.net

© Vervuert Verlag 2008
Elisabethenstr. 3-9
D-60594 Frankfurt am Main
info@iberoamericanalibros.com
www.ibero-americana.net

ISBN 978-84-8489-380-6
ISBN 978-3-86527-403-8
Depósito legal: B. 13.456-2008

Diseño de la cubierta: Michael Ackermann
Ilustración de la cubierta: Mariano Procopio
© ForLaBB, 2008

Composición: Anneliese Seibt, Instituto Ibero-Americano, Berlín
Este libro está impreso íntegramente en papel ecológico blanqueado sin cloro

Impreso en España por Book Print Digital S.A.

# Contents

Ineke Phaf-Rheinberger/Tiago de Oliveira Pinto

# Introduction: About the Project "AfricAmericas"

This book presents several stages of a work in progress in Berlin that started with the series of lectures, *AfricAmericas*, in the Fall and Winter of 2004-2005. The series was organized with the support of the Humboldt University (Institute of Romance Languages, Seminar for Africa Sciences), the University of Potsdam (Institute of Romance Languages), the Free University (Latin America Institute), the Brazilian Cultural Institute in Germany (ICBRA), and the Ibero-America Institute, Prussian Heritage Foundation. Nine specialists gave their interpretations of the link between Africa and Latin America, which dates back to early modern history.

These lectures, some of them based on important research already published elsewhere, formed only the beginning of a larger project on cultural exchanges between Africa and America. Several seminars were organized at the Humboldt University, in which basic knowledge of this matter was imparted to students. Thereafter, Flora Veit-Wild (Seminar for Africa Sciences) assumed responsibility for organizing a student excursion with us to Brazil, with a summer school on "Studies on Africa in Brazil and Germany" at the Federal University of Pernambuco in Recife, from March 12-16, 2007. Subsequently, we visited religious centers, like *xangô* and *afoxé* in Recife, *quilombo* movements and villages in the interior of the State of Pernambuco, and finally the home region of *samba de roda* and Candomblé in the sugar cane- and tobacco plantation area of Bahia State – the *Recôncavo* – to get in touch with the dynamics of the African presence in present-day Brazil.

The focus on cultural exchanges across the Atlantic Ocean, between Brazil and Africa in particular, requires breaking through academic boundaries that hold the continents apart and ignore the millions who have gone back and forth for centuries on this main route of the slave trade. This mass movement comprised people from different countries all over the world. Historians disagree about the numbers of enslaved Africans, but diligently reproduce the myriad of maps indicating the sea routes taken by the sailing vessels. That these water masses did not necessarily suppress human contacts has received less attention. The *Imperial Eyes* (Pratt 1992: 1-11), the viewpoint of the colonizer, systematically has neglected the cultural impact of this no-madic move and its "contact zones" on both sides of the ocean.

At present, in the course of the current globalization, this situation is changing rapidly. It was not by coincidence that the series of lec-tures on *AfricAmericas* was launched in the House of World Cultures in Berlin in October 2004, almost simultaneously with the program *Black Atlantic* (2004), for which Paul Gilroy was responsible. *Black Atlantic* consisted of exhibitions, panels, concerts, lectures, and theater performances. In the eponymous catalogue, Cheryl Finley (2004: 248-263) describes how the "Slave Ship" entered in the visual imagination as an icon since the founding of the Plymouth Committee in 1789 under the leadership of the Quaker Thomas Clarkson. A poster was designed to make a plea for the abolitionist campaign and became famous for showing the overseas transportation of people, as objects for the commercial market. The "Slave Ship" became a theme for poetry in the nineteenth century, when Castro Alves of Brazil, Heinrich Heine of Germany, Pierre-Jean Béranger of France, and John Greenleaf Whittier of the United States wrote about this maritime journey from a more emotional, subjective point of view (Silva 2006). In the twentieth century, anthropology, linguistics, and history increasingly investigate the mutual bonds between Africa and America. In 1993, the UNESCO Slave Route Project places them within a broader framework, whereas references to the slave trade have become a standard issue in cultural studies in academia. Although this issue is mostly discussed in relationship to English- and French-speaking countries, the role of the Portuguese-speaking world is receiving more attention now. Caryl Phillips, for example, in his subchapter on "El Mina: The Encounter" in *The Atlantic Sound* (2000: 128-133), extensively describes the details of the negotiations between the Portuguese deputy Diego de Azambuja and the African king, Caramansa on Saturday, January 20, 1482, concerning the construc-tion of the fortress El Mina on the coast of what is now the Republic of Ghana.

Brazil was the last American country to officially abolish slavery, in 1888. However, as in many other cases, emancipation was not accompanied by an infrastructural reorganization that assured the possibility of social mobility of the "free" in Brazilian society. African influences and African cultures were at the bottom of the society's self-awareness, and this only recently has begun to change. This is documented by the increasing amount of anthologies and critical research on African literatures published in Brazil. It is also promoted by Federal Law 10,639 from 2003, which prescribes that African influences in Brazil, as well as African history in general, are obligatory in the secondary school curriculum. Pioneers like Rita Chaves, Tania Macêdo, Laura Cavalcante Padilha, Carmen Lúcia Tindó Secco, Maria do Carmo Sepúlveda, Maria Teresa Salgado, and Zuleide Duarte have demonstrated that research on African literatures exists. Some of them collaborated on a recent issue of *Research in African Literatures* (2007), edited by Lúcia Helena Costigan and Russell G. Hamilton, and dedicated to literature from Angola, Mozambique, Cape Verde, São Tomé and Príncipe, and Afro-Brazil.

In quantitative matters, an important development of the past two decades undoubtedly refers to academic programs devoted to African literatures, history, linguistics, and ethnomusicology. This last field of study saw the most booming increase, observed at different universities with their own ethnomusicology programs. At the third conference of the Brazilian Ethnomusicological Association (ABET) in São Paulo, in November 2006, approximately 200 papers were delivered. At least forty percent of them dealt in one way or another with African and Afro-Brazilian musical cultures. Besides a few colleagues from Africa, this research was delivered by scholars and students living, studying, and researching in Brazil.

One of the forerunners of cultural studies on *AfricAmerica* is Alberto da Costa e Silva, a poet and historian, who served as Brazilian ambassador to Nigeria and Benin, as well as to other countries in Europe and Latin America. Silva always concentrates in his research on the links between Brazil and Africa. He published *Um rio chamado Atlântico* (A River Called Atlantic, 2003), a collection of sixteen essays previously published between 1962 and 2002. He analyzes Africa as seen from Brazil and Brazil as seen from Africa. The book also includes reviews of important books on this topic. Silva gave the inaugural address of our summer school in Recife, during which two students of the Humboldt University, **Paul Bräuer** and **Philip Küp-**

**pers**, interviewed him on the status of Afro-Brazilian cultures in Brazil. This interview, entitled "It is necessary to construct a new type of difference", is reproduced at the beginning of this book. With this sentence, Silva expresses the hope of the possibility to understand ethnic differences as a cultural issue that transcends racial boundaries, so intensively discussed today among sociologists and ethnologists in Brazil.

## 1. Itineraries

We will not summarize current academic debates on racial boundaries in social life in Brazil in this volume. Instead, our goal is to elaborate historical standards in research and cultural practices in relationship to Africa and America. For that, it is important to take a closer look at specific regularities in this complex transatlantic horizon. The first section is called "Itineraries" to underline our Berlin-based point of departure. In the opening essay, **Flora Veit-Wild** and her collaborator **Anja Schwarz** report about the private archive of Janheinz Jahn (1918-1973), a German specialist on "black" literature from different continents. Jahn collected, analyzed, translated, and interpreted "black" cultures just as interest in "black" literature was emerging in Europe and the United States in the 1950s and 1960s. His private archive was acquired by the Library of Asian and African Studies at the Humboldt University. Jahn also broadcast radio programs and performed the poems aloud, paying special attention to rhythm and sound; his work with different media was unique. He left his personal correspondence with many authors, which recalls how complicated it was at that time for authors born in European colonies to integrate local perceptions in writing. In those decades, the clash between the "imposed" European language and the local experiences expressed in other African languages was a crucial point in a writer's' career. Not only in Africa, but also in the Caribbean, did the antagonistic concepts of rhythm, movement, and sounds have traumatic results that stimulated creative processes and new genres.

An illustrative example is Frank Martinus Arion, whose poetry, translated into German, is included in Jahn's *Black Orpheus* (1964: 219). Arion was born in Curaçao, an island in the Netherlands Antilles. The native language is Papiamentu, a Creole language that developed in close proximity to the slave route between Africa and America. In his first volume of poetry *Stemmen van Afrika* (Voices of Africa, 1957), Arion conceptualizes the "black" *tambu* musical practice in the Antilles within the context of "white" globalization. The enthusiastic reactions in the Dutch press astonished him. One critic even called him the Black Virgil, a qualification that irritated him so much that he decided not to publish poetry in Dutch anymore. He wrote five novels in Dutch instead. In their plots, the local perception versus the "imperial eye" is a crucial dilemma. Arion himself returned to his home island and started supporting institutions for the development and integration of Papiamentu on every educational level.

In the same way, language politics are of utmost importance in many African and Caribbean countries at present. It concerns the delimitation of different perceptions of history and cultures, and Jahn is a pioneer in paying attention to this issue.

Historian **Silke Strickrodt** discusses another move, which was mentioned in Hugo Zöller's report on his visit to Africa in 1884. Zöller was a secret agent of the German government in Berlin in the same year the Congo Conference took place, from 15 November 1884 to 26 February 1885, during which the European countries "divided" Africa among themselves. In his report, Zöller wondered about the "Portuguese" people he observed on the West African Coast and Silke Strickrodt gives an overview of the rich academic research on these Brazilian returnees in the nineteenth century, in many cases after having been brought to America as slaves. They introduced a "Brazilian" style of living in the English colonies, which today still has an impact on daily life.

Visual artist **Christine Meisner** was struck by this lifestyle when she visited Lagos in 2002 and wondered about the Brazilian-looking architecture in this city. She was so intrigued that she developed the video project *Recovery of an Image* (26 Minutes, 2005), in which she reconstructs the story of one of the returnees in the nineteenth century, João Esan da Rocha. He was brought to Salvador da Bahia as a ten-years old child and returned to Lagos as a free man after thirty-one years of domestic slavery on a sugar plantation near Salvador. Meisner also found information about Rocha's life in Salvador, and was encouraged to realize her project in Lagos by a descendent of another returnee family, Tunde Emanuel Balthasar de Silva. The text published in this volume is the exact transcription of her video *Recovery of an Image*, a fictional account narrated by a Lagos-born actor and illustrated with Meisner's drawings.

## 2. Dialogues

One of the important cultures in Nigeria, the Yoruba, has been influential in many regions of Latin America and the Caribbean and is well documented. Much less well known is the long-term and older connection between the Bantu (Angola, Congo) and Portuguese cultures in Brazil. Therefore, all three contributions in the second section of this book discuss this question in-depth as a continuing performance of "Dialogues".

**Yeda Pessoa de Castro** is a distinguished professor of linguistics at the Federal University of Bahia and has maintained contacts with several German universities. She was one of the first Brazilians to study languages at an African university, earning her PhD at the University of Kinshasa, Lubumbashi campus, in 1974. Besides living in Congo (formerly Zaire), she lived in Nigeria in the 1960s. In her essay, she summarizes her own research on the influences of Bantu languages on Brazilian Portuguese. By pointing out the relevance of these influences, Castro equally makes a plea to set up a project within a broader perspective that comprises Ibero-America as well as the Caribbean.

The Swiss scholar **Martin Lienhard** at Zürich University specializes in colonial Spanish American and Portuguese African chronicles. In his more recent work, he links his historical expertise to the lusophone world in Brazil and Angola. Lienhard edited several volumes on popular cultures on both sides of the ocean and, in the essay included in this book, reconstructs the "dialogue" of the local populations with the colonial expansion in Congo and Angola in Portuguese writings of the seventeenth century. Accordingly, Lienhard succeeds in filling up the so-called "empty spaces", according to which the colonized are not supposed to speak. His analytical readings of some texts of that period enables him to find ways to show that the Africans always conducted an active "dialogue" with the Europeans during colonial expansion.

The next essay "Myths on Early Modernity" follows up on research showing that the Dutch Caribbean was culturally developed as a part of the South Atlantic trade route in the seventeenth century (**Phaf-Rheinberger** 2008). According to historian Luiz Felipe de Alencastro (2000), this development is constitutive of the formation of Brazil in early modern history. Port cities on the Atlantic coast, such as Luanda, Rio de Janeiro, and Recife, have been agencies and their cultural mapping is linked to the concept of *The Lettered City* (1984), coined by the late literary critic from Uruguay, Ángel Rama. For him, it was crucial to connect contemporary expressions of cultural democratization with the patterns inherited from the colonial past, in which the basis was laid for an unequal exchange among the different levels of public life.

The Dutch philosopher Gaspar Barlaeus was one of the *letrados* of this South Atlantic urban network, laying the foundation for understanding its commercial and military goals from the Christian moral viewpoint in Amsterdam. He presented its contours in the volume *Rerum per octennium in Brasilia* (1647) addressing the Dutch occupation of Brazil and Angola. This period is restaged in recent novels from Angola and Brazil that aim to display its long-term consequences and to balance its asymmetric social and cultural impact. From this point of view, the "dialogue" with the past is still a problem for contemporary fictional writers and underlines the overall impression that we are only starting to see its deeper dimensions.

## 3. Sounds

The term *AfricAmericas* is entangled with the Islamic world, as Silke Strickrodt shows in her essay on the returnees. Such a term merely indicates the importance of a focus and does not imply a theoretically closed-concept. Alberto Mussa, for instance, presented as a Brazilian writer of Arab descent in *ArabAmericas* (Ette/Pannewick 2006), also has an African component that he describes in his prose narrative on Rio de Janeiro. His *O trono da rainha Jinga* (The Throne of Queen Jinga, 1999), resolving the riddles associated with the enigmatic meaning of a *canto*, provides a clue to the organization of the plot, and the importance of this in-depth dimension is touched upon in this third section on "Sounds".

Studying cultural diversity through music and sound has become a real challenge in Afro-American cultural studies. To deal with this topic, the concept of "soundscapes" is borrowed from Murray Schafer (1976). In the transatlantic world, specific soundscapes emerge and are to be understood as synonymous to a musical landscape in terms of the rich variety of different musical styles and expressions coexisting in a common area or country, in connection with one another or independently. As much as landscapes are characterized by different components and environments, so are the so-called transatlantic soundscapes manifold and diverse. Therefore, when speaking of Brazilian musical structures and contemporary African musical performance production, the authors are referring to single aspects of a complex and factual panorama.

While social sciences have for long limited African cultural presence in Brazil, contemporary studies on music show a much more diverse and broader panorama (Mukuna 1979; 1999; Pinto 2007). The musical dimension always returns as central in studies on the cultural exchanges between Africa and America. This section on "Sounds", starts with a conversation between **Gerhard Kubik** and **Tiago de Oliveira Pinto** about an ethnomusicologist's difficulty in classifying the samba. This genre represents the essence of structural patterns and social meanings in historical terms that evince concepts of a mutual body and sound language that persisted on both sides of the Southern Atlantic Ocean. Kubik and Pinto call attention to the playful aspect of its creative performances, which recall Johan Huizinga's *Homo ludens* (1938). This Dutch cultural historian argued, however, that this playful-performance pattern responds to a pattern of local rules, which always underlie changes and are never static.

Pinto's collaboration with Gerhard Kubik dates back to 1984, when Pinto was conducting field research on music, culture, and religion in the Recôncavo region of Bahia State in Brazil. This research was published in *Capoeira, Samba, Candomblé* (1991) and then elaborated in many essays, lectures, and recordings. "Crossed Rhythms" was first presented as a paper at the LASA 2006 conference in Puerto Rico and summarizes some main points that surface when trying to formulate the African influences on Brazilian musical performances, and on the samba in particular. Kubik's essay is grounded in his personal involvement in jazz-based musical creativity in southeastern

Africa. It is the report on a period of painful transition, from July 2000 to September 2002, in Chileka, Malawi. One of its most eminent musician-composers, Donald J. Kachamba, was passing his art on to the younger musicians he had trained. The essay provides intimate insights into the many ways African-American music of North America, South America, and the Caribbean has inspired local African talent in the twentieth century, giving rise to startling new developments in the twenty-first. As a performer and observer, Kubik possesses the results of meticulous data gathering, especially in the form of diary notes, musical notations, photographs, and audio and video recordings. Most important for him are the human musical mind, the concepts, the burst of ideas, the hidden meanings of word play, and the personal histories of his partners within the larger musical family.

The different layers addressed in the sections "Itineraries", "Dialogues", and "Sounds" reflect upon the potential to trace crucial points of the numerous "contact zones" back and forth over the Atlantic Ocean throughout history. They provide subjective insights through interviews, conversations, video tales, visual material, and short summarizing introductions, whereby some essays develop a more academic point of view from the perspective of different academic fields.

We would like to express our gratitude to everyone who helped to make this publication possible. In the first place, Ottmar Ette (University Potsdam), who coined the term *AfricAmericas*, and Peter Birle (Ibero-American Institute, PK), always supportive in resolving any practical problem. Flora Veit-Wild "adopted" this project in the Seminar for African Sciences at the Humboldt University, whereas Dieter Ingenschay and Werner Thielemann were sympathetic at the Institute for Romance Studies. Carolyn Vines-van Es carefully revised the English texts. And, last but not least, we are very grateful for the collaboration with Christoph Osterdorf, director of the Cultural Center of Brazil and Germany (CCBA) in Recife, whose diplomacy and permanent interventions made the *AfricAmericas* a project, in which students of the Humboldt University became actively involved and were able to encounter actual research and performing practices in Brazil in March 2007.

The Editors
November 2007

# Bibliography

Alencastro, Luiz Felipe de (2000): *O trato dos viventes. A formação do Brazil no Atlântico Sul. Séculos XVI e XVII*. São Paulo: Companhia das Letras.

Arion, Frank Martinus ([1957] 1978): *Stemmen uit Afrika*. Rotterdam: Flamboyant.

Chaves, Rita/Secco, Carmen/Macêdo, Tania (eds.) (2006): *Brasil/África. Como se o mar fosse mentira*. São Paulo: Editora UNESP.

Costigan, Lúcia Helena Costigan/Hamilton, Russell G. (guest ed.) (2007): *Research in African Literatures* (vol. 38, nr. 1, Spring 2007).

Duarte, Zuleide (ed.) (2003): *África de África*. Recife: Programa de Pós-graduação em Letras/UFPE.

Ette, Ottmar/Pannewick, Friderike (eds.) (2006): *ArabAmericas. Literary Entanglements of the American Hemisphere and the Arab World*. Madrid: Iberoamericana/Frankfurt am Main: Vervuert.

Finley, Cheryl (2004): "Erinnerung verpflichtet. Die Ikone des Sklavenschiffs in der Vorstellungswelt des Black Atlantic". In: Gilroy, Paul/ Kampt, Tina (eds.): *Der Black Atlantic*. Berlin: House of World Cultures, pp. 248-263.

Huizinga, Johan ([1938] 1971): *Homo Ludens. A Study of the Play Element in Culture*. Boston, MA: Beacon Press.

Lienhard, Martin (ed.) (2000): *Discursos sobre (l)a pobreza. América Latina y/e paísesluso-africanos*. Madrid: Iberoamericana/Frankfurt am Main: Vervuert.

— (2006): *La memoria popular y sus transformaciones: América Latina y/e países luso-africanos*. Madrid: Iberoamericana/Frankfurt am Main: Vervuert.

Mukuna, Kazadi wa (1979): *Contribuição Bantu na música popular brasileira*. São Paulo: Global.

— (1999): "Ethnomusicology and the Study of Africanisms in the Music of Latin America". In: Codgell DjeDje, Jacqueline (ed.): *Turn up the Volume. A Celebration of African Music*. Los Angeles: UCLA, pp. 182-185.

Mussa, Alberto (1999): *O trono da rainha Jinga*. Rio de Janeiro: Ed. Nova Fronteira.

— (2006): "Who is Facing the Mirror?". In: Ette, Ottmar/Pannewick, Friederike (eds.): *ArabAmericas. Literary Entanglements of the American Hemisphere and the Arab World*. Madrid: Iberoamericana/Frankfurt am Main: Vervuert, pp. 189-196.

Padilha, Laura Cavalcante (2002). *Novos pactos, outras ficções: ensaios sobre literaturas afro-luso-brasileiras*. Porto Alegre: Coleção Memória das Letras.

Phaf-Rheinberger, Ineke (2008, forthcoming): *The 'Air of Liberty'. Narratives of the South Atlantic Past*. Amsterdam/New York: Rodopi.

Phillips, Caryl (2000): *The Atlantic Sound*. London: Faber & Faber.

Pinto, Tiago de Oliveira (1991): *Capoeira, Samba, Candomblé. Afro-Brasilianische Musik im Recôncavo, Bahia*. Berlin: Museum für Völkerkunde.

— (1994): "Une experience transculturelle. Entretien avec Gerhard Kubik". In: *Cahiers de musiques traditionnelles* no. 7, pp. 211-227.

— (2007): "Music and the Tropics: On Goals and Achievements of Ethnomusicology in Brazil". *Hamburger Jahrbuch für Musikwissenschaft*, vol. 18. Hamburg: Universität Hamburg.

Pratt, Mary Louise (1992): *Imperial Eyes. Travel Writing and Transculturation*. London: Routledge.

Schafer, R. Murray (1976): *The Tuning of the World*. New York: Random House.

Secco, Carmen Lucia Tindó (2003): *A magia das letras africanas. Ensaios escolhidos sobre as literaturas de Angola, Moçambique e alguns outros diálogos*. Rio de Janeiro: ABE Graph Editora/Barroso Produções Editor.

Sepúlveda, Maria do Carmo/Salgado, Maria Teresa (eds.) (2006): *África & Brasil: letras em laços*. Rio de Janeiro/São Caetano do Sul-SP: Yendis Editora.

Silva, Alberto da Costa e (2003): *Um rio chamado Atlântico. A África no Brasil e o Brasil na África*. Rio de Janeiro: Ed. Nova Fronteira/Ed. UFRJ.

— (2006): *Castro Alves*. São Paulo: Companhia das Letras.

**Paul Bräuer/Philip Küppers**

# "It is Necessary to Construct a New Type of Difference": An Interview with Alberto da Costa e Silva[*]

**PP:** Ambassador, what are your thoughts concerning the prohibition and repression of African cultures in colonial Brazil?

**Silva:** You cannot forbid it because Brazilian life was impregnated with African culture: our cooking habits, our daily habits. It was at the center of our homes. What occurred for a long time not only in Brazil, but also in Africa is that the religious Afro-Brazilian practices were forbidden. We are now speaking about the 1930s and 1940s until the legislation was changed, and the Afro-Brazilian practices became considered as a religion just as any other one in daily reality. But I have to make the point that in the period in which these cultures were forbidden and in which they suffered political repression, many prominent politicians in Brazil visited and frequented the houses where these cultures were practiced. That is to say that there was some hypocrisy between the public space and the hidden reality.

**PP:** How should we generally consider the influence of African cultures in Brazil?

**Silva:** Consciousness of the Afro-Brazilian presence is completely natural. People often are even not aware of it. It is part of our daily life and it is always changing because culture is always mobile. It changes with us; a static culture does not exist. A culture is always an exchange between different groups. This exchange is modified throughout time in the sense that, what was valid at the end of the twentieth century is not valid today or only in a relative sense. It is valid to the degree that our analysis considers the passage of time, the new influences that are produced, and the new dialogues that were established, because culture is always in movement, culture is a process. It is never

---

[*] Transcription Tiago de Oliveira Pinto.

finished. The same counts for culinary recipes: it is impossible to prepare the same dish today as that in the nineteenth century. The ingredients have changed and not only that, but the quality, the nature of the ingredients has changed. Therefore, everything is a process. People have the tendency to consider cultural facts as something that is crystallized, so-to-speak, and congealed in time. This is not true because culture undergoes permanent mutations.

**PP:** How do these concepts of being black or white function?

**Silva:** Let's not generalize; it is neither one nor the other. In the first place, this distinction between black and white does not exist as such. In Brazil you have gradations ranging from blond with blue eyes to African black. But the majority of the Brazilian population is considered white; if they've been in Brazil for more than three generations, they also generally have black origins. The same happens with the so-called blacks. In general the majority of them have some white influence. Therefore, you have a process that is quite complicated. Here and there people deny, of course, that they have this heredity, but Brazil is not an African or European country, nor an Amerindian country. Brazil is all this and something else. And this consciousness of being something else is gaining terrain in the country; but that has not always been the case. There was a time in which we thought that being black was a problem we had to resolve. And how would we be able to 'resolve' the black problem? Maybe through miscegenation, through mixing, through whiting up, through exclusion? How should we resolve the black problem? Thus, there was a moment in which it was stated that nobody was black in Brazil, that we were all Brazilians, and that we all had the same color. This is a historical and sociological fact. Well, there will be people who deny the black inheritance or others who deny the white inheritance. But this denial is useless because this being together does not happen intentionally. We behave at home, on the streets, and in our social contacts in, let's say, a mestizo way, in a way that accepts the behaviors of other people because it is impossible to live separated from each other. Of some specific cultural products it is impossible to say that this is white and this is black, this is African and this is Portuguese, this is German and this is Italian or Japanese. These distinctions are extremely difficult to make because everything is summed up and everything mingles. And it is very difficult to separate one thing from another. And besides, it is just as difficult as separating the life of all people, of all nations, of all human groups. All human groups are formed through contact with other groups of humans. Sometimes it seems that we are only one, unique reality but when we start verifying the history of these people, we witness a composition of numerous different inheritances. For example, look at Portugal. Since the twelfth century Portugal was already conceived as it is today, with the frontiers of today. That notwithstanding, when we look at its history we discover that many different and distinct people have formed Portugal, sometimes in conflictive situations. These situations have nevertheless produced the harmonization of a people that seems homogeneous, although its origin is heterogeneous.

**PP:** Are Afro-Brazilians discriminated against economically and socially in Brazil?

**Silva:** This point concerns class relations and the distribution of wealth in relationship with different social groups or, let's put it this way, "racial" groups. The situation of a person who looks black – because, certainly, what is important in Brazil is appearance – is not due to heredity. When you have a black grandfather but look white, then you are white; when you have three white grandfathers and a black one, but you look black, then you are black. Well, higher social levels are basically composed by white people, and to the degree that you descend the social ladder people become darker, right? This is something that everybody sees; you only have to walk down the street. And why is this the case? Because of slavery! The transition of the Afro-Brazilian toward the status of a free man has always been difficult. That is to say, the former slave starts his life as a free man with tremendous difficulties. The abolition of slavery in Brazil coincided with the arrival of huge groups of European immigrants. We should not forget that Brazil received within the time span of a hundred years six million immigrants from Portugal, Spain, Italy, Germany, Russia, Ukraine, Switzerland, and Greece, in addition to the Arabs, who also came in great numbers from the Middle East. And what happened? At the same moment the slave left his work on the land, and the urban slave, who was the foremost producer of furniture, utensils, clothes, the artisans, and woodcarvers began to suffer the competition of the immigrant. Immigrants bring new fashions, thus the slave who was a carpenter or cabinetmaker, now a free man with his own carpentry business accustomed to making furniture in the old Portuguese style, suddenly is confronted with a wealthy population that does not want furniture in the old Portuguese style; it wants the English style, it wants the French style. And who will make this furniture for them? The European immigrant, who thus displaces the free, the Afro-Brazilian, the mulatto, from the traditional crafts he had worked as a slave or a free man during the colonial period. It must not be forgotten that upon abolition, the majority of Brazil's black population was already free. She was already free, already had her crafts; now she is displaced from these crafts and marginalized.

**PP:** And what happens with the fusion of religious or cultural elements?

**Silva:** No, we don't make this difference, no! It is important not to confound – sometimes people confound things – a cultural aspect, which is the religion, with other cultural aspects. Evidently, you have an Afro-Brazilian religion or various Afro-Brazilian religions (there is more than one), which compete with the other religions that come from all over the world. Well, when you reflect on it, you have a very interesting phenomenon here. The religion of the *orixas*, for example, the religion of the Nagot, of the Yoruba; the religion of the cult of the *orixas*, this religion was that of a small parcel of the African population, of a determined geographic space in Africa, which is the Southwest of Nigeria and the Southwest of the Republic of Benin. Some eighteen million people are living there. They practiced a religion of this region, in which it was a national religion. In the same way as Judaism was the religion of a people, and Islam was that of an Arab group. This Yoruba religion continues being practiced in Africa; it is a religion that does not expand in Africa. It then comes to Brazil; it comes to Cuba; and it comes to Venezuela. And what happens there? It is transformed into a universal religion. So we have this phenomenon of a local religion transformed into a universal religion, which we've been witnessing permanently in Brazil in the last hundred years. And the last fifty or sixty years it became even more visible. That is to say, we are witnessing a process similar to the expansion of Christianity, to the expansion of Islam. A local religion, the religion of a certain people, of an ethnic group is transformed into a universal religion. So this makes … it is evident that the believers of this universal religion are distinct, are different and aim to affirm their personality and independence and singular face, for example, in comparison with the Catholics, the Evangelistic, the Muslims or whatever other religion. And as with every religion, it does not limit itself to rituals; it also affects all aspects of daily life, culinary habits, behavior, customs, of family education, and everything else.

**PP:** What measures are being taken to protect and maintain those cultures in the future?

**Silva:** I cannot foresee the future. I can only say what I wish for the future, which in my opinion, is that for which the majority of Brazilians strives. Yesterday we spoke about racial democracy. Racial democracy does not exist in Brazil, but an aspiration toward racial democracy in Brazil does. And the important thing is our aspirations. It means we aspire to have a country in which all groups are equal and relate to and support each other in a harmonious way. It means if you went to a popular quarter in Brazil, you would find that, on the level of the people, on the level of the masses, this would be a reality. The spirit of neighborhood would work and there would be a sense of togetherness that goes beyond color differences and religious differences or ideological differences. I am speaking of a Brazilian aspiration. I have the impression that there exists some confusion concerning this concept of racial democracy. It is not that we should think that we are a racial democracy but that we always wanted to be a racial democracy. That is to say that it is on the level of aspirations that things place themselves for us.

All societies are imperfect and will always be imperfect. Well, what you wish is that they would not be so conflictive. What you wish is that the differences would be accepted, that they pull themselves together, support each other, and construct new differences. It will never be possible to achieve unanimity. But it is necessary to construct a new type of difference, an apron that goes beyond difference.

**PP:** Ambassador, thank you very much for this interview.

Recife, 14 March 2007

# Itineraries

Flora Veit-Wild/Anja Schwarz

# Passionate and Controversial: Janheinz Jahn as a Mediator of Cultures Among Europe, Africa, and America

Janheinz Jahn (1918-1973) was one of those few and unique Europeans who played an eminent role in the formation of bridges between black cultures from all over the world and Western cultures, people who assisted in the development and promotion of African literatures at an early stage and changed the perspectives on such literatures in their home country. Ulli Beier, with whom Jahn founded (in 1957) and co-edited the journal *Black Orpheus*, was another mediator of that sort. Driven by some streak of craziness and geniality, such innovators go where no one goes and do what no one does. Some sort of historical and biographical coincidence singles them out for their specific destiny and destination. Hence they produce unusual, atypical, chequered biographies, and do not normally earn the esteem of official academia. Despite all his great merits and international recognition, especially in the United States of America, Jahn never found a place in the German academy – the relationship was rather one of mutual disdain.

Some kind of blind impulse made Jahn find "Africa" and "Africa" find Jahn. From early on, Jahn was a man of the world and a man with a worldview. Born in Frankfurt in 1918 into a well-to-do family, he studied art history, drama, Arabic, Italian and German literature in Munich and Perugia. During World War II he was recruited by the German army but managed to escape a direct military involvement by writing sketches, plays and songs, which he staged with soldiers at the front ("Front-Theater"). Because of the many languages he spoke and his worldly manners he was also deployed as a guide and interpreter for Wehrmacht officers on vacation in Italy. After the war, without completing a university degree, he tried his luck as a lecturer in adult evening classes, freelance journalist and writer – he was also a founding member of the "Group 47", and a member of the German section of PEN – when in 1951 the decisive moment arrived: He attended a lecture on "Negro poetry" by Léopold Sédar Senghor at the Institut Français in Frankfurt. He was so impressed that he gatecrashed the private reception afterwards organized by the writer and translator Erica de Bary and introduced himself to Senghor. Through this encounter Jahn found his vocation: from then on he devoted his life to collecting, translating, and editing black poetry from Africa and the Americas: The famous anthology *Schwarzer Orpheus* (Black Orpheus, 1954) was followed by numerous other anthologies and translations as well as by his works on the history of African writing, African thought systems, his biographical guide *Who is Who in African Literature*, and bibliographies.

## 1. The Jahn Estate

Jahn was a maniac. In a feverish but also systematic way, he collected black writing from Africa and the Americas. Ulla Schild was his partner in life and work since 1968 and she remembered how "shelf after shelf filled up with books" in his house in Messel near Darmstadt, "until the corridor had to be used as well" (Schild 1970). Schild's bibliography of Jahn's published works (1974) contains 150 titles, including books, essays, and radio features. At the time of Jahn's death of a heart attack in 1973, his library included 3,000 books, most of them rare species, works of the very early days of African literature, often signed by their authors, including a large corpus of works in almost 50 different African languages. In 1975, Jahn's library was bought by the University of Mainz, where it was continuously expanded, under the guidance of Ulla Schild until her death in 1998; it then comprised 17,000 titles and represents one of the most important collections of African literatures in Europe.

Jahn was not only fanatic in collecting literary material; he was also manic and meticulous in keeping a record of everything he did. Hence he left behind a large personal estate, which was purchased by the Departmental Library of Asian and African Studies of the Humboldt University of Berlin in 2005 from Schild's widower Godehard Czernik (thanks to the financial aid of the Thyssen Foundation). These huge stacks of material give witness to Jahn's voracious passion for literature, music, and art, as well as for people – in fact everything creative and beautiful. It contains numerous short stories, plays, essays, radio features, many translations of works from writers from all over the world, a voluminous correspondence with publishers, politicians, translators, authors, literary critics – Wole Soyinka, Léopold Sédar Senghor, Abiola Irele, Ulli Beier among them – unpublished manuscripts by African writers, as well as an extensive collection of photographs and audio material. Based on this archive, a research project has been launched at the department in April 2007, a project that aims to evaluate Jahn's role in promoting African literatures in German speaking countries.

## 2. The Universality of rhythm

One of Jahn's major means of promulgating "the word" of black literature was the radio. In the year 1954 alone he wrote around 30 radio scripts, in which he presented and commented on poetry from writers like Paul Vesey, Aimé Césaire, Léopold Sédar Senghor, Léon Damas; from West Africa to Cuba, Brazil and the USA; African philosophy and medicine, Negro spirituals and Voodoo culture. It was the musicality of black poetry that fascinated and moved Jahn above all, and it was this that he wanted to get across to his German audience. "Writing poetry means making music with language",[1] he said reiterating again and again how black poetry lived through its rhythm, how it had to be chanted, danced, performed with music. While valid for black poetry from all parts of the world, this is especially true of Caribbean poetry, according to Jahn: "Whether the poets write in Spanish, French, English or Dutch, the rhythm knows no language barriers."[2] Thus it is no wonder that Jahn's foremost objective in his translations was to preserve the original rhythm of the poems and transpose it into his language. This, for him, was more important than sticking close to their content, as a remark in a letter to the translator and publisher Friedhelm Kemp proves: "Within some poems I've tried to maintain the rhythmic flow, including the internal rhyme. This meant that I had

---

1    Jahn, Janheinz: *Rumba Macumba – Afrocubanische Lyrik*. Jahn Archive, file
     Funk 1-29b, no. Fu 8, p. 18. All translations from German by the authors.
2    Jahn, Janheinz: *Rhythmische Antillen*. Jahn Archive, file Funk 1-29b, no. Fu 6,
     p. 7.

to translate the text more freely, of course."[3] Some of the translators who worked with Jahn found his unconditional dedication to the rhythm very questionable. Thus Kemp wrote to Jahn:

> Regarding the rhythm I can't help feeling that you chase after a chimera. Where the reader will read nothing but clumsy lines, you hear the African rhythm. You sacrifice the animated breath of the German language [...], neglect the exactness of meaning and imagery, just for the sake of obtaining three syllables without stress.[4]

Jahn's insistence on the predominance of the rhythm of black poetry reflects, of course, his close affiliation to the spirit of Negritude and its representatives. Replying to Kemp, he wrote: "In all his writings, Senghor underlines the utmost importance of these rhythms and regards it as his main achievement to have brought African rhythms to the French language."[5]

Jahn had a tendency to universalize poetry and art from the black world and thus to familiarize it for the German audience. Rhythm was one such universal quality of black poetry for him. He found another universal quality in black poetry from South America. In one of his broadcasts on South American poetry he says:

> In South American poetry we find dungeon and dance, hunger and drunkenness, death and laughter side by side. Nowhere else the polarity of life is drawn in such sharp contrasts; possibly it is this richness in contrast that is the only common trait of Negro poetry on that continent.[6]

And he continues with a remark that is astounding in the light of today's emergence of a black movement in Brazil but is symptomatic of the 1950s, when race was not an apparent matter of concern for Brazilians:

> In South American poetry you hear little about the differences between the races, which usually marks Negro poetry. There is hardly any race discrimination though more Negroes live there than in the United States. [...] In the anthologies of South American poetry, you cannot make out

---

3    Letter from Janheinz Jahn to Dr. Friedhelm Kemp, 18.12.1962. Jahn Archive, file Korrespondenz Inland L-Q.
4    Letter from Dr. Friedhelm Kemp to Janheinz Jahn, 06.01.1963. Jahn Archive, file Korrespondenz Inland L-Q.
5    Letter from Janheinz Jahn to Dr. Friedhelm Kemp, 18.12.1962. Jahn Archive, file Korrespondenz Inland L-Q.
6    Jahn, Janheinz: *Meine schwarzen Puppen – Südamerikanische Negerlyrik*. Jahn Archive, file Funk 1-29b, no. Fu 4, p. 9.

the color of the writers; in Brazil you don't get any such information
even if you ask for it.[7]

## 3. Schwarzer Orpheus

The anthology *Schwarzer Orpheus*, which comprised John's translations of black poetry from Africa, the Antilles, South America and
North America, was the first manifestation of the sense of universality
that he discovered in these texts. Thus he defines his own achievements in the publication of the first extensive anthology of so called
neo-African poetry:

> I could show that the black poets who wrote in French possessed no mo-
> nopoly, that there were writers in English and Spanish erupting with the
> same spirit of innovation and that also in African countries the spark had
> caught fire (Jahn 1964: 293).

The first edition made known the hitherto unheard voices of 82 black
poets in 161 poems; the second enlarged edition contains 256 poems
from 133 authors (Jahn 1964: 295). Besides poems from English-,
French- or Spanish-speaking regions, Jahn collected and published
authors writing in Dutch and Portuguese. However, the number of
poems deriving, for instance, from Brazil, Angola or Suriname is very
limited, for a variety of reasons. First, and ironically, despite the absence of race as topic that he observed and his emphasis on universality, Jahn wanted to publish black poets exclusively. This somehow
biased attitude was perceived by some of his contemporaries as doc-
trinaire and prescriptive (see below). However, as he did not know the
skin color of many Latin American poets, he did not know whom to
approach.[8] Secondly, it was not easy for him to get translation rights
(Jahn 1964: 297). Thirdly, he could not translate Portuguese or Dutch
texts on his own and thus had to rely on other translators.

The numerous reactions of the German literary public to *Schwarzer Orpheus* ranged from great praise for Jahn's pioneering work,
which overcame previous prejudiced concepts ("Dealing with poems
such as these, the notion of a primitive Negro culture is no longer

---

7    Jahn, Janheinz: *Meine schwarzen Puppen – Südamerikanische Negerlyrik*. Jahn
     Archive, file Funk 1-29b, no. Fu 4, pp. 14-15.
8    Letter from Richard Katz to Janheinz Jahn, 23.07.1953. Jahn Archive, file Kor-
     respondenz Ausland A-D.

sustainable"[9]), to a romanticizing eulogizing attitude of this poetry and
its cathartic effect on the European:

> [...] the blooming luminosity of this poetry, an all embracing liturgy:
> saying yes, singing yes, affirmation of a positive existence, of a positive
> meaning of creation, in the midst of all the brutalities, of death, of de-
> cline. [...] The European, particularly the affected, anxious and oddly
> helpless man of the occident, should read this collection.[10]

Reading such reviews of the early 1950s today, one is struck by their
quaint over-emphatic diction. While a few German reviewers could
not find any access to what they perceived as a confused, alien literary
idiom, and some read aggressive, racist undertones in it, others criti-
cized Jahn's tendency to romanticize the "otherness" that he heard in
the poems.

## 4.  Jahn's reception in Africa

Despite such differing reactions, Jahn's extraordinary achievements in
revealing the unknown treasure of African literature to a German audience and readership stand beyond doubt. While at the home front he
challenged the prevalent backward and reactionary perception of black
literature as primitive and inferior (Schild 1970), he was just as out-
spoken in his communication with the African counterparts. How
were his ventures received on "the other side of the bridge" – that is,
in Africa and the Americas themselves? Some clues to this question
can be found in the numerous files of his correspondence with African
and Afro-American writers and critics. When collecting poems for the
second edition of the anthology *Schwarzer Orpheus* he got in touch
with the Nigerian poet Akin A., to whom he wrote on 13 August
1957:

> I have read your poems with keen interest. And I feel the need to say to
> you something about your poems, but I see the difficulty too: you do not
> know me, I know very little of you, and you might take wrong all I say.
> To me the easiest way out would be writing to you "Dear Sir, I appreci-
> ate your poems, but I am sorry that I do not have the possibility to pub-

---

9   Unknown (1954): No Title. In: *General-Anzeiger der Stadt Wuppertal*. Jahn
    Archive, file Rezensionen/Presse zu "Schwarzer Orpheus" 1, no. 59.
10  Unknown (1954): "Schwarzer Orpheus. Moderne Dichtung afrikanischer Völker
    beider Hemisphären. Ausgewählt und übertragen von Janheinz Jahn, Carl-Han-
    ser-Verlag". In: *Magnum*. Jahn Archive, file Rezensionen/Presse zu "Schwarzer
    Orpheus" 1, no. 49.

lish them for lack of space etc.". But that would not be true. The truth is that I do not think they are good. I think they are not worth being printed. You may call me an arrogant man who has no right to say so, but having exposed your verses to my eyes you have the right to know my real opinion about them, not merely some void flattery. [...]

An example: BLUE NIGER: there is nothing of the spirit of this river, all you say everybody can see on a map. Even poems such as MY VISION lack all reality, there is no image, there is not even any necessity in your adjectives: the word WAVES includes THUNDERING, WINDS are always HURRYING, your verses are collections of commonplaces.[11]

"But there is still hope", Jahn continues, and suggests that his addressee should read a book by Tutuola and think of what Senghor recently said, whom he quotes:

[...] the best Negro artists and writers of to-day [...] get their inspiration from the Negro-African culture, they elevate themselves into international rank; whenever they turn their back to mother Africa, the [y] degenerate and get boring, flat and dull.

"Are you going to write me again?" Jahn concludes his letter.

Mr. A. did write again. He did not mistake Jahn's upfront criticism and advice as "an argumentum ad hominem", and a long-lasting exchange of over 10 years ensued, in which, among other things, Jahn extracted from Akin A. detailed information on various points regarding Yoruba language and culture; A. also suggested doing a translation for Jahn of a work by Fagunwa. Being aware of the intricacies of an adequate "cultural translation", Jahn was always keen to learn as much as possible about the cultural context of the works he was translating. While he was using his correspondents as informants on languages and cultures he was not familiar with, he simultaneously insisted – imperiously – that they "stick to their roots". This was also a message he put across to Abiola Irele, with whom he shared a close friendship and exchange – also on very personal issues – which lasted from 1960 until Jahn's death. On 25.11.1960, he wrote to Irele, who was at the time studying French and Spanish language and literature in Paris (he later also learnt German). Jahn told him:

I find it good and worthwhile that you are learning so many languages, but please do not neglect Yoruba. I think that for a specialist of neo-African writing it is necessary to know some African languages. You are

---

11   Letter from Janheinz Jahn to Akin A., 13.08.1957. Jahn Archive, file Korrespondenz Ausland K-O. Written in English.

a Yoruba and you should study your own language very carefully now so that there will be <u>one</u> specialist in the world who will be able to study and to analyze Yoruba literature competently.[12]

Not everybody seemed to accept the – typically German – bluntness of Jahn as amiably as Akin A. and his friend Irele. Particularly after the publication of his book *Muntu: An Outline of Neo-African Culture* (1961 – German original in 1958), his dogmatic and patronizing inter-ventions on the African literary scene seemed to provoke antagonistic and adversary reactions. From Nigeria, Jahn's compatriot Gertrud Mander made the following comment:

> Africa enthusiasts like Janheinz Jahn with his "desk-theories of neo-African culture" are very suspect here [in Nigeria] and give a false – because too general and speculative – idea of the situation. In Africa there are at least as many cultural differences as in Europe, and you cannot ignore the European influences on the African continent (Mander 1963).

In the same article, Mander praises Ulli Beier, Jahn's counterpart and friend, for his engagement and his appreciation of the cultural and literary diversity in Nigeria. A glance into Jahn's extensive correspon-dence with Beier, with whom he founded and edited the first issues of the journal *Black Orpheus*, reveals that Beier tried to explain to Jahn, why Jahn's position as co-editor of the journal was no longer desirable at the time of Nigeria's Independence in 1960 and the new Nigerian government's move to Nigeria's cultural life. Instead of limiting his role to analyzing and describing African literature – as would be ap-propriate – Jahn was perceived as imposing his views and trying to push African writing in a certain direction.

***

Being a man of strong views and marked idiosyncrasies, Jahn tended to antagonize people. Despite his great merits and recognition, he remained a solitary figure. Curiously, he appears to have been much more popular in the United States, for instance, than in his home coun-try. Maybe his missionary zeal and dramatic character did not fit into the sober tone and wariness against hyperbole of the German post-war

---

12  Letter from Janheinz Jahn to Abiola Irele, 25.11.1960. Jahn Archive, file Korres-pondenz Ulli Beier – Abiola Irele.

literary scene. However, one of Jahn's great achievements was the exploration and representation of cultural connections between Africa and the Americas. Within his concept of a neo-African culture, he shed light upon the affinities of black poetry from all over the world.

## Bibliography

Jahn, Janheinz (1964): "Nachwort". In: Jahn, Janheinz (ed.): *Schwarzer Orpheus*: *Moderne Dichtung afrikanischer Völker beider Hemisphären*, Neue Sammlung. München: Carl Hanser, pp. 293-297.

— (ed.) (1954): *Schwarzer Orpheus: Moderne Dichtung afrikanischer Völker beider Hemisphären*. München: Carl Hanser.

Mander, Gertrud (1963): "Afrika ist ganz anders". In: *Stuttgarter Zeitung*, no. 159, 13.07.1963.

Schild, Ulla (1970): "Sammler neoafrikanischer Literatur: Porträt von Janheinz Jahn, der den Übersetzerpreis der Darmstädter Akademie erhielt". In: *Die Welt*, 04.10. 1970.

— (1974): "A Bibliography of the Works of Janheinz Jahn". In: *Research in African Literatures*, vol. 5, no. 2, pp. 196-205.

## Map of the South Atlantic Route and the West African Coast

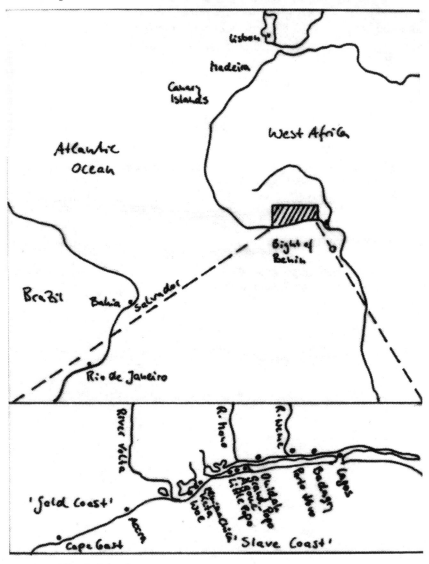

Drawing: Silke Strickrodt.

Silke Strickrodt

# The Brazilian Diaspora to West Africa in the Nineteenth Century

> For the cultural historian, there is nothing more interesting than that class of people which is particularly numerous at Agué and Weida and which calls itself Portuguese (Zöller 1885: I, 182-183).

In 1884, when the scramble among European nations for colonies in Africa had just begun, the German journalist Hugo Zöller visited the coastal settlements in today's Togo and Benin. This visit was part of an extensive trip during which he explored the potential of the West African regions that Germany was interested in, officially as a journalist commissioned by the *Kölnische Zeitung* but secretly as a German government agent. At Agoué and Ouidah, which were soon to become part of the French colony of Dahomey, Zöller was struck by the existence of a group of people who, although heterogeneous in appearance (from "the pure yellow-white of the Southern European to the darkest brownish black" of the Africans), distinguished themselves from the rest of the local population by particular cultural traits and social aspirations. Not only did they describe themselves as "Portuguese", but they were lusophone, adhered to the Roman Catholic Church and had the "easy, agreeable manners" of Southern Europeans (Zöller 1885: I, 182-183). Zöller's observations, however, are nothing exceptional. Other European visitors to the coastal parts of present-day Togo, Benin, and Nigeria in the nineteenth and twentieth century have also noted these people, describing them variously as "Portuguese", "Brazilians", "Afro-Brazilians" or "Aguda". Traces of their cultural influence can be found in the region even today, in the form of Portuguese family names and a particular Brazilian heritage, including the architectural style of many buildings, religious practices, dishes such as feijoada, kousido and mokeka, as well as the memory of ancestral links to Brazil.

This Brazilian diaspora on the West African coast was a reflection of the close trade relations that had existed between this region and Brazil, particular the latter's Northeastern province of Bahia, during the era of the slave trade. It had resulted from several waves of immigration experienced by the West African coast during the nineteenth century, involving people of various backgrounds and motivations. Some were slave traders who had settled on the coast in order to engage in the "illegal" slave trade. Most, however, were ex-slaves from Brazil (and, to a lesser extent, from Cuba) who had returned to West Africa after the Male revolt in Bahia in 1835 – in fact, they were still returning by the time Zöller visited the coast in 1884. By the end of the century, these disparate groups of people began to form a coherent community, unified by the Portuguese language, the Roman Catholic religion, and the practice of intermarriage that was common among them (Law 2004c: 185-187). In this paper, I will discuss the origins and the evolution of this Brazilian diaspora on the West African coast and its impact on the local societies in the nineteenth century.

In this discussion, I use the term "Brazilian" to refer to these communities, as it reflects their strong cultural link to Brazil. However, it should be noted that in the period the people did not usually identify themselves in this way. This term, as well as the term "Afro-Brazilian" which is widely used in the academic literature, is purely a scholarly designation imposed on them retrospectively. From the contemporary documents, including Zöller's report, it appears that if these people identified themselves as a group, then as "Portuguese". This is a reflection of the colonial ties that existed between Portugal and Brazil until 1822, the year of Brazil's independence from Portugal. Even after this date, many Brazilians continued to identify themselves, culturally, as Portuguese. This, at least, was evidently the case in West Africa. However, as will be discussed in greater detail below, the "Brazilians" on the West African coast were a highly heterogeneous group and it is not clear whether a common sense of identity existed before the end of the nineteenth century (Law 2004c: 185; Law/Mann 1999: 324).

The indigenous societies on the West African coast in the nineteenth century used a number of names to refer to the Brazilians. In the area of Dahomey and Yoruba land, the term "Aguda" was used (and is still common in the Bight of Benin today). It was applied to the

Portuguese in general, including Brazilians, and referred to Portuguese and Brazilians of European as well as African descent (Law 2004a: 350). At Lagos, they were called "Amaro". This is a Yoruba term, which according to Kopytoff commonly meant "those who had been away from home" (1965: 87). A variant of this term, "Maro", also appears as the name of one of Ouidah's quarters that was settled by Brazilians. Law has noted that it apparently comes from the interior, where it is documented as the name given to quarters settled by foreign, particularly Muslim, merchants (Law 2004b: 350, 2004c: 182). At Accra (and possibly on the Gold Coast more generally), the Brazilian repatriates were knows as "Tabon". This apparently derived from the Portuguese greeting "Está bom?", which they used (Parker 2000: 14, 40 n. 62).

Most of the Brazilian immigrants settled in that part of the West African coast, which in the pre-colonial period was known to traders of most European nations as the "Slave Coast", but to the Portuguese and Brazilians as "Costa da Mina". It extended from the River Volta, in the west, to the Lagos channel, in the east, and comprised the coastal areas of today's Togo and Benin and parts of Ghana and Nigeria. It roughly corresponded to the Bight of Benin, which is the term often used in the scholarly literature dealing with the Brazilian settlement in West Africa. However, some Brazilians also immigrated into the area to the west of the River Volta, that is the "Gold Coast", which resulted in the formation of a Brazilian community at Accra (Parker 2000: 14). Therefore, in this paper I will use the term "West African coast", by which I mean specifically the coast between Accra and Lagos, as well as "Bight of Benin" when referring to the region from the River Volta to Lagos.

The region between Accra and Lagos was occupied by a number of African groups and states. These were, from west to east, Ga-Dangme, Anlo, Genyi, Hula, Dahomey, Porto Novo, Badagry, and Lagos. The Ga-Dangme, two closely related people, occupied the area to the west of the River Volta, which Europeans in the period usually referred to as the "eastern Gold Coast". Accra, at the western limits of this area, in fact consisted of three Ga towns, Nleshi, Kinka and Osu, which were drawn together to form the city of Accra only in the second half of the nineteenth century under British colonial rule. Each of the three towns was the location of a European trade fort, belonging to

the English, Dutch, and Danes respectively. The coast between Accra
and the River Volta was dotted with European trade forts, mainly belonging to the Danes. To the east of the River Volta, there was Anlo,
an Ewe state. Its major port was at Keta (in present-day Ghana), which
was also the site of a Danish trade fort. Genyi, known to the Europeans as "Little Popo" after its major port town (present-day Aneho,
in Togo), occupied the area corresponding roughly to today's Togo's
coastal parts. Two more port towns, Agoué and Porto Seguro (present-
day Agbodrafo), emerged in this region in the 1820s and 1830s respectively as a result of civil wars at Little Popo. The Hula state,
called Great Popo by the Europeans, was situated around the mouth of
the River Mono, with its port at Grand Popo (in present-day Benin).
The central part of the "Slave Coast" was dominated by the kingdom
of Dahomey, the most powerful state in the Bight of Benin in that
period. Dahomey's major port was Ouidah, which was one of the most
important embarkation points for slaves in the history of the trade,
more than one million slaves having been shipped across the Atlantic
from there. Ouidah was the location of three European trade forts,
owned by the English, the French and the Portuguese respectively.
There were two more Dahomian ports further east, at Godomey and
Cotonou (in present-day Benin). Porto Novo and Badagry were two
independent states that had been founded in the eighteenth century by
refugees from states that had fallen victim to Dahomey's expansion.
At the eastern end of the region described here, there was the Yoruba
state of Lagos (in present-day Nigeria).

   As indicated by its name, the "Slave Coast" had played a major
role in the transatlantic slave trade. With the abolition and criminalisa-
tion of the trade by the European powers, first and foremost the British, after 1807, the trade ended on the neighbouring Gold Coast due to
the British presence and influence there. However, the Bight of Benin
continued to be a major supplier of slaves for the transatlantic trade
for another sixty years, becoming one of the hotspots for the "illegal"
slave trade. The British tried to suppress this trade by posting anti-
slave trade patrols of its navy on the coast as well as by mounting
pressure on the African states in the region. In 1851, they bombarded
Lagos and deposed its ruler in an attempt to end the slave trade there
and established an official presence in the form of a consulate. In 1861
Lagos was annexed. At the western end of the Bight of Benin, too, the

British encroached on African sovereignty in the period. In 1850, they bought the Danish forts on the West African coast, including the one at Keta in the Anlo region. From then on, they gradually extended their influence over Anlo, which in June 1874 was incorporated into the British Gold Coast territory. A month later, the British Crown Colony of the Gold Coast and Lagos was created by Royal Proclamation (Hargreaves 1963: 166-174; Newbury 1961: 49-76). However, apart from these encroachments at its eastern and western ends, the Bight of Benin remained under African control until the European colonial take-over the 1880s.

## 1. Literature review

Zöller has proved prescient with regard to the interest, which the Brazilians on the West African coast have attracted from historians. One hundred and thirty years after his visit to the coast, there is a veritable boom in research done on these people: books, articles, and dissertations have been published by Brazilianists, Africanists, historians, and anthropologists interested in culture, ethnicity, religion, and memory, among others. This increasing interest needs to be seen in the context of the rise of Atlantic history as field since the 1990s, although it should be noted that the pioneering study on the Brazilian diaspora to West Africa, Pierre Verger's *Flux et reflux de la traite des nègres entre le Golfe de Bénin et Bahia de Todos os Santos du XVIIe au XIX siècle* (1968), pre-dated the classic text of Atlantic studies, Paul Gilroy's *Black Atlantic* (1993), by several decades. Verger was the first to discuss the interconnections between Brazil, specifically its Bahia province, and the Bight of Benin during the era of the slave trade. Rather than limiting his discussion to the forced migration of roughly two million slaves from the Bight of Benin to Bahia, he emphasized the bilateral and constant nature of the relations between the two regions, including the return of several thousand liberated slaves to the West African coast in the nineteenth century.

Strictly, however, Verger was not the first to write about the Brazilians in West Africa, although his tome, comprising some 700 pages, was unprecedented in scale as well as regards the wealth of archival material that it presents. First, the history of the Brazilian settlement in the Bight of Benin had been the object of study of local historians in

Africa before. The result of these studies includes two manuscripts
dealing with the Brazilian community at Agoué by the French missionary Pierre Pelofy, who between 1911 and 1946 was curate of the
French Catholic Mission at Agoué (Pelofy 2002), and a booklet of the
Lagosian Anthony Laotan, *The Torch-Bearers or Old Brazilian Colony in Lagos*, dating from 1843. Second, there are some short works
by scholars, such as the essays by Lorenzo D. Turner (1942) and J. F.
de Almeida Prado (written in 1849). A mine of information – if not a
strictly "scholarly" work – is Antonio Olinto's memoir of his two-year
sojourn in Lagos in the early 1960s as cultural attaché at the Brazilian
embassy in Nigeria, entitled *Brasileiros na Africa* (1964). Olinto was
a friend of Verger (who also was in Nigeria at the time writing his
*Flux and Reflux*) and they shared the interest in the Brazilians on the
West African coast. Two of his book's chapters are devoted to the
Brazilian community at Lagos, describing its history and cultural life.
Most fascinating, he gives much information concerning the life and
family histories of individual members of the Brazilian community
who he had met (mainly, but not exclusively) at Lagos, including individuals who had made the passage from Brazil to West Africa in the
early 1900s. In the 1960s, there also appeared a number of articles
dealing with the life and career of prominent members of the Brazilian
community in the nineteenth century: Domingos Martins (Ross 1965),
Geraldo da Lima (Amenumey 1968) and Felix Francisco de Souza
(Ross 1969), who were all notorious slave traders.

Following the publication of Verger's study, another important
milestone in the historiography of Brazilian settlement in the Bight of
Benin was Michael Jerry Turner's unpublished PhD thesis on the impact of the Brazilian immigrants on the West African coast (1975).
Turner focuses on the part of West Africa that became the French
colony of Dahomey at the end of the nineteenth century and is now
the Republic of Benin. In its structure, his thesis follows the return
movement of the ex-slaves from Bahia to the West African coast,
discussing the situation of slaves and emancipated slaves in Brazilian
society, the Male revolt, their passage to Africa and their integration
into coastal society. The particular value of this study lies in the large
number of oral family traditions, which he had collected from the
descendants of the Brazilians in the early 1970s.

In 1985, two more, important studies appeared. Manuela Carneiro da Cunha's monograph, *Negros, estrangeiros: os escravos libertos e sua volta à Africa*, discusses the settlement of Brazilian ex-slaves at Lagos. Her focus is on the evolution of their cultural identity during the colonial period, with one chapter being devoted to the importance of the Roman Catholic religion for the settlers and the latter's role in the establishment of Roman Catholicism on the West African coast. In the same year appeared a study by Marianno Carneiro da Cunha, her husband, on the Brazilian architecture in the Yoruba area of Nigeria and Dahomey. This essay was published posthumously, Marianno having died in 1980, and was accompanied by an introduction by Manuela Carneiro da Cunha and photographs of Brazilian architecture by Pierre Verger and reproductions of historical photographs of buildings and Brazilian individuals. Both these studies are based on research done in Nigeria during eight months in 1875.

Studies dealing with the history of the Brazilians on the West African Coast have abounded since the mid-1990s. They include articles dealing with the careers of prominent individuals (Amos 2000; Law 2001b; 2004a), particular settlements (Akibode 1988-1989; Law 2001a; 2004c: 155-188; Lindsay 1994; Soumonni 2003; 2005; Strickrodt 2004) and particular aspects, such as ethnicity (Law 2004b; Matory 1999) and cultural identity (Guran 2000; Yai 2001). Only one study shall be pointed out here. This is an article, co-authored by Robin Law and Kristin Mann, on the links and reciprocal cultural influences between Brazil and West Africa during the era of the slave trade (Law/Mann 1999). Using the concept of an "Atlantic community" and taking up the thread where Verger left it thirty years ago, they were able to build on the research that has been done in the meantime for their comprehensive discussion of the interconnections between the two regions, including the Brazilian diaspora in West Africa. Nevertheless, there still are gaps in the historiography. One area that remains understudied is the Brazilian settlement in the coastal parts of present-day Ghana (research having so far focused on the immigration to Togo, Benin and Nigeria), with the exception of an article by Alcione Amos and E. Ayesu, which however focuses on the twentieth century (Amos/Ayesu 2002). Another notable absence in the historiography is studies on the role of the Brazilians in the establishment of Islam on the West African coast.

## 2. The Bight of Benin and Brazil in the era of the slave trade

The Brazilian diaspora on the West African coast was a highly heterogeneous group of people in terms of race, class, and geographical origins. They included Brazilians of African origin who had been liberated from slavery and returned to the West African coast, descendants
of (white) Brazilians by African wives, free Africans who had been
educated in Brazil and Africans who acquired the Portuguese language and Brazilian cultural mores in Africa. Moreover, the "Brazilian" community also absorbed the descendants of immigrants from
outside Brazil, not only from metropolitan Portugal and other lusophone territories but also from non-lusophone territories, such as
Spain and Cuba. However, the Brazilian influence was the strongest
and assimilated the others, due to the overwhelming numbers of Brazilian immigrants in the nineteenth century.

Why was the (re)immigration to West Africa from Brazil so much
greater than from elsewhere? Two factors explain this overwhelming
Brazilian influence in the Bight of Benin and shall be discussed in the
following. These were, first, the close connection of the two regions in
the transatlantic slave trade and, secondly, the relatively easy access
for slaves to manumission in Brazil. The close link between West
Africa and Brazil in the transatlantic slave trade becomes clear already
from the sheer numbers of slaves transported from the one region to
the other. Over the whole period of the transatlantic slave trade, about
1,900,000 million slaves were exported from the Bight of Benin. Of
these, about 1,400,000, that is roughly 60%, were taken to Brazil. This
compares to around 20% of slaves who were taken to the French Caribbean, mainly to Saint Domingue (the present-day Haiti), and 1%
taken to the British Caribbean (Eltis/Richardson 1997: 20-21; cf. Law
2004c: 126; Law/Mann 1999: 312). Within Brazil, the Bight of Benin's orientation was predominantly to the northeastern province of
Bahia with its main port Salvador. One reason for this was the geographical closeness of the two regions. Another one, according to
Verger, was the important role-played by a certain kind of Bahian
tobacco in the trade. This tobacco, which was of inferior quality and
therefore prepared in a special way, was much requested in the Bight
of Benin and gave the Portuguese/Brazilian traders an advantage over
their European competitors there (Verger 1964: 7-9; 1968: 28-38).

A more detailed analysis of the volume of the trade shows that the Bight of Benin's orientation towards Bahia was particularly marked from the 1790s to the mid-nineteenth century. In the second half of the eighteenth century, only that of the French rivalled the Brazilian trade in the region. However, French involvement in the slave trade was ended by the slave insurrection in St. Domingue of 1791 and the subsequent abolition of the slavery in the French territories. Moreover, the closure of the slave market in St. Domingue boosted the Brazilian influence in the Bight of Benin not only because with the French the main rival had left the coast, but also because it caused a sugar boom in Bahia which until then had been a backwater of sugar production. Between 1791 and 1830, almost 390,000 slaves were imported into Bahia, the largest part of whom came from the Bight of Benin (Eltis 1987: 243-244; Lovejoy 1994: 154-157).

Significantly, this trade was carried out directly between the Bight of Benin and Brazil, rather than metropolitan Portugal. The Portuguese fort at Ouidah, the Bight of Benin's major port, was administered by the Viceroy of Brazil and staffed by personnel from Brazil. Even the communication between the Bight of Benin and Portugal went via Bahia, as did the Bight of Benin's communication other Brazilian ports, such as Rio de Janeiro. Robin Law and Kristin Mann, and Pierre Verger before them, have emphasized the bilateral and regular nature of the relations between the Bight of Benin and Bahia during the era of the slave trade. These were not just commercial networks, but the trade also fostered social relations and cultural exchange between the two regions:

> Just as slaves carried African religions and Islam as well as material culture and ritual practices into the Americas, so slave traders introduced literacy, numeracy, Christianity, European languages, new consumer goods, artisan knowledge, and building styles to the Slave Coast (Law/Mann 1999: 313, 314; Verger 1968: 127-245).

During the period of the illegal slave trade, the Brazilian influence in the Bight of Benin had increased even further, both in real and relative terms. From the 1790s, the European nations that had traded in the Bight of Benin one by one abolished the trade. The Spanish and the Portuguese were the last to do so, but by the mid-1820s all interested European nations (including Brazil, which had seceded from Portugal rule in 1822) had officially banned the trade on the West African coast. As a consequence of the abolition of this trade, the French and the English abandoned their forts at Ouidah in 1797 and 1812 respectively. The authorities from the 1800s neglected the Portuguese fort at Ouidah, but unofficial agents from Brazil soon filled this gap and continued the trade illegally (Law 2004c: 160-163). Thus, due to the absence of the other Europeans, the Brazilian influence in the Bight of Benin became more pronounced in relative terms in the nineteenth century.

However, the Brazilian influence in the region also increased in real terms. This was due to the different operation of the illegal trade as compared to the period when it was legal. Due to the efforts mainly by cruisers of the British navy to suppress the trade by patrolling the African coast and capturing suspected slave vessel, the trade became a highly risky enterprise. On the Brazilian side, this led to a concentration of the trade in the hands of a few Bahian firms. On the West African coast, it made necessary the presence of agents on the spot, as it became vital for the slavers to load the vessels quickly before the cruisers of the British anti-slave trade squadron could detect them. Therefore, slaves were bulked on shore and whole shiploads were held in readiness to be loaded within a few hours (rather than as before, when the filling of a ship could take several weeks or even months, depending on the arrival of slaves from the interior). The greater need for coordination made necessary the presence of agents on the spot, causing an influx of Brazilian traders into the Bight of Benin in the early nineteenth century (Law/Mann 1999: 322-324).

The second major factor that helps to explain the overwhelming scale of the Brazilian (re)immigration to West Africa in the nineteenth century is internal to Brazilian society. This was the relatively easy access for slaves to manumission, as compared to other slave societies in the Americas. While slavery in Brazil was just as exploitative and harsh as elsewhere, Brazilian slaves stood a much higher chance than slaves on North American or Caribbean plantations of ending their days in freedom, either by being manumitted by their masters or by purchasing their freedom themselves. The latter option, the purchase of their freedom, was a possibility particularly for urban slaves, who enjoyed greater independence than plantation slaves and therefore had more opportunities to earn and save money. Moreover, urban slaves organized themselves in self-help cooperatives, ethnic associations and religious brotherhoods, which worked as banks and lending institutions and assisted them in purchasing their emancipation. While most of the slaves who gained their freedom in this way were Creoles, which means that they had been born in Brazil, emancipation was also a possibility for African-born slaves. Due to the greater facility of achieving emancipation, there were a large number of ex-slaves living in the urban centres in Brazil, who earned their living as artisans (bakers, tailors, coopers, carpenters, and masons), petty traders and merchants. It was mainly from among these people that the "returnees" came (Turner 1975: 11-12, 26-27; Lindsay 1994: 25; Lovejoy 1994: 154; Verger 1968: 515-542).

## 3. Pioneers of Brazilian settlement in West Africa: The slave traders

The origins of the Brazilian diaspora on the West African coast lie in the large-scale immigration of ex-slaves from Brazil from the 1830s. However, individual Portuguese and Brazilian traders settled in the region already from the late eighteenth century. Although they were comparatively few, these traders became an important factor in coastal life and prepared the ground for the settlement of the ex-slaves. As discussed above, following the legal banning of the slave trade there was an influx of greater numbers of traders who acted as agents for Brazilian firms. Initially, these new agents came from Brazil and other lusophone territories. From the 1820s, with the rise of the Cuban slave trade, Spaniards and Cubans joined them. On the coast, the traders concentrated at Ouidah and Lagos, which were the main ports of the slave trade on the West African coast in the period.

At Ouidah, the illegal slave trade and the Brazilian settlement centred around one particular individual. This was Francisco Felix de Souza (d. 1849), the most notorious of the traders, who has fascinated contemporary observers and historians alike. De Souza was a Brazilian who had come to the West African coast around the turn of the century. For a few years in the 1800s he had been employed as an official in the Portuguese fort at Ouidah, but had then established himself as an independent trader in the illegal trade to Brazil and Cuba. In 1818, following a dispute with the Dahomean monarch, Adandozan, he supported the latter's brothers, Gezo, in a successful coup d'état by

which Adondozan was deposed. Gezo became the new ruler of Dahomey and rewarded de Souza by making him his agent for the slave
trade at Ouidah, an office that came to be referred to as "Chacha".
This privilege, together with his international commercial connections, became the basis for de Souza's domination of the illegal trade
and his great influence in the Bight of Benin until the 1840s. He
worked in association or competition with other Brazilian, Portuguese
and Spanish traders at Ouidah, such as Joaquim Telles de Menezes,
who married one of de Souza's daughters, and Juan José Zangronis, a
Spaniard from Havana (Law 2004a: 190-200; 2004c: 165-179). De
Souza founded three quarters in Ouidah, Brazil (today's "Blézin"),
Zomaï and Maro. The Brazil quarter was the location of his family
home and until today is settled by his descendants and those of his
free clients and slaves. Zomaï is remembered to have been built as his
country home and storehouse for goods, and is still settled by the descendants of his slaves. The Maro quarter was settled by returned ex-
slaves, as whose patron he acted (Law 2004c: 183-184). Besides these
quarters in Ouidah, he also owned places elsewhere that were settled
by members of his extensive family and by slaves, such as Adjido at
Little Popo and Zomaï at Agoué, attesting to his influence beyond
Ouidah's (and Dahomey's) boundaries (Strickrodt 2004: 218-220).

In the 1830s and 1840s, Lagos overtook Ouidah in the volume of
slave exports. This was due to the destruction of the Oyo Empire in
the interior in the early nineteenth century, which was followed by
wars that generated large numbers of slaves, mainly Yoruba, who
were sold into the transatlantic trade. This booming slave trade attracted many Portuguese, Brazilian and Spanish traders, of whom
some twenty-two were documented at Lagos during the 1830s (Law/
Man 1999: 324, citing House of Commons Sessional Papers 1831-
1839). The leading trader among them was José Domingos Martins
(d. 1864), a Brazilian who had come to the West African coast in early
1830s. He was said to have arrived destitute, as part of the crew of a
slave vessel that had been captured by the British navy and put on
shore at Ouidah. He had first at Ouidah on de Souza's charity for a
few years, but in the late 1830s had moved to Lagos where he prospered in the trade (Ross 1965: 79; Law 2004a: 203).

A major change occurred in the settlement pattern of the slave
traders in the Bight of Benin in the 1840s with the decentralization of

the trade from Ouidah. This was caused by new legislation employed by the British in their effort to suppress the trade, specifically the Equipment Act of 1839. This act enabled the British navy to detain suspicious Portuguese slave vessels that carried equipment for the trade (such as water containers, wood for slave decks and chains), while before 1839 vessels actually had to have slaves on board to be liable to capture. In reaction to this new legislation, the traders dispersed from Ouidah, which was under close surveillance from the anti-slave trade patrol, to the settlements to the east and the west. There, they established secondary bases from where to ship slaves with less risk. Most of the slaves still came from Dahomey via Ouidah, from where they were transported to the respective points of embarkation by canoes along the coastal lagoon that connected most of the port towns. To the west of Ouidah, slave traders are documented from the 1840s at Little Popo, Agoué, and Grand Popo, and, to the east, at Godomey, Cotonou, Porto Novo and Badagry. Among them were Isidore and Antonio de Souza, two of Francisco Felix de Souza's sons, who established themselves at Little Popo and Agoué in the early 1840s. Several other traders are documented at Little Popo and Agoué in the 1840s and 1850s. They include the Brazilian José Francisco dos Santos, nicknamed "Zé Alfaiate" (José the tailor) because after his arrival on the coast he had worked for de Souza as a tailor, and Domingo Mustiche, a Spaniard. However, the most prominent trader at Agoué in the 1840s was Joaquim d'Almeida (d. 1857) alias "Zoki Azata", a liberated slave from Brazil. He was a Mahi from Hoko, to the north of Dahomey, who as a child had been captured by the Dahomeans and sold into slavery to Bahia. He had been bought by a Brazilian slave captain, Joaquim Manoel d'Almeida, who traded between Brazil and the West African coast. Joaquim d'Almeida was also employed in this trade. He served his master well and assumed the latter's name. After his liberation, he continued in the trade. In 1845, he finally returned to the West African coast, settling at Agoué (Strickrodt 2004: 221; Turner 1975: 102-105). Grand Popo became a secondary base of Joaquim Antonio, a Spaniard established at Ouidah, and a "Senôr Carvallio" was reported at the neighbouring village of Hévé in 1852 (Strickrodt 2004: 222). To the east of Ouidah, Francisco Felix de Souza shipped slaves from Godomey and Cotonou. After his death in 1849, his sons Isidoro and Antonio assumed control of theses two places (Law 2004a: 199-200). From 1846, Porto Novo became the base of José Domingos Martins, who had formerly traded at Lagos. Following de Souza's death, he became the leading slave trader in the Bight of Benin (Law 2004a: 203; Ross 1965: 83).

Furthermore, slave traders were active at the far eastern end of the Slave Coast, in the Volta region. In 1844, the Governor of the Danish settlements on the Gold Coast passed along the Slave Coast on his return home and noted Portuguese flags flying at Woe and Atoko, two settlements in the Anlo region to the east of the River Volta. Woe was the base of José Mora. According to Danish reports he was a Spaniard, although this does not tally with the Portuguese flag flying at Woe or with local traditions recorded in the late nineteenth century, which remembered him as a "Portuguese" (Carstensen 1965: 5-6, 10, 15; Greene 1996: 74; Spiess 1907: 207). Atoko was the base of João Gonçalves Baeta, a trader from Bahia, between 1840 and 1850.

In the 1850s, several important developments affected the illegal slave trade and the Brazilian community in the Bight of Benin. First, due to the increasingly aggressive anti-slave trade measures of the British, the trade in the Volta region and at Lagos ended and many of the slave traders located to the ports on the central Slave Coast. In the Volta region, the British took over the fort at Keta from the Danes in 1850. By the following year, Baeta had left Atoko for Elmina Chica, some miles to the east of Keta. By 1856, he had relocated to Agoué (Strickrodt 2004: 59). Mora had left Woe for Ouidah already in 1845, following a dispute with the Danish (Jones/Sebald 2005: 49-50, no. 1.47). Lagos dropped out of the slave trade after the bombardment of the town by the British in December 1851 and the installation of a British consulate (Law 2001a: 30).

Second, in 1850 the Brazilian slave market closed due to effective legislation ending the illegal importation of slaves. This materially affected the traders on the coast. Some of them turned to legitimate trade, such as Francisco dos Santos at Ouidah. Others left the coast and returned to Brazil. An example is João Gonçalves Baeta, who became an agent for dos Santos in Bahia, where he took care not only of the latter's business but also of his elderly mother (Verger 1952: 53-100). Nevertheless, the illegal slave trade in the Bight of Benin continued for another decade or so, due to the revival of the Cuban trade in the 1850s. This trade was differently organized. It was controlled by firms in the US that used American vessels. It also used new agents, mainly Portuguese, who arrived in the Bight of Benin in the 1850s where they replaced the old ones. Sometimes even in a literal sense: Francisco José Medeiros (d. 1875), a Portuguese from Madeira who established himself at Agoué in the 1850s, is remembered to have occupied Baeta's house. De Medeiros worked in association with João Soares Pereira, a Portuguese. One of the old traders who managed to enter this new trade was Samuel Costa Soares (d. 1894), Portuguese by origin and a natural citizen of the United States who was based at Ouidah (Law 2001a: 30-31, Strickrodt 2004: 224). Another old-established trader working in the Cuban trade, if perhaps only in a subordinate role, was Francisco Olympio da Silva (d. 1907), a Brazilian who had formerly worked for Baeta in the Volta region. In the early 1860s he was established at Porto Seguro, a small port to the west of Little Popo which in the period was used as an embarkation point for shipments of slaves (Borghero 1997: 124-125; Strickrodt 2004: 222).

Although comparatively small in numbers, the Brazilian, Portuguese, and Spanish traders played an important role in the creation of a Brazilian diaspora in the Bight of Benin. They were an important factor in the economic, political and social life of the region, establishing extensive trade networks along the coast as well as across the Atlantic Ocean. The most successful and prosperous of them had large entourages of followers who became part of the Brazilian community. They founded large families, marrying polygamously and fathering large numbers of children with African women. Francisco Felix de Souza had 63 children baptized and Joaquim d'Almeida 82 (Souza 1992: 109; Verger 1992: 47). They also had many slaves who often assumed their master's name and – if offered the chance – embraced their master's lifestyle. A well-documented example is Geraldo da Lima (d. 1904), who was a domestic slave of Cesar Cerqueira da Lima (d. 1862), a Brazilian trader in the Volta region. Following his master's death, Geraldo assumed his name, inherited the part of his fortune that was left in Africa, including his wife, and continued the business very successfully (Amenumey 1968; Claridge 1915: i, 548; Greene 1996: 127-134). Some of these slaves had been brought from Brazil, such as José Paraiso who was Domingos Martins' barber, but most were Africans who had never left Africa (Law 2004b: 355; Turner 1975: 120-123). Furthermore, the slave traders attracted free

African dependents and clients who also became assimilated into the Brazilian community. For example, Pedro Felix d'Almeida of Little Popo was brought up in the de Souza's household, where he learnt to speak and write Portuguese. He eventually returned to Little Popo, where the family home remained, and prospered in trade. According to family tradition, he sent two of his sons to Portugal to be educated there (Law 2004c: 185; Souza 1992: 72; Turner 1975: 108-111). Another case is that of Pedro Kodjo alias Pedro Pinto da Silveira, who was a descendent of one of the ruling families of Little Popo and Agoué. According to family and Ouidah traditions, he entered the service of Francisco Felix de Souza and trained as a cooper. He returned to Agoué, where he unsuccessfully competed for the chieftaincy and started a civil war in the 1860s, and finally settled at Little Popo. One of his sons, Domingo Francisco da Silveira, worked for José Francisco dos Santos at Ouidah (Strickrodt 2003: 223-234; Turner 1975: 111-112).

## 4. The return of the ex-slaves

Some few ex-slaves from Brazil had arrived already in the late eighteenth and early nineteenth centuries (Law/Mann 1999: 318-319). However, a large-scale immigration of emancipated slaves from Brazil occurred only after the slave insurrection in Bahia in 1835, which became known as the "Male" revolt. There had been a number of slave revolts in Bahia between 1807 and 1835, reflecting the growing discontent among slaves suffering from increasingly harsh working conditions during the sugar boom. In the Male revolt, both slaves and freed slaves had been involved. Following its suppression, harsh punishments were meted out to those who had participated or were thought to have participated in the revolt. There was a backlash particularly against the ex-slaves living in Bahia, who were increasingly regarded as a security risk by the authorities. Some of them were deported to West Africa, while those remaining found themselves targeted by a number of repressive measures, including the imposition of a head tax, curfews and prohibition of land purchases. Freed slaves had always been discriminated against, but this backlash prompted many to re-immigrate to West Africa.

This voluntary return movement (as distinguished from the deportations) of Brazilian ex-slaves lasted until the early decades of the twentieth century, although most of it occurred in the nineteenth century. The precise volume of this movement is not known, due to the lack of exact statistical material, and the estimates of scholars vary greatly. Turner assumed the number of returnees to be about 4,000 (1975: 85). According to Manuela Carneiro da Cunha, 3,500 ex-slaves returned to West Africa between 1820 and 1850, and 4, 578 individuals (3,000 Africans and 1,278 Creoles) between 1850 and 1899 (Carneiro da Cunha, Manuela 1985: 213). Turner shows that although most of the freed people in Bahia were Creoles, that is Brazilian-born individuals of African extraction, African-born ex-slaves made up roughly three-fifths of the returnees between 1850 and 1880. This shows that for African-born slaves in Brazil, their allegiance remained with their African home societies and cultures, while for slaves born in Brazil, the return to a country which they knew only from the reports of their parents and fellow slaves was a much more daunting step. In fact, many of the Creoles who left for West Africa were children accompanying their parents. According to Turner, relying on data from passport applications, in the period between 1850 and 1860 the average age of applicants was approximately 35 years. In the later nineteenth century, the average age (computed from passengers' lists and ship's registries) was much higher, close to 55 years. This indicates a difference in the motivation for re-immigration to West Africa: while the younger immigrants in the mid-nineteenth century went to West Africa to start a new life, the elderly returnees in the late nineteenth-century went to there in order to die and to be buried in the land of their ancestors (Turner 1975: 67-69).

In West Africa, some of the ex-slaves returned to their homelands in the interior. Most, however, remained on the coast where they tended to concentrate in certain towns, with Agoué, Ouidah, Porto Novo and Lagos becoming major centres of Brazilian settlement. As already noted above, some returnees also landed on the Gold Coast to the west of the River Volta. For example, in 1836 the captain of the Nimrod landed his passengers, more than 160 voluntary returnees, at Elmina and Winnebah, both on the Gold Coast, as well as at Agoué (Verger 1968: 361). Accra also became host to a community of Brazilian ex-slaves, with the first immigrants from Bahia, mainly Muslim deportees, arriving in 1836 (Parker 2000: 14).

There are several reasons for the ex-slaves' settlement on the coast rather than the interior. First, a return to their homelands in the interior would have meant exposing themselves to the risk of being enslaved again (Carneiro da Cunha, Manuela 1985: 107). Secondly, the coastal settlements offered them better opportunities to make a living, given that most of them had formerly lived in urban Salvador as artisans or traders (Turner 1975: 76-77). Thirdly, it could be argued that it was precisely presence of the Brazilian, Portuguese and Spanish slave traders that made the coastal settlements attractive to the ex-slaves, given the cultural affinity between the two groups, most importantly the shared Portuguese language and the Catholic faith, and the patronage and employment offered by the traders.

From our point of view, this affinity between slave traders and former slaves may seem ironic and difficult to understand, just as the fact that many of the returned ex-slaves engaged in the slave trade. However, it was not ironic. As has been pointed out by historians, the ex-slaves were inherently pragmatic and tried to make a living and better their situation under very harsh conditions. For most, the return to Africa meant the arrival in a strange country, where they suffered abuse and extortion from the local African authorities and risked not only their property but often enough their freedom and even their lives (Lindsay 1994: 28-29; Turner 1975: 134; Verger 1968: 613-615). In Brazil, their ethnic identities had been important, although not as important as their religious affiliation. There, they had been Africans, and specifically Yoruba, Hausa, Fon, etc. On the West African coast, they became Brazilians, as their language, religion and culture unified them with the white traders and set them apart from the African population of the countries that they had "returned" to, even if they often retained a sense of their specific African ethnicity.

The fortunes of these people on the West African coast depended on a number of factors. According to Turner, those who arrived earlier in the century tended to prosper while those arriving later in the century were less successful and often had to eke out their living. This can probably be explained partly at least with the fact, referred to above, that the latter were predominantly elderly people who came to Africa to end their life rather than start a new one. Another explanation, however, is the fact that those arriving in the mid-nineteenth century experienced a period when the illegal slave trade was still flourishing and the Brazilian, Portuguese, and Cuban slave traders prospered and had great influence. This was before the take-over of coast's external trade by European firms in the 1860s and 1870s, which ended the Brazilians' ascendance and the Bight of Benin's commercial orientation towards Brazil. Another factor that affected the ex-slaves' careers on the West African coast was the location, as conditions differed significantly in the various coastal settlements.

Ouidah, Dahomey's port, was strictly controlled by African authorities. It is documented to have been the destination of 200 deportees after the Male revolt in 1835 (Reis 1993: 220). In 1845, the British explorer Duncan noted the presence there of "numerous" ex-slaves from Brazil, most of whom had been expelled due to their involvement in the revolt (Duncan 1968: i, 185, 201-202). Francisco Felix de Souza is remembered to have been the patron of the ex-slaves, who settled mainly in the Maro quarter. Even today, there live several families in this quarter who trace their origins to Brazilian ex-slaves (some recognizable by their names, such as Toubiaz and Neves, while others have African names, such as Oloubon, Ougidan and Dangana). Some few ex-slaves also settled in de Souza's quarter as his clients (Law 2001a: 26-27; 2004c: 179-183).

Agoué was a relatively young settlement. It had been founded only in the 1820s and played an important role in the slave trade in the 1840s and 1850s. According to local traditions recorded in the 1930s/1940s, the first ex-slaves arrived there during the reign of chief Toyi (Yaovi Siko), who is said to have ruled from 1835 to 1844 (Pelofy 2002: 6-7). In 1863, the Catholic missionary Francesco Borghero visited the place and reported that there were "some hundred Christians, all returned from Brazil after their liberation" (Borghero 1997: 123). In a striking difference to the Brazilian settlement at Ouidah, the ex-slaves at Agoué founded several quarters where they settled largely according to their ethnicity. Fon, Mahi and Yoruba settled at Fonkome, (Muslim) Yoruba at Diata (or Idi-Ata) and Hausa, Mahi and Yoruba at Hausakome. Apart from these three quarters, there was Zokikome, which belonged to Joaquim d'Almeida, the most prominent and prosperous of Agoué's Brazilians. Then there was Yakome, the quarter of Iya Francesca Mondukpe (d. 1899), a Yoruba slave who became assimilated into the Brazilian community through her successive marriages to two ex-slaves from Brazil, Antonio Pereira Santos and Manuel dos Reis (Guran 2000: 56-57; Pierucci 1953: 24; Westermann 1935: 230-231). These quarters were known collectively to contemporary European observers as "Portuguese town", which was distinguished from the "English town" settled by returnees from Sierra Leone (Strickrodt 2004: 225-229).

Porto Novo, to the east of Ouidah on the Ouémé River, also became a centre of Brazilian settlement, but it is not so well researched as Ouidah, Agoué, or Lagos. It appears that the settlement occurred there only later. By 1884, there were about one hundred repatriates there, mostly Brazilians but including some Sierra Leoneans (Law 2004a: 55). According to Turner, life in the Porto Novo kingdom was more difficult for the Brazilians than in Agoué or Ouidah because they were barred from engaging in agriculture and were thus restricted to commercial pursuits. As few of the ex-slaves were able to compete with the European commercial firms that had established themselves on the coast by the 1880s, many ex-slaves occupied the roles of artisans or mechanics (Turner 1975: 137-139).

Lagos boasted the largest Brazilian community in the Bight of Benin. According to the British governor, in 1889 there were about 5,000 returnees from Brazil and Cuba (Lindsay 1994: 27, citing Moloney 1889: 268-269). They settled mainly in the Brazil quarter (just as at Accra). The situation for the Brazilian ex-slaves at Lagos differed from that at Ouidah and Agoué due to the British influence at the former place after 1851. On the one hand, life was easier for the returnees in the British protectorate as they were not so prone to extortion and abuse. This probably explains why there were such a large number of immigrants there. On the other hand, there was great competition from Sierra Leonean immigrants, that is former slaves who had been captured by the British navy's anti-slave trade squadron on slave vessels, had been taken to Sierra Leone and liberated there. The majority of these slaves were Yoruba, who from the mid-nineteenth century returned to Yoruba land, many of them settling in Lagos. Being Anglophone, Protestant and trained in the British system, they fitted in better with life under British. This situation put the Brazilians at Lagos under great pressure to assimilate, as is indicated, among others, by the fact that many anglicised their names (as did the Brazilian immigrants at Accra who also lived under British rule) (Carneiro da Cunha, Manuela 1985: 101-151; Lindsay 1994; Soumonni 2003; 2005; Turner 1975: 140-151; Verger 1968: 612-632).

## 5. The impact of the Brazilians on West African coastal society

The Brazilians became a major factor in the economic, political and cultural life of West African coastal society in the period before the European colonial take-over. Their influence on the regions' economic life is obvious. Until the end of the illegal slave trade in the Bight of Benin in the mid-1860s, they dominated the region's export trade. They were able to do this due to their extensive trade networks across the Atlantic. These, of course, were the white slave traders, although there was one major exception: Joaquim d'Almeida at Agoué, a former slave who became a shipper of slaves. Indeed, a British naval officer who visited the Bight of Benin in 1850 referred to Agoué as "a slave-port, almost a monopoly of José [sic] d'Almeida" (Forbes 1966: i, 102). However, the returned ex-slaves also became a major influence in the regions' economic life. At Agoué, Borghero noted in 1863 that they "tend to become masters of the trade" (1997: 124). By this he presumably referred to the trade in agricultural produce, although many of the ex-slaves also dabbled in the slave trade, if only in small-scale, buying and re-selling slaves as opportunity offered (Pierucci 1953: 16). As regards the produce trade, this involved palm oil for export as well as provisions. Both were produced on farms by means of slaves. According to Turner, land and the plantation economy that was associated with it became the basis for status identification within the Brazilian community (Turner 1975: 138). The most prosperous of the returnees owned a large number of slaves. For example, the will of Antonio d'Almeida (d. 1890), a Yoruba ex-slave who in Brazil had belonged to the same master as Joaquim d'Almeida, shows that his farm (roça) at Agoué that was worked by eighteen male slaves and six female slaves (Verger 1992: 123; cf. Strickrodt 2004: 226-227). Iya Francesca Mondukpe, already referred to above, is remembered in local traditions to have grown rich and influential in Agouè society from selling the produce of her plantations that were worked by many slaves (Westermann 1935: 230-231). However, as noted before, not all of the ex-slaves prospered on the West African

coast. The Brazilian community was socially and economically strati-
fied. Ownership of land and agricultural pursuits were important particularly for the Brazilians at Agoué and Ouidah, while those at Porto
Novo and Lagos often found themselves restricted to (petty) trade and
the crafts. The Brazilians played an important role in the introduction
of a range of crafts to the West African coast because many the returned ex-slaves were trained or semi-trained artisans. Among the
men, there were stone masons, master builders, carpenters, cabinet-
makers, tailors, gold smiths and barber-surgeons, while the women
were renowned needle workers and cooks ("quituteiras") (Carneiro da
Cunha, Manuela 1985: 136).

Due to their control of the trade, their wealth and, resulting from
this, their ability to attract followers, the Brazilians also became a
major factor in the political life in the Bight of Benin, particularly in
Dahomey and Genyi. Again, this is most obvious in the case of the
slave traders, particularly the most prominent ones, Francisco Felix de
Souza and Domingos Martins, who are also best documented. In de
Souza's case, several instances are documented where he actively
interfered in local political conflicts and were his support is remembered to have secured victory for his allies. Firstly, in 1818, he supported Gezo in the coup d'état by which the Dahomean ruler, Adandozan, was deposed (Law 2004c: 165-166). Secondly, in 1823, he
supported the African trader George Lawson alias Akuété Zankli in a
civil war at Little Popo, which resulted in the defeat and expulsion of
Lawson's adversary from the town (Strickrodt 2004: 188-200). Domingos Martins, too, is recorded to have attempted to influence local
politics. In 1846 or 1847, he sent an army of followers to Lagos in
support of the deposed ruler Akitoye, but this effort failed. Both de
Souza and Martins played an important part in the formulation of Dahomey's relations towards Europeans, due to their role as the king's
advisers on trade, which was the basis of Dahomey's relations with
the Europeans (Ross 1965: 80). The slave traders sometimes strength-
ened their relations to local political authorities by marriage. For example, one of de Souza's wives, the mother of his eldest son Isidoro,
was the daughter of a chief at Little Popo. In Dahomey, some of the
wealthy traders, such as de Souza, Domingos Martins and Francisco
dos Santos, were officially made "caboceers", i.e. chiefs, and their
political role thus became formalized. However, even where the Bra-

zilians did not gain official positions in the local political hierarchy, they became an important political factor in the coastal towns – although of course this differed according to the local political conditions at the respective settlements. At Agoué, a relative young and small settlement whose economy depended on the slave trade, the Brazilians had much clout, while at Lagos, under British rule, they had very little influence.

The cultural impact of the Brazilians on West Africa coastal life has been widely discussed in the literature. Three aspects are particularly interesting: the introduction of Christianity and Islam to the coastal settlements, the establishment of schools and the Brazilian influence on architecture. The Brazilians pioneered the introduction of Roman Catholicism and of Islam to the coastal settlements. Many returned ex-slaves were Roman Catholics, having been baptized in Brazil. They brought their religion with them and established the first chapels, prior to the arrival of Catholic missions from Europe. According to local interpretations, the first Catholic chapel at Agoué was established in 1835 by a female ex-slave from Brazil (Bouche 1885: 266). In 1845, another chapel was opened there by Joaquim d'Almeida, for the use of his family. Francesco Borghero, a missionary of the French Société des Missions Africaines that had arrived at Ouidah in 1861, was impressed by it. According to him, the chapel "was lavishly decorated for this country, nothing was missing". D'Almeida "had brought or made come from Brazil all that is necessary for establishing a church, even the bells" (Borghero 1997: 123, 251). D'Almeida had reportedly planned to establish a larger chapel for public use, but he died before being able to do so. At Lagos, too, a Roman Catholic chapel was established by a Brazilian returnee before the arrival of the first ordained Catholic missionary in 1863 (Carneiro da Cunha, Manuela 1985: 162-170; Turner 1975: 169-174).

However, the French missionaries were generally critical of the Brazilians' practice of Christianity. Borghero was

> very pained to see that these black and white Portuguese who call themselves Christians live exactly like the pagans for the most part. The whites from Portugal just as all the other Europeans are polygamous, their descendants, who have become almost black, have as their religion a monstrous blend of paganism, Christian practices and fetishist superstitions (Borghero 1997: 46 [my translation]; Law 2004b: 358).

The Brazilians had a syncretistic understanding of religion, mixing Christianity with elements of their African ancestral religions, as they had done in Brazil. There were typical Brazilian, and specifically Bahian, traits in their Catholic worship. Furthermore, they adapted to local African practices, as shown by the fact that Francisco Felix de Souza and Joaquim d'Almeida were buried in their houses rather than the Christian graveyard, following local African custom rather than Christian rites (Verger 1992: 45-46, 48).

The Brazilians also played a pioneering role in introducing Islam to some of the settlements, such as Accra, Agoué, and Ouidah (Law 2004b: 359-360). There were many Muslims among the returned ex-slaves, who after the Male rebellion in Bahia were perceived to be a particular threat and therefore more liable to deportation. At Accra, the arrival of Brazilian ex-slaves, mainly deportees, in 1836 represented the first influx of Muslims. According to Parker, they settled in the Brazil quarter and integrated into Ga society while retaining a distinct identity due to their adherence to Islam. By contrast, Hausa traders and other Muslim groups which subsequently joined them from the interior settled in a different quarter, Zongo, and remained aloof from local Ga society (Parker 2000: 83, 164-165). Likewise, local tradition at Ouidah recalls that some Brazilian ex-slaves who settled in the Maro quarter introduced Islam. Muslims from the north arrived only later, during the period of French colonial rule (Law 2004b: 359; 2004c: 182). At Agoué, Zöller noted the large number of Muslims in 1884. By the early twentieth century, there were mosques in two of the quarters settled by Brazilians, Idi-Ata, settled mainly by Yoruba, and Hausakome. The "great mosque", in Idi-Ata, was built in 1905, "a beautiful building of 8 x 10 metres [...], surrounded by a beautiful covered veranda, and all in bricks; a roof of corrugated iron covers the whole ensemble, which looks very nice" (Marty 1926: 119; Pierucci 1953: 11-12; Strickrodt 2004: 227). At other places, however, such as Porto Novo and Lagos, Islam already existed before the arrival of the Afro-Brazilians, having been introduced directly from the interior. Nevertheless, Brazilian Muslims were prominent in these communities, too, particularly the family of José Paraiso in Porto-Novo (Law 2004b: 359-360; Turner 1975: 120-123).

As Catholicism became an important badge of Brazilian identity, Muslims sometimes had their children baptized. This is illustrated by the information given in the baptismal registers of the Catholic Missions at Agoué. They list 60 ex-slaves from Brazil (heads of families) who had settled at Agoué, of whom 8-10 individuals were Muslims who nevertheless had been baptized. It was nothing unusual to have Catholics, Protestants and Muslims all in one family. Manoel Geraldo's family was reported to comprise "Muslims and some rare Christians", while João do Rego, a Hausa, left "a large family of Muslims, Catholics, and Protestants". This attests to the spirit of religious tolerance that existed in the Brazilian community on the West African coast.

The Brazilians also established schools for the instruction of their children as they valued education highly. Of particular importance for them was the teaching of the Portuguese language, not only because it was their own language but also because it was the *lingua franca* in the Bight of Benin und therefore fundamental for a successful commercial career. At Agoué, a school, attended by 30 children, is documented in 1863 (Borghero 1997: 276). It was funded by Francisco José de Medeiros, a locally based slave trader from Madeira, and was staffed by a schoolmaster from Brazil, Micer Gonsallos, "a black Brazilian priest [...] who occupied himself mainly with the catechism and the Portuguese school". He died about 1870, "leprous and venerated by all" (Pelofy 2002: 7, 22). Borghero was unimpressed by school, complaining, "alas, the children... did not know one prayer or one article of the catechism" (Borghero 1997: 276). This indicates that education at the school was secular rather than religious.

Another aspect of coastal cultural life that was influenced by the Brazilians – and which has been discussed extensively in the literature – is architectural style (Carneiro da Cunha, Marianno 1985; Law 2004b: 187-188; Soumonni 2003: 186-187). Many of the principal buildings in the coastal communities, such as trader's houses, chapels and mosques, were built in the Brazilian, and particularly Bahian, style. Characteristically, the houses (called "sobrados") had two stores, a portal, shutters and ornaments. The knowledge and skill for this had been brought to West Africa by ex-slaves from Brazil who had been trained as carpenters and masons. Some of the prominent Brazilian traders on the coast also sent African slaves to be trained as artisans to Brazil. The Brazilian-style houses were noted by contemporary visitors. For example, in 1850, João Gonçalves Baêta's house at Atoko was reported to stand in "strange contrast" to the "beehive huts" of his neighbours, as it consisted of two stores with five upper rooms, was made of clay and surrounded by a clay wall that enclosed a front and a back yard. Even more impressive was Isidoro Felix de Souza's house at Little Popo in the 1840s. According to a British visitor, it contained

> a large hall, or principal apartment, beautifully arranged in the Spanish *[sic]* style, and richly furnished with European materials. Round this apartment were arranged prints, in rich gold frames, of Napoleon in his principal battles, as well as his disinterment at St. Helena, and second funeral in France ... (Duncan 1968: i, 102).

However, this house was destroyed in an accidental fire in 1849 and not rebuilt as Isidoro left Little Popo for Ouidah to succeed his late father as "Chacha" (Jones/Sebald 2005: 119-120, no 1.225).

The construction of Roman Catholic churches and mosques by Brazilians is not surprising, given their pioneering role in the establishment of these religions in the region. For example, two Brazilian master builders, Lázaro Borges da Silva and Francisco Nobre, built the Cathedral at Lagos, the Holy Cross Church, inaugurated in 1881. Parts of its interior were fitted out by another Brazilian, Baltazar dos Reis, a famous carpenter who won a bronze medal at the Colonial Exposition of 1886 for an inlayed table (Carneiro da Cunha, Manuela 1985: 136, 156-158). The first Catholic church in Lomé was also built by a returnee from Brazil, Jacintho da Silva (Amos 2000: 183-184). A prominent example for a mosque in the Brazilian style is the central mosque at Porto Novo, which was constructed in the twentieth century. It was the source of conflict between the Brazilian and the indigenous Yoruba members of the Muslim community. The Brazilian Muslims managed to assert themselves, with the result that the mosque resembles the Brazilian model of the Roman Catholic Church that inspired it (Soumonni 2003: 187, 191 fig. 9.4).

The Brazilian architectural style still characterizes many buildings at Agoué, Ouidah, Porto Novo and Lagos these days. However, as has been noted elsewhere, it is uncertain whether any of these buildings date from the nineteenth century; most seem to have been built only later (Law 2004b: 187-188; Law/Mann 1999: 325).

## 6. Epilogue: the Brazilians in West Africa after the ending of the illegal slave trade

The illegal slave trade in the Bight of Benin ended in the 1860s, the last successful shipment of slaves being made in 1863 from Godomey. With the ending of the slave trade, some of the traders disappeared from the coast, while others switched to the palm oil trade. This in itself was not a major change, as the two trades had been carried on simultaneously by a number of traders for some time. However, the end of the transatlantic slave trade entailed a weakening of the ties with Brazil, as the main market for palm oil was industrial Europe. Moreover, the increasing dominance of European firms on the West African coast the 1860s and 1870s spelled the end for the Brazilian's ascendance and their economic independence (Law 2001: 31-32). Many of the children of Brazilians became agents of European commercial firms. The son of José dos Santos became an agent to the British firm of Swanzy, as did three of the sons Francisco of Olympio da Silva (who after the end of the slave trade shortened his name to "Olympio", deleting the "da Silva"). Another of the latter's sons worked for Miller Brothers. In the 1880s, a son of Francisco de Medeiros, Julio de Medeiros, served as agent to the firm of Goedelt, while Chico d'Almeida, of the D'Almeida family at Little Popo, worked for the German firm Hansa Faktorei (Amos 2000: 182; Law 2001a: 31-32; Zöller 1885: I, 169). Law has summarized this development succinctly, noting that the Brazilians

> were drawing upon their existing social capital, making their linguistic and commercial skills and their local contacts available to serve the interests of others, rather than being able any longer to sustain independent accumulation (Law 2001a: 31-32).

Following the establishment of colonial rule on the West African coast in the 1880s, the Brazilians maintained this position of middlemen between the Africans and the Europeans. Being pragmatists and well educated, they prospered under colonial rule. Many entered colonial service, others worked in the commercial sector or as artisans. Those who could afford it sent their children to Europe to study law or medicine. The colonial period was more difficult for them culturally, as the colonial powers did not tolerate the continuing Luso-Brazilian influence in their territories. For example, in 1882 the British at Lagos prohibited the use of any language other than English for instruction in schools, a measure aimed mainly at the suppression of Portuguese (da Cunha Carneiro, Manuela 1985: 174). However, in spite of this – and perhaps because of this – it was in this period that a collective Brazilian identity developed, helped by the widespread practice of intermarriage and the foundation of cultural associations aimed at preserving the Brazilian heritage. Antonio Olinto, who stayed in Lagos a few years after the end of colonialism, has given a fascinating description of this community at a time when the last surviving returnees with first-hand experience of Brazil, by then septuagenarians and octogenarians, were slowly dying off, and with them the knowledge of the Portuguese language. For some of them, the memory of Brazil had become tinged with a yearning for the return to the country of their childhood – just as their parents, who in the nineteenth century had made the passage from Africa to Brazil as slaves, had yearned for a return to their homelands (Olinto 1964: 161-256).

## Bibliography

### Archival Sources

Pierucci, Jean ['Histoire d'Agoué'] (ms, 1953, 48 pp.). In: *Archives Mgr Robert Codjo Sastre*. Lokossa, Benin.

### Government Documents

House of Commons Sessional Papers (1831-1839), Class A. Correspondence with British Commissioners [...] relating to the Slave Trade.

Parliamentary Papers ([1171] 1850 XXXVIII), Papers Respecting the Cession to Great Britain of the Danish Possessions on the Coast of Africa, 5: Journal of Governor Winniett, 10 March 1850.

### Books, Articles and Dissertations

Akibode, Imbert O. (1988-1989): "Contribution à l'étude de l'histoire de l'ancien royaume Agoué (1821-1885)". Unpubl. mémoire de maîtrise. Bénin: FLASH, Université Nationale du Bénin.

Amenumey, D. E. K. (1968): "Geraldo ad Lima: A Reappraisal". In: *Transactions of the Historical Society of Ghana*, 9, pp. 65-78.

Amos, Alcione M. (2000): "Afro-Brasileiros no Togo: A história da família Olympio, 1882-1945". In: *Afro-Ásia*, 23, pp. 175-197.

Amos, Alcione M./Ayesu, Ebenezer (2002): "'I am Brazilian': History of the Tabon, Afro-Brazilians in Accra, Ghana". In: *Transactions of the Historical Society of Ghana*, 6 (new series), pp. 35-58.

Bethell, Leslie (1970): *The Abolition of the Brazilian Slave Trade; Britain, Brazil and the Slave Trade Question 1807-1869*. Cambridge: Cambridge University Press.

Borghero, Francesco (1997): *Journal de Francesco Borghero, premier missionaire du Dahomey 1861-1865*. Mandirola, Renzo/Morel, Yves (eds.). Paris: Karthala.

Bouche, Pierre (1885): *Sept ans en Afrique Occidentale: la Côte des Esclaves et le Dahomey*. Paris: Plon.

Carneiro da Cunha, Manuela (1985): *Negros, estrangeiros; os escravos libertos e sua volta à África*. São Paulo: Editora Brasiliense.

Carneiro da Cunha, Marianno (1985): *Da Senzala ao Sobrado; Arquitectura Brasileira na Nigéria e na República Popular do Benim/From Slave Quarters to Town Houses: Brazilian Architecture in Nigeria and the People's Republic of Bénin*. São Paulo: Nobel Edusp.

Carstensen, Edward (1965): *Governor Carstensen's Diary 1842-1850*. Legon: University of Ghana, Institute of African Studies.

Chatwin, Bruce ([1980] 1982): *The Viceroy of Whydah*. London: Pan Books.

Claridge, W. Walton (1915): *A History of the Gold Coast and Ashanti*. London: John Murray.

Duncan, John ([1847] 1968): *Travels in Western Africa in 1845 and 1846*, 2 vols. London: Frank Cass.

Eltis, David (1987): *Economic Growth and the Ending of the Transatlantic Slave Trade*. New York/Oxford: Oxford University Press.

Eltis, David/Richardson, David (1997): "West Africa and the Transatlantic Slave Trade: New Evidence of Long-run trends". In: *Slavery & Abolition*, 18, 1, pp. 16-35.

Forbes, Frederick E. ([1851] 1966): *Dahomey and the Dahomans*, 2 vols. London: Frank Cass.

Greene, Sandra (1996): *Gender, Ethnicity and Social Change on the Upper Slave Coast. A History of the Anlo-Ewe*. Portsmouth, N.H.: Heineman/London: James Currey.

Guran, Milton (2000): *Agudás: os "brasileiros" do Benim*. Rio de Janeiro: Nova Fronteira.

Hargreaves, John D. (1963): *Prelude to the Partition of West Africa*. London: Macmillan.

Jones, Adam/Sebald, Peter (eds.) (2005): *An African Family Archive: The Lawsons of Little Popo/Aneho (Togo) 1841-1938*. Oxford: Oxford University Press.

Kopytoff, Jean Herskovits (1965): *A Preface to Modern Nigeria: The "Sierra Leoneans" in Yoruba, 1830-1890*. Madison/Milwaukee/London: The University of Wisconsin Press.

Laotan, Anthony B. (1943): *The Torch-Bearers or Old Brazilian Colony in Lagos*. Lagos: The Ife-Loju Printing Works.

Law, Robin (1994): "The White Slaver and the African Prince: European and American Depictions of Pre-Colonial Dahomey". In: Gray, Martin/Law, Robin (eds.): *Images of Africa: The Depiction of Pre-Colonial Africa in Creative Literature*. Stirling: Centre of Commonwealth Studies/University of Stirling, pp. 22-41.

— (2001a): "The Evolution of the Brazilian Community in Ouidah". In: *Slavery & Abolition*, 22, 1. Special Issue: Mann, Kristin/Bay, Edna G. (eds.): *Rethinking the African Diaspora: The Making of a Black Atlantic World in the Bight of Benin and Brazil*, pp. 22-41.

— (2001b): "A carreira de Francisco Félix de Souza na África Ocidental". In: *Topoï: Revista de História*, 2, pp. 9-39.

— (2004a): "Francisco Felix de Souza in West Africa, 1820-1849". In: Curto, José C./Lovejoy, Paul E. (eds): *Enslaving Connections: Changing Cultures of Africa and Brazil during the Era Of Slavery*. Amherst: Humanity Books, pp. 187-211.

— (2004b): "Yoruba Liberated Slaves Who Returned to West Africa". In: Falola, Toyin/Childs, Matt D. (eds.): *The Yoruba Diaspora in the Atlantic World*. Bloomington/Indianapolis: Indiana UP, pp. 349-365.

— 2004c): *Ouidah: The Social History of a West African Slaving 'Port'*. Athens: Ohio UP/Oxford: James Currey.

Law, Robin/Mann, Kristin (1999): "West Africa in the Atlantic Community: The Case of the Slave Coast". In: *William and Mary Ouarterly*, 56, pp. 307-334.

Lindsay, Lisa A. (1994): "'To Return to the Bosom of their Fatherland': Brazilian Immigrants in Nineteenth-Century Lagos". In: *Slavery & Abolition*, 15, 1, pp. 22-50.

Lovejoy, Paul E. (1994): "Background to Rebellion: The Origins of Muslim Slaves in Bahia". In: *Slavery & Abolition*, 15, 2, pp. 151-180.

Marty, Paul (1926): *Etudes sur l'Islam au Dahomey: Le Bas Dahomey – Le Haut Dahomey*. Paris: Éditions Ernest Leroux.

Matory, Lorand J. (1999): "The English Professors of Brazil: On the Diasporic Roots of the Yorùbá Nation". In: *Comparative Studies in Society and History*, pp. 72-103.

Moloney, Alfred (1889): "Cotton Interests, Foreign and Native, in Yoruba, and Generally in West Africa". In: *Journal of the Manchester Geographical Society*, 5, pp. 255-276.

Newbury. C. W. (1961): *The Western Slave Coast and Its Rulers*. Oxford: At the Clarendon Press.

Olinto, Antonio (1964): *Brasileiros na África*. Rio de Janeiro: Edições GRD.

Parker, John (2000): *Making the Town: Ga State and Society in Early Colonial Accra*. Portsmouth, N.H.: Heinemann/Oxford: James Currey/Cape Town: David Philip.

Pelofy, Isidore (2002): *Histoire d'Agoué (République du Bénin)*. Ed. Byll-Cataria, Régina. Leipzig: University of Leipzig Papers on Africa [ULPA], History and Culture Series no. 8.

Prado, J. F. (Yan) de Almeida (1956): "Bahia e as suas relações com o Daomé". In: *O Brasil e o colonialismo europeu*. São Paulo: Companhia Editora Nacional.

Reis, João José (1993): *Slave Rebellion in Brazil: The Muslim Uprising of 1835 in Bahia*. Baltimore/London: The Johns Hopkins University Press.

Ross, David A. (1965): "The Career of Domingo Martinez in the Bight of Benin, 1833-1864". In: *Journal of African History*, 4, 1, pp. 79-90.

— (1969): "The First Chacha of Whydah: Francisco Felix de Souza". In: *Odu*, 2 (3rd series), pp. 19-28.

Silva, Alberto ad Costa e (2003): *Um rio chamado Atlântico: a África no Brasil e o Brasil na África*. Rio de Janeiro: Nova Fronteira: Ed. UFRJ.

— (2004): *Francisco Felix de Souza, mercador de Escravos*. Rio de Janeiro: Editora Nova Fronteira & EdUERJ.

Soumonni, Elisée (2001): "Some Reflections on the Brazilian Legacy in Dahomey". In: *Slavery & Abolition*, 22, 1. Special Issue: Mann, Kristin/Bay, Edna G. (eds.): *Rethinking the African Diaspora: The Making of a Black Atlantic World in the Bight of Benin and Brazil*, pp. 61-71.

— (2003): "Afro-Brazilian Communities of the Bight of Benin in the Nineteenth Century". In: Lovejoy, Paul E./Trotman, David V. (eds): *Trans-Atlantic Dimensions of Ethnicity in the African Diaspora*. London/New York: Continuum, pp. 181-194.

— (2005): "The Afro-Brazilian Communities of Ouidah and Lagos in the Nineteenth Century: A Comparative Analysis". In: Curto, José C./Soloudre-La France, Renée (eds.): *Africa and the Americas: Interconnections during the Slave Trade*. Trenton, N.J./Asmara, Eritrea: Africa World Press, pp. 231-242.

Souza, Simone de (1992): *La Famille de Souza du Bénin-Togo*. Cotonou: Les Éditions du Bénin.

Spiess, C. (1907): "Ein Erinnerungsblatt an die Tage des Sklavenhandels in West afrika". In: *Globus: Illustrierte Zeitschrift für Länder- und Völkerkunde*, 92, 13, pp. 205-208.

Strickrodt, Silke (2003): "Afro-European Trade Relations on the Western Slave Coast, 16th to 19th Centuries". Unpubl. PhD thesis. Stirling: University of Stirling.

— (2004): "'Afro-Brazilians' of the Western Slave Coast in the Nineteenth Century". In: Curto, José C./Lovejoy, Paul E. (eds.): *Enslaving Connections: Changing Cultures of Africa and Brazil during the Era of Slavery*. Amherst: Humanity Books, pp. 213-244.

Turner, Jerry Michael (1975): "Les Brésiliens – The Impact of Former Brazilian Slaves upon Dahomey". Unpubl. PhD thesis. Boston: Boston University.

— (1995): "Identidade étnica na África-Ocidental: o caso especial dos afro-brasileiros no Benin, na Nigeria, no Togo e em Gana nos séculos XIX e XX". In: *Estudos Afro-Asiáticos*, 28 (October), pp. 85-99.

Turner, Lorenzo D. (1942): "Some Contacts of Brazilian Ex-Slaves with Nigeria, West Africa". In: *Journal of Negro History*, 27, pp. 55-67.

Verger, Pierre (1952): *Les afro-américains*. Dakar: IFAN, pp. 53-100.

— (1964): *Bahia and the West African Trade, 1549-1851*. Bembo, Nigeria: Ibadan University Press for The Institute of African Studies.

— (1966): "Retour des 'Brésiliens' au Golfe du Bénin au XIXème Siècle". In: *Études Dahomeennes* (Octobre), pp. 5-28.

— (1968): *Flux et reflux de la traite des nègres entre le golfs de Bénin et Bahia de Todos os Santos du XVIIe au XIX siècle*. Paris: Mouton.

— (1992): *Os Libertos: Sete caminhos na liberdade de escravos da Bahia no século XIX*. São Paulo: Corrupcio.

Videgla, Michel (1999): "Le royaume de Porto-Novo face à la politique abolitionniste des nations européennes de 1848 à 1882". In: Law, Robin/Strickrodt, Silke (eds.): *Ports of the Slave Trade (Bights of Benin and Biafra)*. Stirling: Centre of Commonwealth Studies, University of Stirling, pp. 135-152.

Westermann, Diedrich (1935): *Die Glidyi-Ewe in Togo: Züge aus ihrem Gesellschaftsleben*, supplement to *Mitteilungen des Seminars für orientalische Sprachen 38*. Berlin: Universität Berlin.

Yai, Olabiyi Babalola (2001): "The Identity, Contributions, and Ideology of the Aguda (Afro-Brazilians) of the Gulf of Benin: A Reinterpretation". In: *Slavery & Abolition*, 22, 1. Special Issue: Mann, Kristin/Bay, Edna G. (eds.): *Rethinking the African Diaspora: The Making of a Black Atlantic World in the Bight of Benin and Brazil*, pp. 72-82.

Zöller, Hugo (1885): *Das Togoland und die Sklavenküste*, vol. 1 of his *Die deutschen Besitzungen an der westafrikanischen Küste* (4 vols.). Berlin/Stuttgart: W. Spemann.

— (1930): *Als Jurnalist* [sic] *und Forscher in Deutschlands großer Kolonialzeit*. Leipzig: Koehler & Amelang.

# Christine Meisner

# Recovery of an Image: A Video Tale

This narration is the transcription of the video *Recovery of an Image*, a twenty-six minute film about the life of João Esan da Rocha, who was captured in 1840. He was brought from Nigeria to Brazil as a ten-year-old child and returned as a "free" man to Lagos after thirty-one years of domestic slavery on a sugar plantation in Bahia. Research for the video led to the descendants of Esan — his Yoruba name – in Lagos and Salvador. After talking to them it was possible to trace the different stages of his journey and mind by imagining the shifts in his remembrance and identity. But in the end this story became a fiction – a reinvention of his life, just as memory is always a new tale.

The video is part of Meisner's long-term art project about the transatlantic slave trade calles *what became*. It was combined with a series of drawings entitled *Quilombolisation* in Brazil and with a compilation of notes and sketches. The video, notes and drawings were first exhibited at the *fim de romance* display in the Musée des Beaux-Arts de Nantes, the Pinacoteca São Paulo, and the Museu de Arte Moderna in Recife in 2005 and, more recently in 2007, in the *Uncomfortable Truths* exhibition at the Victoria and Albert Museum London.

The video's narrator is Michael Ojake, born in Lagos. He studied in the United States and lives in Berlin as a professional actor or voice artist. Ojake speaks Lagos English, and the text reproduced below is precisely copied from his narration.

When Amaize was talking about the original of this house, which supposedly stands in Salvador de Bahia, I tried to remember the story of Kakawa Street, or rather, my mind was haunted by the remembrance of another person that did not really belong to me. That all this would become a part of my history at first seemed strange to me. Then I began to believe what I invented, and for a time, I took on the memory of another...

For seven days and seven nights, I rode on a donkey from Ilesha to Lagos. My parents wanted to send me to a school there run by missionaries. I was ten years old. At night, I was stolen out of my uncle's house by the Ijebus. How they got in, I don't know. They took me far away from the city to a village on the lagoon. I was put in hand and foot cuffs, which they had in all sizes. There were already many men, women and children there when we arrived. We traveled by canoe to

**The *Campos* or the square in Lagos**
**where the Brazilians used to celebrate their festivals**

Photo: Christine Meisner.

an island that we all had to cross together. Two large ships were just off shore. We were taken on board, and the men in chains were fastened together. There were several hundred people. The ship then left the coast, and the women were forced to dance naked as the sailors watched. I witnessed one sailor take a small girl and disappear with her, but no one else noticed. The others were concentrated on the women. Then the men and children had to go below deck and we were chained to metal frames. On deck, the women were screaming. Suddenly, it was silent and the women returned to the hold. They said a girl was dead and was thrown overboard, and the sailor was whipped by the captain. A woman attempted to take her own life and was placed in chains.

When I arrived on board, I couldn't imagine what was supposed to happen and why. They handled us like goods that had to be stuffed into the narrow, airless space inside the ship. They developed an attitude to make themselves immune against their actions by defining us as cargo rather than passengers. There was something clandestine about what they were doing. They took us here all the way from Lagos to do something that was forbidden in the city. I lost my dignity in a secret that everybody knew. The air in the hold was sickening. Short breathes, just enough to survive. I was scared of breathing in too much air while sleeping. Yet sleeping was the only thing that helped me overcome the uncertainty of the next moments. I knew nothing about the next day, not even if I would make it that far without going crazy.

The captain was afraid of patrol ships, which is why we had to stay mostly below deck. Once the men received pipes and tobacco and we were allowed to move and had to dance on deck. After a few weeks, they began to shave and wash us and rub palm oil on us. Then they freed us from the chains. Many had died since the start of the journey and had been thrown overboard. We were given blue fabric for loincloths. We reached another coast. Just before approaching the harbour, we were washed and rubbed with palm oil again. An agent came on board to have a look at us, and then we went on land, chained together. It looked like where I had come from, but no one told us where we were. We had to walk to a large market located very close to the harbour. There was a large house filled with human beings for sale, and at first, we were kept in the cellar. After a few days, I was sold to a man named Da Rocha. He was the one who changed my name and baptized me. I became Catholic. I never forgot my name: Esan.

We became the hands of the New World idea. Somewhere, there was a plan that we had no part in creating. We were there simply to fulfil what had already been established. The change of my name and what I believed in should have brought me closer to their kind, but in reality, they didn't really want that. Who was I, I wondered, when would I become this name? I simply did what came to me.

It all became so routine that there was no room for possibilities. I always took everything with me; I had nothing anywhere. I was occupied only in doing what they had planned for me. I was in Brazil and worked as an *escravo doméstico* on a sugar cane plantation in Candeias. I was an *aristocracia escrava*, a privileged worker. From a very young age, I had to help the baron in the mansion. He actually treated me well; he only beat me sometimes, though I never knew why. The other slaves were treated more brutally. I worked closely together with the baron in his office; eventually I had to do quite a bit for him. Somehow he trusted me. I learned things from him: to speak Portuguese, to read, to write, and how to do business. The windows were open wide most of the time to catch the cool of the breeze. You could see the slave barracks from the mansion, and there was a wide view over the bay. The plantation was surrounded by jungle; plants ran riot everywhere. The baroness had a garden with roses. When there was no sugar being produced in the evening and on Sundays, everything was quite still. There were no sounds other than the soft crash of the waves and the birds, numberless different kinds of them, singing in the trees by the house.

The air carried the smell from the nearby sugar mill into the mansion. In my memory, this smell probably meant something quite different to me than it did to the baron. Both of our existences here in this country were founded in such different and absurd ways. Time was my only luxury. I ran in circles without exit. I was nonexistent in time; I had no part in the calculation of time. I simply did not appear in the writing of history. Things never would be as I wanted them. Finally, I gave up imagining what I would like to have. Sundays, after attending the service in the chapel next to the mansion, I went to the bay and swore to myself never to get on a distant point of view where I would be resigned watching the ships disappear into the horizon. I was afraid that I would accept the whole situation, that I would see my position as fixed. I never wanted to give up imagining myself on all these ships. I always wanted to go back, but to somewhere else.

People in the city said that in Africa, you had the chance of a better life. You could be independent, your own boss. The English had abolished slavery, and you could live as a free person in Lagos. Here we had learned many things: how to make fine crafts and to trade. We were the most dependable workers, responsible, and trustworthy people.

I often had to go to the city for the baron. I always made a visit to the "Sociedade" next to the San Francisco church to speak with the head of the brotherhood about buying my freedom. The baron knew I was a member there. By the time I was 30, enough money had been collected in the casket at the "Sociedade" for another raffle. All the pieces of paper with names of the other candidates were tossed on the big table. The director pulled one piece of paper from the pile, the piece with "João Esan da Rocha" on it. That's how I was called. They opened the three locks on the casket with the three keys and bought me from my master. At this time, I didn't know what I really was. An African trained to be Portuguese but now Brazilian? I had distanced myself from me and spoke of myself in the third person. I wanted to go back to what I was at the beginning. In the beginning, I was a child able to be taught anything. Africa promised me the chance to be something else. In Brazil, I was forever separated from the status of others by the mark of slavery.

After being purchased from my master, I lived with my wife, Louisa Angelica, in the Rua da Forca until our departure. My son Candido was born here. There was another woman I had children with. She stayed in Salvador. The journey to Africa was risky. Often passengers were not taken to their desired destinations. Sometimes people were immediately seized and sold again or were taken against their will to another destination. It was better to take an English ship; it was safer. The Portuguese ships reduced you back to slavery again. The captain spat on the wooden deck. Hopefully it was clear to him where I wanted to go ...

The last sentence that she placed into my memory when I left her behind in Bahia ... On the way to Brazil, I lost my orientation. On the way to Lagos, I lost my ability to forget. I had always hoped to one day wake up and be at my destination. Half my life I had spent adjusting to an existence in Brazil – had spent time there, absorbed much and made the most out of it without losing all self-respect. Every day something of myself went into this country without ever coming back to me. But I wasn't afraid anymore. What would be would be; what happened, happened. I was tired, but still I wanted to continue. The long journey home finally gave me time.

More than 1,000 returnees lived in Lagos. You could immediately recognize the newcomers by their dress. Angelica, too, wore a white dress from Bahia. After 31 years, we went back. No one knew anything about my family in Lagos; perhaps they had all died. We returnees from Brazil were assigned to receive a quarter in the city center from Governor Glover, so I moved into the area around Campos Square. You could still see slave traders on the streets with their mulatto children from their former servants and slave ship captains. There was a curious mixture of Catholic belief, but no one was bothered by it. We quickly gained an advantage with the skills we brought with us to Lagos from Brazil. Our community stood between the Africans and the English. The indigenous people of Lagos were jealous of our accomplishments, but despite their mistrust, they let us be.

I returned to the country that had sold me. I never stopped suspecting that my parents were the ones who sold me. I didn't really want to find them. During the first four months I felt a sense of joy about my return, but the novelty quickly faded and I began to think back to Salvador. The past always appeared to me, more and more often, until in the end, all that was left was an essence of a memory, and I began to believe in this lie. My return was no mistake, but I created a new identity that was more at home in the remembered place Bahia than in Lagos, where I really lived. This is about promises, not changes.

I built the Waterhouse in Kakawa Street in the Brazilian style. Inside was a fountain that gave our house its name. It was the first fountain inside Lagos' city center and people came from all over to buy its water. Even the Oba drank from it. When you went inside the house, the birds greeted you by chirping and singing. The red parrot on its ebony stand always called my name. We had aviaries as large as rooms in the garden with crown birds, turkeys, guinea fowls, pigeons, and partridges. We had every kind of animal – cats that I fed with expensive fish boned myself. We had tortoises, and plants, and flowers. I grew roses. If they weren't careful around them I scolded my grandchildren in Portuguese. When I was upset, I always spoke Portuguese, even when the British stopped using translators by doing business with us.

Africa was a word. A promise. I knew that I could live a life like the one I had seen in Brazil but would never have been able to realize. In Brazil, I only had a past that added nothing more to what I always was there. Here, I had no past and was free to invent my own future. We were considered to be a new kind of white, with color and without classification. I am Brazilianized, Bahianized. In Brazil, I cultivated my African individuality, but upon my return to Lagos, I affirmed my attachment to the manners and customs of Bahia. It was better to come to Lagos ... Is it important to link the people with their history?

I traded textiles, all sorts of trinkets and groceries. Later I dealt in gold. I sold to Brazil and Europe as well. I had our clothes made in Britain. We set ourselves up well in Lagos. We didn't want any mixing; my children had to marry within the Brazilian community. Discipline, honesty, and obedience – those were our values that I wanted to pass on to them. "Never lie, always tell the truth, and don't lose character. Be confident and generous, upstanding and loyal – the blood is straight." Back then, when a child was difficult, you gave him to the Brazilians. There was a lot of pride in the Brazilian community. Even though the people who had sold us into slavery thought they did something bad, they actually did something good. We were not the same anymore after slavery. After our experience in Brazil, we couldn't simply go back to Africa where we came from. This quickly became clear to us in Lagos. We had developed differently than those who had stayed here. We began to see advantages in this. We defined ourselves as a new class, even as a new kind of ethnic group.

I had a restaurant called "Bonanza" in Custom Street. I had breakfast there every Saturday and made sure everything was in order. Next to the large window on the street, there was a table that was always reserved for me. I had a clear view of the street from there. I smoked an El Arte cigar and drank a glass of Dry Monopol Ayala. Afterwards I went to the horse races, where I had horses running for me named "Tempest" and "Vampa". I watched them win every week.

I was in heaven as I sat in the Holy Cross Cathedral in Catholic Mission Street. Suddenly, it became dark outside, and a violent rainstorm poured down upon the church. The rain was so loud that the speech of the provost faded into the background. I didn't understand him when he thanked me for the donation I gave to the church to build the three chapels. I often helped this church so that it could become big and beautiful and allow Catholicism to find a home in Lagos ... like a church in Bahia. I forbade my children from kneeling before the Elders. I said to them, "You shall only kneel before God". The first Saturday in March was reserved for thanking God for the safe return of those who had left slavery and returned home. This day was known as "Nossa Senhora de Bom Fim". The da Rochas always went to this festival. All the Brazilians came together to attend a church service and then we went through the center of town to go to Agege in the countryside and have a picnic. We had Brazilian dishes like *leite de coco*, *feijoada*, *mocaca de peixe*... It was a huge party where we also enjoyed dancing samba. We celebrated it every year.

I never wanted to be treated like a "Negro". With time, we formed a kind of bourgeoisie, which with its dignity and its refinement, belonged to another time. We had become conservative in this way.

# Dialogues

Yeda Pessoa de Castro

# Towards a Comparative Approach of Bantuisms in Iberoamerica[1]

Professor-doctor Nina Rodrigues in Salvador, the capital of the state of Bahia, initiated African studies in Brazil in the last decades of the nineteenth century. Bahia state is located in the northeastern region of Brazil, and the city of Salvador, besides having been its first capital from 1549 to 1763 was the largest and most important trade centre for the transatlantic trade in Portuguese America. Today, Salvador is the third major city of Brazil with a population of more than 2,700,000, eighty percent of which is of African descent.

At the time of Rodrigues's research, the majority of the city's black population was composed of slaves and free men of African origin working in urban and domestic jobs. Among them a majority of Yoruba-Nagots maintained direct contact with the Gulf of Benin through merchants sailing from Lagos (Nigeria) several times a year carrying the so-called *products-of-the-coast* (clothes, collars, shells, fruits, etc.). This type of trade was destined to meet the demands of the local population as it concerned the products necessary to maintain African religious cults or used in the Candomblé houses condemned by the press of that epoch as *noisy cults frequented by persons of all classes* (*Pelourinho Informa* 1980: 35-37). This trade, on the other hand, promoted the return of Africans and their descents born in Brazil, the *agudás*, to Africa, where they founded the Brazilian communities of Benin and Nigeria keeping their Portuguese family names such as Rocha, Pereira, Souza, Olímpio, among others. The last of those voyages took place in 1898. Thereafter, the English authorities in Nigeria, fearful of the cholera epidemic that had broken out on board, dissolved the boat line Brazil-Lagos, or rather, Bahia-Lagos in 1903 (Pessoa de Castro 1964: 41-56; Verger 1968).

---

1  This is a revised version of my contribution to the volume *Kilombo*, Ngowe, Nicholas (ed.). Libreville: Cerafia (2001: 29-35). Translation from Portuguese into English by Ineke Phaf-Rheinberger.

According to the testimony of Rodrigues, the Yoruba language, whose written literature was established by the circulation of journals such as *Ewe Irohin Eko* (Lagos Journal) in Nigeria, was taught to the blacks of Bahia by other blacks, who had learned it in school from the missionaries in Lagos. This was, incidentally, the case of the teacher and *babalaô* (Candomblé priest) Martiniano Elizeu do Bonfim, who in his eighties died in Salvador (Carneiro 1948). Moreover, the necessity of communication in the trade and in daily life among different African speakers concentrated in an urban centre supported the emergence of a vehicular language that Rodrigues denominated "Nagot dialect". According to him, it was a mixture of Portuguese and African languages and, as we can imagine, certainly had an important Yoruba-based vocabulary preserved and related to religious and liturgical practices. Unfortunately, Rodrigues did not bother to register them as he did with the other five African languages (Tapa, Grunce, Fulani, Hausa, Djedje-Mahi), probably because only a few survivors in that city spoke that language when he conducted his research. Therefore, this "Nagot dialect" was not meant to thrive in the Yoruba language, as many researchers seem to think. In fact Yoruba's in Brazil were traditionally known as Nagots, derived from the kingdom of Ketu in the present-day Republic of Benin.

Impressed by this overall presence, Rodrigues erroneously concluded that the Yoruba's were the most numerous and influential Africans in Bahia although his research only comprised the city of Bahia and not Congolese and Angolans who lived there, as Rodrigues declared himself (1945: 193). In addition the Yoruba had at their disposal a literature that conferred on them, from an occidental viewpoint, a certain prestige comparable to the European languages. Considering that many of their speakers practiced Islam and followed the Koran, Rodrigues ended with excelling the Yoruba supremacy in Brazil, attributed accordingly this same parameter to the superiority of the culture of its people in comparison with other black Africans.

## 1. Methodological and pioneering continuity

In the 1930s the posthumous publication of Rodrigues's work *The Africans in Brazil* was organized by Homero Pires and awakened a major interest in Afro-Brazilian studies. With the exception of the pioneering efforts of Renato Mendonça (1935) and Jacques Raimundo (1933) on the influence of African languages on the Portuguese of Brazil, the majority of published works concentrated on religion, attracting to Bahia foreign researchers with an international reputation, among them Roger Bastide and Pierre Verger.

Notwithstanding the existence of otherwise oriented scientific studies, all follow in Rodrigues's steps. They concentrate their research on the Candomblé houses in the city of Salvador, in which the rites and myths of the Yoruba pantheon can easily be distinguished empirically. This is also the case, although not with such intensity, with the religious manifestations of Ewe-Fon based languages in São Luis, in the state of Maranhão, as well as in Northeast Brazil. The result of this methodological continuity was the development of an erroneous tendency to reduce the history of the Africans in Brazil to the history of the Yoruba people, a scientific panorama Valdés Acosta repeated for Cuba (2002: 3). Consequently, all African traditions were explained through a Yoruba optic. Allsopp (1996: 130), for example, attributes a Yoruba origin to the Bantuism *calalu*, current in Caribbean English to designate a soup of vegetables. Ortiz (1991: 56) commits the same error with the origin of another Bantuism, *bilongo*, medicament, magic, both registered in Brazil with the same meaning. Edison Carneiro (1937), author of a book dedicated to the Bantu blacks in Brazil, admitted the cultural inferiority of these people, a standing stereotype in Brazilian historiography. It suggests that Congolese (including those in the English-speaking Caribbean) and Angolans are less intelligent and lazy according to Allsopp (1996: 167).

Already in the 1960s, with the policies of cultural relations of Brazil with Africa, the Brazilian Portuguese was taught in universities in Senegal and Nigeria. The universities of Bahia and then São Paulo also began offering practical courses of Yoruba via their recently created centres of African studies. From there, conceiving the African continent as one singular country, a "unique" Africa, of Yoruba language and culture, became popular in Brazil meanwhile relegating the participation of other black African people equally expressive in the process of configuring the profile of representative language and culture of Brazil to a second plan.

In this sense, with my doctoral thesis *De l'intégration des apports africains dans les parlers de Bahia au Brésil* presented at the National

University of Zaire in Lubumbashi in 1976, a new stage was inaugurated in Afro-Brazilian studies signifying the rediscovery of the importance of the Bantu world and its repercussions in Brazil. For the first time, the field research in the city of Salvador was extended to Africa from the Gulf of Benin to Güthries' linguistic zones H (Kikongo/Kimbundu) and R (Umbundu). At that same moment, through the exchange with the National University of Zaire, the Centre of Afro-Oriental Studies of the Federal University of Bahia offered the first course of Kikongo and Bantu linguistics in Brazil. This last course, with a more academic orientation, was discontinued due to a lack of interest, whereas the Kikongo course was continued, having attracted members of the Congo-Angola religious community of Bahia, thanks to the efforts of a former student and his teacher, the unforgettable Tata Raimundo Pires, also a member of that community (Pessoa Castro 1997).

These efforts reflected a methodological reorientation in ethno- and linguistic research, whose objective was to study the African way of speaking in Bahia, which was communication using lexical (morpho-semantic) systems of African languages spoken in Brazil and modified by the Portuguese influence. The goal was to study the mechanisms of its integration into the regional Portuguese of Bahia as well as in the Portuguese repertoire of Brazil. The point of departure was the analysis of the Afro-Brazilian liturgical languages, by its own nature closer to its original models (Pessoa de Castro 1998; 2005).

## 2. Results of research

Taking into consideration that the living language of the people is the most vivid testimony of its history, the existing information was extended and enriched through knowledge of the language, religion, and popular cultures of Brazil. This research revealed the Bantu presence as the oldest and superior in number and geographic distribution in the Brazilian territory under the colonial slave regime. It must be noted that the human trade to Brazil was just as consistent as the trade Portugal had already conducted with the Kingdom of Congo in the sixteenth century. The striking presence of the African element returns in the Portuguese literature of that period when Gil Vicente reproduces the black speech of Lisbon in his short, satirical theatre pieces, such as "Bitter Love" and "The Clergyman from Beira".

Regarding Brazil, the Bantus people were initially brought from the Kingdom of Congo, then from port settlements along the Angolan coast, and later from Mozambique. A relevant testimony of this fact is the nomenclature of the Republic of Palmares in the seventeenth century, the largest and longest-standing *quilombo* in Brazilian history (Moura 1959), whose most important leaders were Ganga Zumba and Zumbi, titles of indubitable Bantu origin. Its topography – Dembo, Macaco, Osengo, Cafuxi, and the word *quilombo* (kilombo) itself, meaning a settlement of black people – are of Bantu origin, as is the African vocabulary associated with the regime of slavery: *senzala* (slave hut), *mucama* (female servant), *moleque* (black child), *carimbo* (stamp), *banzo* (sadness). Another evidence is the larger number of Bantu toponyms in comparison with others of African origin in rural as well as in urban zones, such as Bacanga, Gandu, Caçanje, Catete, Moçambique, Mombaça, Cambuta, the equivalent of Cambute, related by Ortiz to Cuba.

The word Zumbi is a title that refers to the function of constructor, assistant, or chief of a village also found with the variants *zuma* and *zumba*, as in *Gangu Zuma* or *Zumba*, the Big Constructor. These words are confused in Brazilian studies with a form convergent in Portuguese from another verb-derived substantive of the Bantu word *zumbi*, or "nvumbi/nzumbi", spirit of the dead, phantasm. With the same significance in the written variant "zombee" or "zombi", it is also used in American Spanish and English to demonstrate that the geographic extension of Bantu influence exceeds the language and cultures of the Ibero-American world. In Haiti, for instance, among the African religious traditions that influence the life of its population, those dedicated to the Voodoo culture from Dahomey are most studied. This explains that their former dictators were addressed as Papa Doc and Babe Doc, titles of political-religious leadership with a mystical character, whereas the second element is the Bantu vocal "ndoki", the master of healing, the healing doctor, which phonetically is confused and understood with the reduced form of "doctor" in English, or "docteur" in French, the official language of that country. From this same Bantu is derived the name Mandrake, the famous magician-sorcerer and hero of the comic strips (Pessoa de Castro 2005: 274).

The use of the vocals of Bantu origin for religious purposes is predominant for different local practices. The oldest known is the *calundu* in Bahia that Nuno Pereira described in *O peregrino das Américas* (The Pilgrim of the Americas) in 1728, whereas the most famous are *Candomblé*, *Umbanda*, and *Macumba*, this last one also registered in Cuba by Fabelo and as "mayumba" in the work of Fernando Ortiz. Another important testimony of the antiquity of this presence is the so-called *Candomblé-de-caboclo* in Brazil, a product of the direct contact of Bantus with Brazilian Amerindians, the *caboclos*, a fact that can be proved by the Bantuisms *cafuzo*, in Portuguese, and *zambo*, in Spanish and English America to characterize the mestizo of black and Amerindian descent.

Moreover, it is worth mentioning that the principal characteristic of the vocabulary spoken by the *pretos-velhos* or *baculos* (Bantu "bakulu", old people) during the religious ceremonies is the use of Bantu words modified by the initial increase of the morpheme [zi-], an old demonstrative that subsists optionally in Kikongo and Kimbundo and ends up contaminating Portuguese words, such as "zipai" (pai, father), "zifio" (filho, son). This phenomenon is also known in Cuba, under the form [si-], in the glossary of Afro-negrisms of Ortiz and of the Conga language residual enlisted by Fabelo, with the examples of *zingoma/singoma* (tambor) and *zimbomba/simbomba* (insipid) (Pessoa de Castro 2005: 90).

## 3. The Bantu legacy

The perdurability of the favoured presence of the superior number of the Bantu element in the demographic composition of colonial Brazil can be learned from its concentration in rural zones, isolated and certainly conservative, where in the past liberty meant escape to the *quilombos*. These zones were important factors of social and geographical order, which recalled the extensive and persisting Bantu influence in the configuration of the representative culture and language of Brazil. Moreover, the contributions of Bantu origin were integrated into the national patrimony as symbols of *Brasilidade*, which does not mean that the average Brazilian was conscious of its African, and even less of its Bantu, origin.

The most notable manifestations are of Bantu origin and appropriated as authentic Brazilian, such as the *rhythm of the* s*amba*, the playfight of the *capoeira of Angola* with its beats from the *berimbau* or *urucungo,* and songs in honour of *Aruanda* (Luanda) in the sense of a mythical Africa inhabited by gods and forefathers. Similarly, the *ganzá* and the *cuíca* are characteristic of Brazilian music and indispensable instruments in the percussion of the samba schools of carnival in Rio de Janeiro. The names of typical Latin American dances also are of Bantu origin: besides the Brazilian *samba* and the Argentincan *tango*, there is *mambo, merengue, rumba, conga* accompanied by the *marimba* and the *bongo.* Another important testimony of the amplitude of this presence is the play dance or drum beat largely distributed in Spanish America called *calinda/kalinda.* This word is found in the English of Trinidad/Tobago where the dance is also performed (Codallo 1983). In Brazil it is called *maculele,* also a Bantu-based denomination.

The historical importance of the kingdom of Congo is still reflected in dramatic representations of Brazilian folklore in numerous regions, through specific popular performances called *congos* and *candombe.* The latter is celebrated in Minas Gerais and is a popular manifestation of black origin in Argentina and Uruguay. The *Manicongo* (lord of Congo) is always remembered in verses such as "The old Cabinda arrived/ and the king of Congo spoke". The same memory is also registered for Queen Jinga or Zinga of the old kingdom of Matamba in present-day Angola. It is important to realize that the term *candombe* does not derive from the etymon "ndombe", black, as has been explained erroneously (Montaño 1995: 440). It concerns the Bantu lexem "kandombe", derived from "kulomba", to pray or to ask for the intervention of the gods, similar to the word Candomblé in Brazil (Pessoa de Castro 2005: 195-196).

Significant traces of the Bantu lexical system are found in work songs performed during the harvest of beans and corn, the so-called *batas* (Bantu "kubata", to fan) in popular storytelling, whose thematic structure is populated with fantastic beings of the Bantu world, among them *calunga, quibungo, tutu moringa*, and *cafuringa*, equivalent of "moringa" and "cafunga" of the Afro-Cuban folklore (Ortiz 1991).

Interestingly enough, *Bambi* and *Dumbo* or *Jumbo*, the roe and the elephant of the animated designs of Walt Disney, have Bantu names, whereas in Portuguese, the most dandyish of the seven dwarfs of Snow White is *Dunga*, another Bantuism.

In reference to the influence of the African languages on Brazilian Portuguese, Bantu speech was indubitably the most significant in social interaction in colonial Brazil, in contact with the old Portuguese, and, on a minor scale, with indigenous languages. It configured the process of differentiation that removed the language from its spoken matrix in Portugal. Innumerable isolated rural speeches that preserve a Bantu lexical system are still found today, which are probably traces inherited from old *quilombos*, such as those found in the states of São Paulo and Minas Gerais, among others (Pessoa de Castro 2005).

Otherwise, to the degree that the synchronic profundity reveals a diachronic antiquity, this influence becomes evident because of sizeable: 1) of lexical Bantu-based contributions completely integrated into the Portuguese linguistic system, for example of the verbs in the first conjugation (ar), like *chuetar*, to ridicule (Kik. "tyetela"); 2) of Portuguese derivations formed from the same Bantu root through prefixes or suffixes, such as in "nleke", child, youngster = *moleque* = *amolecar* (to behave as a child), *molequinho* (little boy), *molecote* (little boy), or also, prefixes like – eiro, in *marombeiro*, sorcerer, marimba dancer or – dor in *chuetador*, one who ridicules.

In the majority of cases it concerns current words on all levels of the languages and some known in Portugal *(cachimbo, cachaça, carimbo, miçanga, moleque)*, only that the Brazilian speaker in general is incapable of distinguishing whether they are of African or Amerindian descent or even not of Portuguese descent. Examples are *tanga, sunga, cacimba, calunga, maconha* or *diamba, (ma)riamba*, the same root as "marijuana" in Spanish- and Angloamerican. In some cases the Bantu lexem completely replaces the equivalent Portuguese word, like *caçula* for benjamin, *corcunda* for hump, *moringa* for water jar, *marimbondo* for wasp, *cochilar* for to fall asleep, *bunda* for buttocks. According to the glossary of Ortiz (1991), the cases of derivation mentioned here also happen in Cuban Spanish as the examples mentioned above have demonstrated and only differ slightly in form but with the same meanings as in Brazilian Portuguese.

Among the Afro-Brazilian religions of Congo-Angola descent, besides preserving a Bantu-based lexical system such as is the case of the "Congo language" of Cuba (Granda 1973; Fabelo s.d.), persist of beliefs and rites of the pantheon of the old kingdom of Congo. That notwithstanding, many of them have the tendency to grade their symbolic structure by the patterns of the Nagot-Ketu Candomblé with the worship of their *orishas*, due to the social prestige they have in Brazil, also exported to Argentina, Uruguay, and Portugal. Such prestige results from the fact that these Candomblés were the object of specialized studies in Afro-Brazilian religions since Nina Rodrigues. They have attracted an increasing number of intellectuals, artists, and politicians, who eventually occupied important functions in the socio-religious hierarchy of the group. This was the case for Nina Rodrigues, Roger Bastide, and Pierre Verger.

Meanwhile, despite the exploration of the image of Yoruba *orishas* and their publicity executed in the benefice of governmental institutions and tourist spectacles, the *congo-angola candomblé* is resistant to this impact and conserves a Bantu-based liturgical language that is also found in Cuba. This resistance is more explicit at this moment because their followers become increasingly conscious of the rediscovery of the greatness of the Bantu world and its contributions to the culinary traditions, flora and fauna, customs, and habits of daily life of Brazilians. Moreover, Bantus were the principal agents and transmitters of Portuguese on the Brazilian territory under the colonial slavery system, i.e. e. for three consecutive centuries.

In summary, in spite of the importance of the Bantu influence, we must consider that, historically, Brazilian language and culture are the result of an implicit movement of Africanisation of the Portuguese and, inversely, the increasing influence of Portuguese on African languages. The pre-existing and local Amerindian languages in Brazil also have had their impact. The major or minor grade of acceptance of these multiple and reciprocal influences or of the resistance against them is a question involving the historical and socio-cultural order.

Although this process of Africanisation is indebted to the territorial expansion and occupation, demographic density, and the antiquity of the Bantu people in colonial Brazil, "bantuizing" Brazil as a counterpoint to the "Yoruba-centrism", which has prevailed in Afro-Brazilian studies is not an option. I think that this is also valid for Afro-

American studies since there is a general tendency of privileging the old kingdom of Congo, its people and languages to the disadvantage of others that were equally active in the process of consolidation of the Bantu legacy in Brazil and in the Americas.

I am referring here to the Ambundo and Ovimbundu. The latter presence was characteristic in the State of Minas Gerais where they worked in the mines. Today this region still registers a large number of localities where certain special languages are known based on a lexical system of Umbundu (Machado Filho 1944). Kimbundu was certainly one of the most frequently spoken languages in Brazil because of the dense commercial ties that were established with the ports along the coast of Angola in the seventeenth century. The name Angola remained registered in one of the manifestations considered among the most representative of Brazilian culture: the Angolan play-fight of *capoeira*. At that time speakers of Congo and Angola were so numerous in the city of Bahia that in 1697 the Portuguese missionary Pedro Dias published *A Arte da Língua de Angola* (The Art of the Language of Angola) to facilitate the Jesuits' indoctrination of the 25,000 Africans in that city without speaking Portuguese, as witnessed, in that period, by Padre Antonio Vieira (Silva Neto 1963: 82).

The question, though, is how to identify those people when the historical documentation about the trade is insufficient and unreliable regarding ethnic origins. Considering African languages and religions have developed since the arrival of the Africans in America, the first proposal is to collect all the Bantuisms in the Afro-American bibliography we have at our disposal, identify probable and possible etymons, precise meanings and most frequent semantic camps, geographic areas and levels of languages in which they appear, to beginning with the liturgical language because of its conservative and archaic aspect (Pessoa de Castro 2005).

The second stage would be to confront written documentation about the transatlantic trade to broaden and deepen our knowledge in a more justified way, in relationship with the importance not only of a specific group of people but also of other ones brought from the Bantu world to the Americas.

This proposal was formulated in my dissertation project in 1976 and should become the point of departure for a project of triangular research. It will reveal aspect still unknown about the Bantu language, not only in Brazil but also in the Spanish American world. The optic of such an interpretation reconstructs the cultures and languages of the Bantu group and will legitimise its role in the configuration of differences that brush aside the official Ibero-American profile from their respective European matrix. We cannot forget that the black African has learned the languages of European colonization as a second language and has contributed to its distribution in the territories of South America and the Caribbean. This African presence, therefore, is as characteristic as the implantation of the official languages, Portuguese, Spanish, English, French, and Dutch in the (former) colonies and contemporary republics on the American continent.

## Bibliography

Allsopp, Richard (1996): *Dictionary of Caribbean English Usage*. NewYork: Oxford UP.

Bastide, Roger (1971): *As religiões africanas no Brasil*, 2 vols. São Paulo: Pioneira.

Carneiro, Edison (1937): *Negros Bantos*. Rio de Janeiro: Civilização Brasileira.

— (1948): *Candomblés da Bahia*. Salvador: Museu do Estado da Bahia.

Codallo, Alfredo (1983): *Selected Works by Holly Gayadeen*. Trinidad: published by the author.

Fabelo, Teodoro Diaz (s.d.): *Diccionario de la lengua conga residual en Cuba*. Santiago de Cuba: Casa del Caribe, Colección Africanía.

Granda, Germán de (1973): *De la matrice africaine de la "langue congo" en Cuba*. Dakar: Université de Dakar, Centre des Hautes Etudes Afro-Ibero-Américaines n° 9.

Güthrie, Malcolm (1948): *The Classification of the Bantu Languages*. London: Oxford UP.

Machado Filho, A. M. (1944): *O negro e o garimpo em Minas Gerais*. Rio de Janeiro: Civilização Brasileira.

Mendonça, Renato (1935): *A influência africana no Português do Brasil*. São Paulo: Editora Nacional.

Montaño, Óscar (1995): "Los afro-orientales. Breve reseña del aporte africano en la formación de la población uruguaya". In: Montiel, Luz María Martínez (ed.): *Presencia africana en Sudamérica*. México, D.F.: Consejo Nacional para la Cultura y las Artes, pp. 414-415.

Moura, Clovis (1959): *Rebeliões da Senzala*. São Paulo: Edições Zumbi.

Ortiz, Fernando (1991): *Glosario de afronegrismos*. La Habana: Editorial de Ciencias Sociales.

Pelourinho Informa (1980): *Alabama 15.11.1864*. Salvador/Bahia: Biblioteca do IPAC, pp. 35-37.

Pereira, Nuno Marques ([1728] 1933): *O peregrino das Américas*. Rio de Janeiro: Academia Brasileira de Letras.

Pessoa de Castro, Yeda (1964): "Notícia de uma pesquisa em África". In: *Afro-Asia* 1. Salvador: CEAO/UFBA, pp. 41-58.

— (1976): *De l'intégration des apports africains dans les parlers de Bahia au Brésil*, 2 vols. Lubumbashi: Université National du Zaire.

— (1978): *Contos Populares da Bahia*. Salvador: Departamento de Assuntos Culturais da Prefeitura Municipal.

— (1995): "Proyección historica y perspectivas de la población negra en Bahia, Brasil". In: Montiel, Luz María Martínez (ed.): *Presencia africana en Sudamérica*. México, D.F.: Consejo Nacional para la Cultura y las Artes, pp. 333-390.

— (1997): "Línguas africanas como objeto de estudo e ensino no Brasil". In: *Lusorama*, 34, pp. 52-60.

— (1998): "Lenguas africanas: factor de resistencia en la Ruta del Esclavo". In: *Del Caribe*, 28, pp. 71-74.

— (2000): "Las religiones de origen africano en Brasil". In: *Revista de Cultura Hispanoamericana*, 11, pp. 19-25.

— (2001): "Para um estudo comparativo de bantuismos na Iberoamérica". In: Nwoge, Nicholas (ed.): *Kilombo*. Libreville: Cerafia, pp. 29-35.

— (2005): *Falares africanos na Bahia*, 2 ed. Rio de Janeiro: Academia Brasileira de Letras/Topbooks.

Raimundo, Jacques (1933): *O elemento afro-negro na lingua Portuguesa*. Rio de Janeiro: Renascença.

Rodrigues, Nina ([1933] 1945): *Os africanos no Brasil*. São Paulo: Editora Nacional.

Silva Neto, Serafim da (1963): *Introdução ao estudo da língua portuguesa no Brasil*. Rio de Janeiro: INL/MEC.

Valdés Acosta, Gema (2002): *Los remanentes de las lenguas bantúes en Cuba*. La Habana: Fundación Fernando Ortiz, Colección Africanía.

Verger, Pierre (1968): *Flux et Reflux de la Traite des Nègres entre le Golfe de Bénin et Bahia de Todos os Santos, du XVII au XX Siècle*. Paris: Mouton.

Vicente, Gil (1965): *Obras completas*. Porto: Lello & Irmãos.

Martin Lienhard

# Milonga.
# The "Dialogue" between Portuguese and Africans in the Congo and the Angola Wars (Sixteenth and Seventeenth Centuries)[1]

Among them there are neither golden nor other metal coins as money, nor is there anything else that responds to that, but they use certain things instead, which have their fixed and regular prices, such as slaves – called *pieces* by us (*Informação acerca dos escravos de Angola*, [1576] 1989: 118).

From these [slaves] the number of those captured in war is nothing in comparison with those who are bought on markets, to which the kings and the chiefs of whole Ethiopia send their slaves for sale. This trade is very old among them, and they always used to handle *pieces* instead of money for buying clothes and whatever else they needed ("História da residência" [1594] 1989: 188).

The money used in this city of Luanda has different qualities and values. The best is *peças de Índias*, which are slaves who are shipped to the Indies [the Americas] for the value of 22.000 *reis*; they also have *pieces* who are boys, girls, bearded blacks, and less valuable blacks, who are meant for the State of Brazil (Sousa [1624-1630] 1985: 310).

And the richest mines in this Kingdom of Angola are the quantity of *pieces* which depart from this port every year, from 7 to 8000 heads of slaves each year (Cadornega [1680] 1972: 243).

The most important trade of the Portuguese and other whites with the inhabitants [of Congo] is the trade with the slaves, who are shipped to the islands of Puerto Rico, Rio Plata, Santo Domingo, Havana, Cartagena, and to the continent, especially to Brazil and other places, where they are forced to work in the sugar mills and in the mines ... And the Portuguese and Spaniards, therefore, owe almost all their wealth in the West Indies to the work of these slaves (Dapper [1688] 1964: 294-295).

---

1   Slightly abridged version of chapter two of Martin Lienhard's *O Mar e o Mato: Histórias da Escravidão* (Luanda: Editorial Kilombelombe, 2005). Translation into English by Ineke Phaf-Rheinberger and the author.

## 1.  European discourse vs. African discourses

In search of a maritime route to India, the Portuguese navigator Diogo
Cão arrived at the mouth of the Zaire (or Congo) River in 1482. That
same year, the Portuguese must have started, although modestly, the
extraction of slaves. Two events occurred in the following two decades that completely transformed the incipient international trade of
African slaves: the Spanish arrival in the Caribbean (1492), as well as
on the American continent (1498), and that of the Portuguese in Brazil
(1500). Based on forced labor, the development of mining in Spanish
continental America and the creation of a sugar industry in the Caribbean and Brazil led to the deportation of an ever-increasing number of
African slaves. For more than two centuries, Central Africa was to be
desolated by the European slave trade. It has to be remembered that
this would not have been possible without the collaboration of local
kings, chiefs, and other agents. Assigned to satisfy the voracity of an
ever-expanding slave market, Angola, at that time, entered world history as a sub-colony of Brazil (Rodrigues 1982: chapter II).

One of the consequences of the eruption of European slave-traders
was the breaking out of a generalized war between the Africans and
the intruders. This war also may be read as a "war of discourses" or a
"dialogue" – certainly asymmetrical – between the European conquerors and their local adversaries. Which sources may we use to study
this "dialogue"? Unfortunately, we are not able to retrieve authentic
African "voices" from this period. No doubt contemporary Africans
tried to shape, in their songs or oral narratives, the trauma caused by
the eruption of European slave traders, but no written testimony of
such literary productions has been preserved. The few written "African" sources are the letters in which local chiefs – called *mani* or
*muene* in Congo and *soba*[2] in the Ndongo (central area of the present-

---

2    In this and the following linguistic footnotes, kmb. means Kimbundu, and kk.
     Kikongo (the two major Bantu languages in the area). Ass. refers to the Kim-
     bundu dictionary by Assis Júnior (1947), and Sw. to the Kikongo dictionary by
     Swartenbroekx (1973). *Muene*. Lord, political title. "Muene puto means in the
     Ambunda language of Angola the Lord of Portugal. And in the maxiconga lan-
     guage mani means lord, and they call the king of Congo Mani Congo or Mueni
     congo" (Cadornega [1680] 1972: I, p. 353). Kk. *mwéné*, pl. *mamwéné*, nobleman,
     free man, lord (Sw.). *Soba*. Kmb. *sôba* (pl. in *ji-*). Generic name of the represen-
     tatives of the local authority in a specific region (Ass.). "They are like counts or
     great lords" (Simões [1575] 1989).

day Republic of Angola) – used to address Portuguese authorities. Eminently diplomatic, such letters – written in Portuguese – do not reveal the real thoughts of their African authors. The remaining sources are exclusively European: chronicles, reports, and letters written by navigators, traders, political agents, governors, and priests, all of them involved in the colonial slave trade. Fortunately for us, not all of these documents represent a purely official or unilateral view of the events. Less marked by the official ideology than their Spanish colleagues involved in the conquest of America (Lienhard 2003), some of these "writers" did little to disguise the real goals of the conquerors or to keep secret the resistance of their adversaries. None of them, however, was really interested to know how the African chiefs or their subjects thought about Portuguese intrusion. For that reason, the historian trying to discover the "discourse" of Africans in documents written mostly by their European adversaries resembles someone listening to a telephone conversation between an individual close by and a distant partner. In such a situation, the indiscrete listener cannot hear the utterances of the distant interlocutor, but is able to imagine them. Thanks to Bakhtine's research on the "dialogical" nature of language, we know that any statement, as an element of a speech chain, refers to a previous utterance and anticipates, in one way or another, the following utterances (Bakhtine 1977). That means an unheard or "lost" utterance may be reconstructed from the preceding and/or the following utterances.

In the Portuguese reports mentioned before, the role of the "distant interlocutor" is performed by the "silent" Africans. We cannot hear their voices, but we can try to imagine their reactions. On this basis, we will analyze letters, chronicles, and reports written mostly between 1580 and 1680 by different actors of the military, economic, and 'spiritual' colonization of the territory the Portuguese named "Angola".[3] Two of these texts are 'classics': *Descrição histórica dos três reinos do Congo, Matamba e Angola* ("Description of the Three King-

---

3   *Ngôla* was the title given to the kings of Ndongo, a kingdom situated in the central part of the present-day Republic of Angola. When speaking about "Angola", the Portuguese, in the early years of their occupation, meant only this kingdom. Later on, "Angola" took approximately the shape of present-day Angola, incorporating, among many other chiefdoms, the central part of the kingdom of Congo.

doms of Congo, Matamba and Angola", [1687] 1965) by the Capuchin João António Cavazzi de Montecúccolo, and the *História geral das guerras angola nas* ("General History of the Angolan Wars", [1680] 1972) by António de Oliveira de Cadornega. Particularly rich in 'echoing' African voices, however, is the lesser-known "Extensive report" (published by Beatrix Heintze in 1985) in which Fernão de Sousa, Portuguese governor of Angola between 1624 and 1630, addressed his sons inviting them "to learn from things that happened to me; I give you a written account of them as of landmarks of government errors in order to allow you to choose" (Sousa 1985: 217). In contrast to the majority of the reports produced during the conquest of the Congo-Angola area, and without excluding the more official writings of the same author, this text manifests an uncommon lack of premeditation. It is a sort of diary in which the governor successively recorded the maneuvers of his adversaries as well as the measures he took to strengthen the Portuguese hegemony in the region. As a diary, this text is rather "spontaneous" and does not obey "political correctness". In a more official document, Fernão de Sousa certainly would have made the effort to reinterpret all the events in the light of the "political" image he wished to give of himself to his principal addressee, the Luso-Spanish Crown. In his "Extensive report", the governor also transcribes or summarizes the correspondence received from his interlocutors: Portuguese officials and African chiefs, allies or adversaries. All of these other "voices" contribute to reinforce the "dialogicity" of this report.

## 2. Slavery and slave trade

The famous "kingdom of Congo" – *Kóngo dia ntôtíla* ("Kongo of the King") – existed before the arrival of the Portuguese expansionists in 1482.[4] The central part of this rather vaguely defined state embraced the *Kongo* 'provinces' or chiefdoms of Sonyo, Nsundi, Mpangu, Mbamba, Mpemba, and Mbata. Its capital, Mbanza Kongo, thereafter baptized São Salvador by the Portuguese, was located in the north of the present-day republic of Angola. During the reign of Dom Afon-

---

4 The best introduction so far to the history and daily events in this kingdom is *La vie quotidienne au royaume du Kongo, du XVI<sup>e</sup> au XVIII<sup>e</sup> siècle* by Georges Balandier (1965).

so I, or Mbemba a Nzinga (1509-1540), the kingdom of Congo, as a vassal state of the Portuguese empire, was a reservoir for slave labor. In the final years of the sixteenth century, the Portuguese, because of the difficulties encountered in obtaining *pieces* in sufficient quantity (Glasgow 1982: 24), transferred their slavery headquarters south to Luanda, but they still considered the king of Congo as their vassal. When demanding his collaboration in expelling the Dutch in the 1620s, for example, the governor of Angola, Fernão de Sousa, recalls the 'benefits' the kingdom of Congo had received from the Portuguese, including 'Christianity' and military support against the *jaga* warriors in 1571 (Sousa 1985: 222).

Officially, the justification for Portuguese penetration in Central Africa was the conversion of the autochthonous kings to Christianity. As a matter of fact, the evangelization of the "savages" was part of the conditions the Pope imposed on the Iberian powers when he divided the "world" among them in the Treaty of Tordesillas in 1494. However, even a superficial reading of the Portuguese reports of the conquest of the Congo-Angola area demonstrates that the actual preoccupations of the conquerors were quite different. The only goal they had in mind was obtaining the greatest possible number of *pieces* for exportation. On account of Portuguese aggression, a permanent war developed in the *matos* and savannas of Angola between the intruders and the local chiefs who tried to defend their sovereignty and, at times, their own position in the slave trade. In the last years of the sixteenth century, the Angola-based Jesuits remarked that

> as you learn by seeing the many slaves shipped to Portugal and in even greater quantity to the State of Brazil and the mines of the Spanish Indies, as well as by considering the high income earned by the economy of His Majesty thanks to the slave trade, the number of slaves obtained each year in Angola is very considerable ("História da residência" [1594] 1989: 188).

Not the conversion of the Africans, but the slave trade was, actually, the context in which the first exchanges between Africans and Europeans took place. Even for the clergy, the evangelization of the Africans was never a priority. In his "Extensive report", Fernão de Sousa brutally stated:

> Until now, the way of baptizing the heathens has been very unsatisfactory, lacking the convenient instruction for the obtainment of Holy Bap-

tism because the priests who came to these parts are more occupied with
the buying and shipping of the negroes than with their catechization
(Sousa 1985: 262).

It is worthwhile to remember that this blame comes from a governor
who never opposed the slave trade. "The slave markets", he writes, are
"the substance of this kingdom" (Sousa 1985: 223). By the way, no
Portuguese writer of that period seems to feel horrified by the trans-
formation of African people into *pieces*.

The moral indifference of the Lusitanians toward the enslavement
of Africans is not too surprising: the use of slave labor was traditional
in the Mediterranean area (Saco 1853; Capela 1978; Maestri Filho
1988a). In spite of that, as if trying to justify the trade, many Portuguese documents of that time declare that the buying and selling of
slaves had been established in Africa long before the arrival of the
Portuguese: "this trade is very old among them: they are accustomed
to making use of *pieces* instead of money to buy clothes, and whatever
else they need" ("História da residência" [1594] 1989: 188). Modern
European or African historians also admit the existence of slavery in
ancient Africa. But what was slavery in the African tradition? Accord-
based on a conjunction of traditional rules. War prisoners, traitors, and
criminals were taken as slaves, but neither noble persons nor women
and children could be sold as *pieces*.[5] Moreover, the sale of slaves
took place only at specific times at markets specifically designated for
such commercial transactions. Sometimes, slaves also could be given
as a tribute to a more powerful chief. Besides, slaves became part of
the family of their master and could not be sold, usually, to anybody
else.

With the intrusion of the Europeans, "traditional African slavery"
was transformed into "colonial slavery" (Gorender 1985). All the consulted documents underscore a European disrespect for the traditional
rules of obtaining slaves. For example, they didn't hesitate to buy
slaves who "had royal blood and were outstanding dignitaries" (Pi-
gafetta/Lopes 1951: 85). According to Fernão de Sousa (1985: 122),
there were also many freed slaves found among the persons shipped to
the Americas. The most noteworthy novelty of the Atlantic trade was,

---

5   Based on "História da residência" (1989), "Informação" (1989), Pigafetta/Lopes
    (1951); Sousa (1985); D. Afonso (1992).

however, the mass deportation of slaves to a distant continent. The voracity of the American markets was to increase the demand for slaves to an unprecedented degree. During the seventeenth century, Brazil alone imported no fewer than 44,000 *pieces* annually (Glasgow 1982: 51).

In the mind of the slaves, to be a slave in Africa or to be deported to the Americas was not the same. In his *Descrição histórica*, the Capuchin Cavazzi recalls the terror felt by Africans threatened with deportation to the Americas:

> There is a big difference between the slaves of the Portuguese and those of the negroes [Africans]. The first do not only obey words, but even signs. They are especially afraid of being taken to Brazil or to New Spain because they are convinced that when they arrive at those lands, they will be killed by the buyers, who, as they think, will make gunpowder of their bones and extract of their brains and flesh the oil that is sold in Ethiopia [...]. The reason they give is that they sometimes find hair in the leather bottles, which in their opinion comes from humans skinned for that purpose. Therefore, out of fear of being sent to America, they get frantic and try to run away to the forest. Others, at the moment of embarking, challenge the blows and kill themselves, jumping into the water (Cavazzi de Montecúccolo [1687] 1965: I. 160).

Aside from such individual acts of resistance, we also know about mass rebellions. In 1798, a Portuguese navigator, Joseph Antonio Percira, tried to obtain a refund from an insurance company in Cadiz for damages to his ship in the port of Cabinda (present-day Angola) by *the rebellion of the 278 slaves he had on board* (my cursive).[6] To be shipped outside of Africa was, according to a Portuguese explorer who wrote during that same year, "the worst of all the punishments you could inflict on a *caffre*" (Almeida [1798] 1989: 113). In fact, besides threatening the "peace" of African households, the so-called 'Atlantic trade' implied radical changes for the African societies. In the words of Jan Vansina (1990: 197),

> the Atlantic trade was a spur, equivalent to the industrial revolution. Its effects must have been equally impressive. However, unlike the industrial revolution, which was home-made, the Atlantic trade was accompanied by foreign values, attitudes, and ideas. It therefore posed even more of a challenge to the old ways than the industrial revolution did in Europe.

---

6     Archivo Histórico Nacional (AHC), Madrid, Consejos, 20257, exp. 2, 1806, 1-5r. e 5v.

### 3.  The *mato* as a refuge

The resistance of the local kings or chiefs against the Portuguese penetration develops mostly in the *mato* ["bush", "forest"]. The history of the resistance of "colonial" slaves begins in the African *mato as well*; it develops simultaneously in the African and the American forests. In his wide-ranging study about the rise of the first states in Central Africa, Vansina (1985) emphasizes the importance of the rain forest in the ancient history of the area. He argues that these states arose in accordance with the regional environment, characterized by the existence of a tropical forest sprinkled with savannas. In Central Africa, the rain forest played a decisive part in the war between Africans and Portuguese. Outside the forest, Africans had only few possibilities to escape Portuguese aggression. In the villages and in the open savanna, their sole options were slavery or death. However, they soon discovered the "bush" as their safest ally. By the end of the sixteenth century, the Jesuits in Angola asserted that,

> the Africans are never on the winning hand in the plain field, but when they take shelter in their strongholds, which are dense forests in times that they have leaves, they make fire without being seen, and they mostly damage our men a lot ("História de residência" [1594] 1989: 190).

Sometimes, the *mato* is a stone "forest". Queen Njinga, "Lady of Angola" (Sousa 1985: 223) and a strong enemy of the Portuguese, often fortified herself in the rocky hills of the interior. Difficult to access, the rain forest was, certainly, the strongest ally of Africans who fought – for different reasons – against the Portuguese. For these men of the Atlantic, the tropical forest was an unknown and unfriendly space or even a military and theological inferno. The *General History of The Angolan Wars* by Cadornega ( [1680] 1972) reveals the obsession the forest aroused in the imaginary of the Portuguese. In virtue of the abundance of its forests, Cadornega calls Angola "a dense land" (Cadornega [1680] 1972, I: 102). In the work of this early historian, the forest becomes the quintessential expression of a hostile continent. It represents everything that hinders the advancement of Portuguese penetration. Referring to the fugitive slaves of a former Portuguese governor of Angola, Fernão de Sousa (1985: 286) assures us that they "hid themselves in the bush with the intention of defending themselves, apprehensive because of the crimes they had committed and the eating of human flesh" (Sousa 1985: 286). What really troubles the governor is, of course, that the hidden slaves are out of his reach. Instead of recognizing the advantage the knowledge of territory offers to the Africans, he disqualifies them by accusing them of grave crimes against humanity. In his narrative, the forest – like in the famous novel by Joseph Conrad – is *the heart of darkness*, the very seat of barbarism. When the Africans discovered that the *mato* inspired such horror in the Portuguese, they made it their habitual refuge, patiently negotiating from there with the intruders. Queen Njinga, in Angola, played this game to perfection, thus provoking the increasing anger of the Portuguese. Referring to the subterfuges the Portuguese governor opposed the liberation of her sister, a prisoner in Luanda. The queen wrote on 13 December 1655: "For these and other betrayals I took shelter in the *matos*, far from my territories" (Cadornega 1972, II: 501). By withdrawing to the forest, the queen was not only obeying a military imperative, but also putting pressure on the Portuguese. If they wanted her to get out of the forest, they had to fulfill a series of conditions. Meanwhile, she would resist: that was, in her political language, the sense of her withdrawal to the *matos*.

Besides its strategic function in the military and political struggle between the Africans and the Portuguese, the forest constituted, in the eyes of the autochthonous, a 'sacred' space. In the *História* of Cadornega, as was mentioned before, allusions to the "dense forests" of Angola are abundant. By repeating observations made by Jesuits almost a century before, the Portuguese historian hints to the religious dimension the bush or the forest had for Africans: "seeing that they could not triumph over us in the open lands, they gathered unwillingly in the sanctuary: their vast and dense *matos*" (Cadornega [1680] 1972, I: 81). By 1586, Father Diogo da Costa (1989: 163) had affirmed that the natives "worship wood and stones". In the same period, Duarte Lopes alluded to the "symbiosis" that existed, in Congo, among humans and the elements of nature: "men and women do not have proper, convenient, and rational names, but are called after plants, stones, birds and animals" (Pigafetta/Lopes 1951: 65). By giving themselves names of plants, stones, or animals, the natives manifested the intensity of their relation with the natural cosmos. The *mato*, concretely, becomes a sacred space in which men receive the protection and the power of their traditional "deities". It is true that in the texts

written by functionaries of the Portuguese empire, the quality of the
relationship the Africans maintained with the *mato* or the forest as a
sacred space is not described precisely. Something that may allow us,
at least to a certain point, to imagine the content of this relationship,
are certain songs – *mambos*[7] – of the present-day Cuban "Congos". A
creation of Cuban slaves, these songs are not strictly "African": it
would be naïve, therefore, to consider them a "source" for the reconstruction of an African *(Kongo)* cosmovision. It is probable, however,
that their "core" still draws upon the *kongo* cosmovision. In the *mambos* I had the opportunity to hear in Havana (1993), an ever-present
word is *(n)finda*[8]. In present-day Kikongo, *mfinda* is "bush" or
"forest". *(N)finda* is invoked by the *palo monte* communities as the
residence of the spirits of the dead and the spirits of nature. It is the
space of origin and tradition. Therefore, we can suppose that by hiding
themselves in the *matos*, the Central African populations not only
tried to escape the persecution of the slavers, but also renewed contact
with their ancestors, their traditions, and their "powers". The *mfinda*
allowed them to recover the energies they needed to keep struggling
against the *mindèlé* ('whites').

For the Africans, the war was never a purely military matter. On
the contrary, they dedicated themselves to it with the whole stock of
their traditional beliefs. Many Portuguese texts suggest that, for the
Africans, all circumstances involving military activity bore religious
meanings: "When some poor soldier in the camp happens, in his
dream, to cry *itá, itá*, which means war, war, the others take that as a
bad omen and cut his head off" ("História da residência" [1594] 1989:
190). Before going into action, the Africans consulted their "deities".
A nobleman "consulted his fetishes before crossing a river. He was
told that crossing the river, he would be killed" (Afonso [1581] 1989:
138). The invoked fetishes were right, but the nobleman was not given
time to take advantage of their advice: "By seeing that he did not
cross, our troops attacked him and took forty women, the most distin-

---

7   *Mambo*. Ritual song in *palo monte* communities. Kk. *màmbù* (pl. of *diàmbù*),
    trade, word, process, story, ritualized conversation (Sw.).
8   *(n)finda*. Also *finda*. "Those dense wood that these people call enfindas" (Ca-
    dornega [1680] 1972: II, 56). "The land of the dead is often called *mfinda*" (Bent-
    ley 1887: 347). Kk. *mfinda* (class i-zi), forest, wood (Sw.).

guished of his house, and killed some of his men" (Afonso [1581] 1989: 138).

Europeans also invoked their "deities": Saint Anthony, the Mother of God, and Santiago, the Iberian holy warrior. A battle that broke out in December 1622 between the Portuguese and the army of Mani-bumbe, a vassal of the king of Congo, was transformed into a battle among rival deities:

> Our Portuguese, in the heat of the battle, called Santiago, and the Muxi-congos[9] did the same. When they realized it, they said 'you have a white Santiago, while ours is black'. But our white one showed to be more powerful (Afonso [1581] 1989, I: 105).

## 4. Languages of violence

The fundamental context for the start of the Luso-African "dialogue" in the Congo-Angola region was, as we already know, the develop-ment of the Atlantic trade. To make contact with African chiefs, the Portuguese would "propose" an agreement of vassalage through which they committed themselves to providing them military help; the local chiefs would have to pay tributes and allow them full commercial freedom. The Africans were not always eager to accept those condi-tions. If they rejected the proposed alliance, the Portuguese, according to "juridical" rules established by themselves, declared war. Any war, whether they were victorious or not, was always an opportunity for the Portuguese to obtain large quantities of slaves. Explicit in this sense is a commentary of Father Baltasar Afonso ([1583] 1989: 142): "There is no war in which our troops do not get rich because they take many *pieces* [slaves] oxen, sheep, salt, oil, pigs, mats."

Besides its military and economic aspects, war was also a means of communication, a "language" based on more or less institutional-ized codes. Through their specific way of making war, the Portuguese sought to demonstrate their superiority and their ambition of total control over the territories. The "signifier" used to transmit this mes-sage was indiscriminate violence:

> It happened here that a father fled with his child from our troops, and seeing that he could not save his son he turned to us and shot all his ar-

---

9     *muxicongo*. Inhabitant of the Kongo kingdom. Kk. *músi* (pl. *bísi*), inhabitant, and *kóngo*, population of the Congo basin (Sw.).

rows until they killed him; he never abandoned his place so that his son could hide, and the father died and went to hell. Another man was in a house with two women and defended himself without any intention to surrender, so strongly that they put fire to the house, and burnt all three of them. This caused such a terror amongst our enemies that the whole of Angola was afraid of us (Afonso [1581] 1989: 135).

This story of an Angolan father's heroism provides evidence of the symbolic aspects of Portuguese violence. By acting with utter cruelty, the conquerors continuously "signified" the futility of any resistance. Another frequent practice of the Portuguese, mass decapitation, was the signifier of a similar message. Around 1620, "conforming to the customs of these kingdoms", the lieutenant-general of the Portuguese in Angola, João Mendes de Vasconcellos, convoked the *sobas* vassals of the Crown for a *maca*[10] – a sort of public trial based on the intervention of witnesses. Officially, the concern was to judge the "betrayal" of these chiefs, allies of Queen Njinga. According to Cadornega, the real goal of this encounter was to stage

> [...] a mass decapitation of black people (not inferior to that which King Xico inflicted on the Abencerrajes in the City of Granada, or to that of the famous duke of Alba in Flanders), who all had to pay with their heads for the betrayal, an event which would remain immemorial for the future of all the heathens of these astonished and fearful kingdoms: only with rigor and terror, we are able to maintain our domination over these indomitable pagans (Cadornega [1680] 1972, I: 92).

To further enhance the impact of such messages, the Portuguese did not hesitate to violate the bodies of their dead enemies: "From another war, [the Portuguese] brought 619 noses of decapitated men, and in another there were so many dead that they said they couldn't avoid walking on them" (Afonso [1583] 1989: 142).

The Africans fully understood the meaning of such messages. According to the stories of their adversaries, they used to respond with verbal violence. In the course of a battle on the Kwanza River, for example, the Africans, "loudly screaming, said they would eat all of us the next day" (Afonso [1583] 1989: 137). It has to be remembered that in European reports of that period, we frequently find allusions to

---

10   *maca*. "Maca is a meeting in a public place where people can expose their arguments" (Cadornega [1680] 1972, I: 91). Kmb. *máka* (pl.), conversations, questions, disputes (Ass.).

African 'cannibalism'. Jerónimo Castaño, a Spanish missionary in Angola, comments in 1599:

> This is the fourth time [the king of Angola asks for peace]. The last time, when Governor Paulo Dias sent presents to him with some Portuguese and [the king] agreed with the peace terms, when they arrived, he ate all of them (Gomes 1951: 60).

Did he actually eat them? In European colonial sources, allusion to cannibalism is always suspect because it is used to justify the so-called "rightful war" against populations who reject colonialism. In fact, far from being based on actual observation, allusions to African cannibalism mostly derive from an inaccurate interpretation of certain African speech patterns. As we heard before, Africans threatened the Portuguese by boasting that they would eat all of them. By saying this, they are not really uttering the intention to eat the Portuguese. By using a speech pattern I call *boasting speech*, they only intend to scare their enemies. Verbal violence against real and unlimited violence: the asymmetry of the "dialogue" between Europeans and Africans is evident.

## 5. Diplomatic languages

In Angola, during the first half of the seventeenth century, the exchange of diplomatic letters was the most prestigious "channel" for the "dialogue" between the Portuguese governor and his African interlocutors, allies or adversaries. It is important to understand that the correspondence between the representatives of the Portuguese crown and their African "vassals" was only an annex to a circuit of communication whose center was located in Europe. The messages exchanged through this channel always bore the mark of the European written tradition and the feudal language used in the Spanish-Portuguese empire. Of course, epistolary communication was radically alien to the local oral tradition. No expression of autonomous African thought would fit in a letter, which respected the rules of feudal correspondence. By writing or dictating a letter, African kings or chiefs implicitly recognized their submission to the Iberian crown. When a Portuguese governor, in a diplomatic letter, offered the status of a "vassal" to some of the local chiefs, the latter, if responding via the same channel, could only declare his acceptance. That means that the channel or medium – diplomatic correspondence, in this case – decisively shaped the content of the message. The famous theory of McLuhan (1967) – "the medium is the message" – receives here an evident confirmation. Of course, African chiefs did not always agree with the Portuguese hegemony. If they wanted to speak out their refusal, they would lay hand on other means like orality, body language, and, last but not least, war.

A letter of Angola Aire, puppet king of the Portuguese "Angola", who had been elected under pressure and in the presence of the Portuguese by a council of autochthonous "electors", in October 1626 offers a good example of what an African lord was allowed to say in a diplomatic letter addressed to a Portuguese authority. In the words of Fernão de Sousa, its author, the "king"

> [...] thanked me for having made him a king, and excused himself for not having sent me what he owed to me for this reason; he [said] he would do it at a given time because in this very moment, he didn't have any properties. He begged me to catch the free maroon negros in order to people with them his kingdom. He explained he could not open the [slave] market for not being ready yet. Arguing that people said that the *jaga* Caza and [the queen] Ginga Ambande were between Zungui Amoque and Andalla Quesua causing great damage and threatening war, he begged for protection and security of life. He asked me for an umbrella and a hat for himself, similar to that worn by the king of Congo, some tambourines and some bells, a carpet and a silk blanket and paper, and he sent me a black woman with hanging breasts, a bearded negro, and four negroes (Sousa 1985: 260).

In this piece of writing, Angola Aire, the new and so grateful "king", is speaking as a "good vassal". A thorough reading of his letter, however, shows that he does not offer anything concrete to the Portuguese. Pointing to the difficult situation of his kingdom, Angola Aire refuses, without saying so explicitly, to create the slave markets and to pay the tributes the Portuguese expect from him. His letter is a refined diplomatic exercise: by simulating his submission, the "vassal" hopes to avoid its consequences. As can be learned from the governor's summary, the puppet king accompanied his epistle with another kind of message. The gift of a "black women with hanging breasts, a bearded negro, and four [other] negroes" does not meet, of course, the expectations of the governor. Without breaking the rules of official communication, the mediocrity of Aire's gift symbolically indicates the limits of his good will. As we will see later on, the puppet king would finally get tired of this role.

In his report, governor Fernão de Sousa transcribes a letter that queen Njinga sent on 3 March 1625 to the *capitão-mor* ("field-marshall") of Angola, Bento Banha Cardoso. Notwithstanding the hate she always seems to have felt for the Portuguese (Sousa 1985: 227), she knew perfectly the rules of diplomatic correspondence:

> With all my heart I appreciate that Your Honour will come to this fort of Embaca, allowing me to give to you, as to a father, an account of how, when I sent some *pieces* to the market of Bumba Aquiçanzo, Aire launched an attack and stole some thirty *pieces* from me. When I gave orders to demand satisfaction from him as my vassal, my warriors found themselves face to face with nine men who were with Tigre [Estêvão de Seixas Tigre] in my territory, and when he pushed these nine men against my troops outside the Pedra [de Pungo Andongo], they were, God willing, defeated by my warriors. The surviving six of them were delivered to me. It made me sad to learn that in Aire's rocks there are Portuguese soldiers supporting Aire. I received them warmly because they are vassals of the king of Spain, to whom I owe obedience as the Christian I am (Sousa 1985: 244-245).

This letter is one of the best examples the report of Fernão de Sousa provides to anybody willing to see to what extent the means (or the "channel") determine the form as well as the content of a message. Through her attack on the Portuguese, the queen, in the transparent language of war, "declared" that she would not tolerate the penetration of the Europeans into her kingdom, and that she did not lack military means to defend her territory. However, as an author of a diplomatic letter addressed to the chief of her enemies, "Dona Ana de Sousa" exposes the same circumstances according to the norms of epistolary communication with a superior. If we read what she actually wrote, it seems that she never attacked the Portuguese: she only sent an expedition to punish one of her vassals, the puppet king, for the hold up he had launched against her slaves. By pretending to ignore the privileged relations that existed between Aire (Aquiloange)[11] and the Por-

---

11  (Aquiloange) Aire should not be confounded with (Angola) Aire. After the death of the father of the future queen Njinga, the Portuguese needed to find a new king for Ndongo or 'Angola'. By maintaining a hostile attitude towards the intruders, Njinga could not be their candidate. Therefore, they chose (Aquiloange) Aire, "the closest family member of the king of Angola" according to Fernão de Sousa

tuguese, she argues that the encounter of her warriors with the troops of the governor was purely accidental. As for the victory of her warriors against the Portuguese, it was, simply, "God's will".

Although the queen's argumentation is absolutely sarcastic, she formally confirms her submission and loyalty to the Spanish-Lusitanian Crown. Throughout her long struggle with the Portuguese, the queen, without abdicating her principles, always showed a great ability in the choice of the "channel": diplomacy or war.

In Angola, diplomatic correspondence was usually conveyed by *macunzes*[12], "ambassadors" of the local chiefs – or of the Portuguese. These messengers were responsible for transmitting oral messages. In the court of the Portuguese governor, the oral messages, recited by the "ambassadors" in some African language (probably Kikongo and Kimbundu), required the help of an interpreter. To what extent could African chiefs choose between oral and written communication? For the *sobas*, written communication was certainly out of reach. Only the kings seem to have had interpreters and scribes at their service. The king of Congo as well as Angola Aire, the puppet king of Ndongo, apparently preferred writing as a way of demonstrating their real or feigned loyalty to the Portuguese. As for the queen Njinga, she systematically alternated letters with oral messages.

On 17 December 1627, Alvaro Roiz de Sousa, captain of the fort of Embaca, informs Fernão de Sousa about the arrival of two *macunzes* of queen Njinga conveying an oral message. In the previous month, the governor had declared an all-out war on the queen (Sousa 1985: 294). In the governor's words

> [...] the [queen's] message contained instructions proposing to submit [the *macunzes*], in her name, to an ordeal they call *quelumbo*[13], in order to prove that the incident which occurred in the Quezos: the death and

---

(Heintze 1985, I: 202). As Aquiloange Aire died of pox in the Portuguese camp, they finally "supported" his half-brother Angola Aire.

12  *Macunze*. "Mukunzes are envoys or ambassadors in the Ambunda language" (Cadornega [1680] 1972, I: 349). Kmb. *múkunji* (class *mu-a*), envoy, prophet, missionary (Ass.). Kk. *nkùnzi* (class *mu-ba*), bearer, ambassador, envoy (Sw.).

13  Kmb. *kilúmbu* (class ki-i), ordeal. Test which serves to assert the truth of the affirmations of the individual. Testers apply white-hot metal to the body of persons suspected or oblige them to absorb some poison.

the imprisonment of several *pombeiros*[14] [catchers of slaves], the robbery of *pieces* and fabrics, had not been ordered by her, and if the said two negroes died because of the ordeal, she would be glad to have her head cut off, but if they did not die with the ordeal, it would be clear that she did not have any responsibility in this incident because she did not join with the Quezos, nor did the *sobas* of Lucala join with her, and she was not at war with any of them. The only wish she had was to be a *piece* and a daughter of mine, and to obtain permission to *tungar*[15] [settle] on the island of the *imbillas*[16] [graveyards] where her brother died, and that for God's sake Angola Aire should be the king, because she wanted to retire for being tired of living in the *matos* (Sousa 1985: 296-297).

According to this summary by the governor, Njinga, by choosing the oral "channel", seems to pursue the same goals as when, in the former example, she addresses the governor by means of diplomatic correspondence. The way she justifies herself and denies any responsibility for the 'crimes' attributed to her by the Portuguese resembles perfectly the way she used in her letters. There are, however, several allusions to another kind of argumentation. One of them is the wish to *tungar* ("settle") on the island that hosts the grave of her brother. If we remember the importance of the ancestor's cult amongst Bantu populations, we understand immediately that the "Christian" queen intends to honor, in that place, the memory of her dead brother. A Congo king quoted by Wing (1921: 285) in the early twentieth century seems to justify the queen's wish: *Ga k'akala nkulu aku ko, k'ulendi tunga ko* ("Don't settle in a place where there are none of your ancestors"). Everybody knew that Queen Njinga never detached herself from a receptacle called *mosete*[17] in which she "enclosed the bones of her forefathers" (Cadornega [1680] 1972, II: 167). In a diplomatic letter, the expression of her wish to continue honoring – in an African way – the memory of her brother certainly would have been perceived as proof of her persistent resistance against Christianity and European

---

14  *pombeiros*. African slave traders in the service of the Portuguese (area Congo-Angola). *Pumbo* or *pombo* "are places and villages in which the slave markets are organized and where they sell our products in exchange of clothes and *pieces* of slaves" (Sousa 1985: 324).

15  *tungar*. "Tungar means to make quarter and houses" (Cadornega [1680] 1972, I: 345). Kmb. and kk. *-tunga*, to build, to construct, to settle.

16  *imbilla*. Name of an island in the Kwanza River (Angola). "They call their graves *imbilla*" (Cadornega [1680] 1972, III: 263). Kmb. *mbila* (plural in *ji-*), tomb, grave (Ass.).

17  Kmb. *músete* (class mu-mi), shrine, bag (Ass.).

values.[18] In an oral message in an African tongue, however, the same expression does not seem to have scandalized the Portuguese governor.

Perhaps the *script* proposed by Njinga for the reception of her oral message – an ordeal – is clearer evidence of her "African way of thinking". Used as a means of diplomatic exchange, the written word is a "weapon", but certainly not the expression of truth. On the contrary, in the African – oral – system of communication, an "ethic code" guarantees, in principle, the sincerity of the speaker as well as the veracity of the transmitted message. This veracity, as we see in Njinga's message, may be controlled through a ritual proof: to certify her sincerity to the governor, she proposes indeed the application of the *quelumbo*, an ordeal, to her *macunzes*. If they died, she explains, "she would be glad to have her head cut off". Based on a non-Christian theology, the proof proposed by Njinga to assert the veracity of her message demonstrates that the Christian faith she professed in her diplomatic letters was merely "diplomatic". Of course, the "authentic" Christian faith of the Portuguese did not allow them to accept the "diabolic" proof proposed by their enemy. As "Christians", the technique they chose to know the "truth" was "Christian". More concretely, it had developed in the jails of the Inquisition. Like the defendants in the trials organized by the Holy Office, Njinga's *macunzes* were considered guilty before they had the opportunity to "confess". In a secret session, the Portuguese decided that "if they were not willing to confess, they would oblige them by torture to declare where [the queen] was, and that this – to prevent negroes from speaking about it – had to be done by Portuguese" (Sousa 1985: 296). The first to pay for his "crime" was the queen's *mani lumbo*[19], who accompanied the two *macunzes*. In a desperate effort to escape death, he offered an apparently full "confession". In spite of that, the Lusitans, declaring him guilty of espionage, condemned him to death. Thus, the

---

18  As it becomes clear from Cavazzi's *Descrição histórica*, the worship Njinga dedicated to the memory of Ngola Mbande, her deceased brother, continued thirty years after her negotiations with Fernão de Sousa, creating a serious strain on the relationship between the queen, officially Christian, and the Europeans – especially the catholic priests – present on her territory (Lienhard 1999).

19  *mani lumbo*. Also *muene lumbo*. "Muene lumbo is the one who has contact with the Royal House and supervises the most valuable things of that house" (Cadornega [1680] 1972, I: 353).

Portuguese, like the Africans, had at their disposal a *quilumbo* of their own: an arbitrary means to test the sincerity of their adversaries. The main difference between the African and the European ordeal is a contrasting attitude toward orality. The African attitude is positive – sacred, the spoken word is considered to be 'true'. Nobody, therefore, minds submitting to a *quilumbo*. For the Portuguese, the spoken word, on the contrary, is essentially deceptive – only violence allows the "truth" to emerge.

## 6.  African rhetoric: *nongonongo*

If we stick to Fernão de Sousa's transcriptions of the oral messages he received from his African interlocutors, it seems that they were free of any rhetorical or poetical artifice. To what degree, however, are these transcriptions reliable? The *makunzes*, without any doubt, recited their messages in one of the local Bantu languages. The governor did not speak any of them; moreover, he does not show any particular interest in understanding the surrounding linguistic culture. The veil that covers the rhetoric of his African adversaries is partially lifted only in a few fragments of his report. As we already know from the letter queen Njinga sent to the governor on 3 March 1625, she had – thanks to God – captured six Portuguese. In a message transmitted by her *mani lumbo* to Sebastião Dias, the captain of the fort of Embaca, the queen made their delivery conditional on several requirements, especially the suppression of the military support given by the Portuguese to Aquiloange Aire, the puppet king she considered her vassal. As the captain did not accept her conditions, the queen sent her *moenho*[20] – private ambassador – to repeat her demands. The dialogue between the queen's emissary and the Portuguese captain developed, in the words of the governor, as follows

> [...] in the message he transmitted from Ginga, the *moenho* said the same by way of the following comparison: "There has been a heavy rain, which has reached some hen and plucked them; they have retired to a house, where they wait now to recover their feathers". Sebastião Dias answered that if she did not want to bring those Portuguese, she had better send them and not retain them as hostages [to be exchanged] for Diungo Amoiza and Aire Quiloange because there might be a thunderstorm and a

---

20   *Moenho*. "This is life" (Cadornega [1680] 1972, III: 265). Kmb. *muénhu* (class *mu-mi*), soul, existence, spiritual force (Ass.).

flash might fall on the house where the hen were recovering their feathers, and burn it down (Sousa 1985: 243).

A missive sent by the six Portuguese to the captain helps to understand the issue of this rather enigmatic dialogue. They wrote that their liberty "would not cost more than to hand over Dungo Amoíza and to ship Aire" (Sousa 1985: 243). The queen pretended, as a matter of fact, to exchange her prisoners for a befriended *soba* prisoner of the Portuguese and to obtain, at the same time, the withdrawal of the puppet king Aire Aquiloange. Through his ironical "comparison", the *moenho* stressed that the queen was prepared to wait until the Portuguese accepted her conditions. His interlocutor, Sebastião Dias, a Portuguese soldier familiarized with this type of verbal exchange, responded in the same way, evoking, with evident sarcasm, the risks the queen would run should she not cede to the pressures of the Portuguese. This apparently strange dialogue may be situated easily within the Bantu tradition of "enigmatic dialogue". Referring to this tradition, our always well-informed Cadornega wrote in 1680:

> These heathens from the province of Quissama [south of Luanda] speak in an enigmatic way, using nicknames and metaphors. He who knows their fashion and their tongue speaks to them and answers in the same style. Thus, he who understands their inventions and their tricks, manages to pay them back in the same coin (Cadornega [1680] 1972, II: 344).

The "metaphorical" rhetoric Cadornega ascribes to the "pagans of Quissama" is, in fact, common in the Bantu area. Among proverbs, riddles, apologues and jokes, it nurtures a gamut of minor literary genders. According to Chatelain, one of the names assigned to the riddle in Kimbundu (the language probably used by the emissary of the queen and the Portuguese captain in their venomous dialogue) is *nongonongo* (Chatelain 1888-1889: 143). In Kikongo, *nóngo*[21] is used for a "pungent saying", for a way to mock the interlocutor through a fable or an apologue. In the following Kimbundu "proverb", recollected by Chatelain (1888-1889: 140), the sarcasm often accompanying the enigmatic rhetoric is evident: *Uanienga xitu, nguma ia jimbua* ("Who carries flesh, is an enemy to dogs"). It is used to criticize a person whose arrogant behavior provokes social reproval. When ut-

---

21   Class *i-zi*.

tered after a person has already suffered "the dog's bite", i.e. the negative consequences of his arrogant behavior, it takes on a clearly sarcastic meaning.

In the seventeenth-century reports of the Portuguese, allusions to the rhetoric used by the Africans in their verbal exchanges with the Europeans are rare. Typically, their authors reduce African speech to its purely denotative aspects. Therefore, the brief dialogue between queen Njinga's *moenho* and the Portuguese captain is one of the rare opportunities we have to imagine the "tone" of the verbal exchanges between conquerors and conquered. Irony similar to that used by Njinga's ambassador in his *nongonongo* can be discovered, retrospectively, in several of the queen's written messages we find in his "diary". If we go back to the letter in which Njinga declares her "compassion" for the six unfortunate Portuguese who fell into the trap laid by her troops (3 March 1625), we now "hear", notwithstanding her perfectly diplomatic language, the verbal perfidy it hides. In fact, the affirmation of her "regrets" for the "divine" punishment suffered by the Portuguese, those "plucked hens", in the oral message of the *moenho*, scarcely cover the expression of the most profound sarcasm.

## 7. African rhetorics: *milonga*

The "journal" kept by Fernão de Sousa contains numerous allusions to another African speech pattern: *milonga*. In Kimbundu, *milónga* (plural of *mulónga*) refers not only to "words", but also to more specific uses of speech: "affirmations", "reasons", "trial", "calumny", "offense". In the text of the governor, *milonga* seems to point to a rather specific speech pattern. According to Fernão de Sousa, Njinga's *milongas* have the power to persuade whole villages to flee to the lands under her control:

> [Njinga] kept temporizing with messages she sent me, and her *macunzes*, on their way back, in this city as well as in [the lands of] the *sobas* along where they passed, persuaded our slaves and our black soldiers, whom they call *quimbares*[22], that they should go to her, and that she would give them land to work and live on because it was better for them to be native lords than to be our slaves; and with such messages, which they call

---

22    Kmb. *kimbari* (class *ki-i*), tenant.

*milongas*, she has such an influence over them that that complete *senzalas*[23] [villages] run over to her (Sousa 1985: 227).

In Fernão de Sousa's report, *milonga* seems to hint at a speech of persuasion based on promises or threats. From the viewpoint of the governor, this sort of speech is essentially treacherous. Africans were not the only ones who knew how to use it. The governor shows that Portuguese also were capable to practice it successfully:

"To dress" is a fashion that was introduced to ask the *sobas* for *pieces* [slaves] in the following manner: the governors sent a *macunze*, who is an ambassador, with a quantity of silk clothes, *empondas* [clothes] and *farregoulos*, which is the clothing of the negroes, and this *macunze* told each *soba* that he was the *macunze* of the governor and that he came looking for *loanda* [tribute], and as the *macunzes* were always persons well trained for this business, they stripped the best they could from each *soba*, obliging them with practices they call *milonga*s to give to the governor, the *macunze*, the interpreter and their companions, the [number of] slaves they could not [really afford to] give (Sousa 1985: 279).

In this case, *milonga* seems to be a speech used to persuade his interlocutor to do or to give something he is not really prepared or willing to do or to give. In the journal of Fernão de Sousa, we can see that the practice of *milonga* often implies using body language, mime and other theatrical means. The Africans as well as the Portuguese seem to know how to use such means for their purposes of persuasion.

## 8. Body language

Body language seems to play a capital role in the Luso-African "dialogue". One day, in order to convince the puppet king, Angola Aire, to support the war against queen Njinga, the Portuguese field marshal reminds him of the duties he has as a vassal of the Portuguese king (Sousa 1985: 328). Conscious that "the kingdom did not belong him", Aire refuses to continue the masquerade. Replying to the field marshal, he stages a curious mime sequence:

[...] he answered that he and Ginga were children of the field marshal, that he did not mind if [the Portuguese] wanted to crown her queen, that he would go to Pedras or to Lembo and stay there, and that they could cut his head off. Then he sat on the ground, stood up, took a straw in his hand and handed it over to the interpreter, so giving to understand that he surrendered the kingdom, and, by turning his back very impolitely,

---

23   Kmb. *sanzala* (plural *ji-*), village, settlement outside the residence of the *soba*.

he left without giving anything to the porters who had asked him for provisions for the war that was being made in his favor and that he had
requested, even if he said he did not (Sousa 1985: 328).

What is interesting about this scene is that Aire, at the exact moment
he gives up his role as puppet king in the service of the Portuguese,
stops talking and adopts non-verbal means of communication, undoubtedly inspired by the "autochthonous" tradition. This way, he
shows that he has resolved to leave definitely the world of the Portuguese. These were quick enough to understand the meaning of this
body language message. The governor had already chosen the person
who, in his opinion, had the capacity to play the role of king or queen
of "Angola": Dona Maria Cambo, sister of Njinga and of Ngola
Mbandi, the former king of Ndongo.[24]

As for the Portuguese, they learned to use mime or body language
to their own advantage. Sousa offers a vivid description of the methods used by Portuguese officials and traders :

> At other times, certain persons offered to realize such missions by con-
> tract for a certain amount of *pieces* [slaves], and some were so devoted
> that they offered to do that on their own cost. When they made the jour-
> ney in such a way they provided themselves with silk and other things,
> went to the provinces, and every time they arrived to [the residence of] a
> *soba*, they sat down on an armchair and performed the role of the gover-
> nor, and by intimidating the *soba*, they obliged him, when he was power-
> ful, to give them at least ten slaves, and when he was less powerful, only
> five, not counting the other ones he had to give them for their needs of
> company, alimentation and lodging, among them sometimes women and
> children of the *sobas*, with a great disrespect they felt deeply. The cap-
> tains of the forts did and continue doing the same by sending *macunzes*
> to the *soba*s in imitation of the governors (Sousa 1985: 279-280).

In these and other similar cases, the use of mimic codes by Portuguese
adventurers creates the fraudulent illusion of the governor's presence.
Fernão de Sousa obviously denounces such simulacra. That notwithstanding, certain stagings realized by the governor were hardly less
spectacular than those of his subalterns. As a great "communicator",
Fernão de Sousa skillfully combined diplomatic writing, body language, and the language of violence. In his answer to a letter the field
marshal sent him on 16 February 1629, Fernão de Sousa (1985: 327)
wrote:

---

24   See Sousa's letter of 25 August 1629 (Heintze 1985, II: 230-231).

> If the imprisoned *sobas* do not submit as vassals, you shall give orders to
> apply to their chests two stamps of mine, and let them go; on account of
> their little value and things that may happen in the future, it is more im-
> portant that they remain marked as my slaves.

This way, the "presence" of Fernão de Sousa would remain "staged"
forever on the bodies of the humiliated *sobas*, compelled from now on
to act as involuntary propagandists of his politics. By marking the
bodies of his adversaries with his stamp, the governor repeats a particularly perverse use of writing, which we know also from other areas
colonized by the Europeans. A missionary-chronicler of the colonization of Mexico wrote, around 1541, that the Spaniards "applied on the
faces [of the Indians] so many inscriptions besides the principal stamp
of the king that they had the whole face written because they had inscriptions of all who had bought and sold them" (Motolínia 1985:
paragraph 50). Imitating cattle branding, this practice expresses, better
than any words, the mentality of the European slavers in Africa and
America.

## 9.  Rumors

In Angola, the communication between Africans and Portuguese was
not always carried out within the "official" circuit discussed above.
Fernão de Sousa's report presents many cases of indirect or "oblique"
communication. I am referring here especially to messages received
by the Portuguese through their prisoners and to the rumors constantly
buzzing around their ears. Some of these indirect messages contain
details about life in African military camps that never figure in the
official messages of the *sobas* nor of the queen herself. How does
"indirect" or "involuntary" communication work? Who, if anybody,
wants to communicate with whom and with what intention? Fernão de
Sousa's journal does not provide explicit answers to such questions.
Who, for example, are the real interlocutors in the following story?

> [...] and the negro [slave of Pedro de Sousa Sotomayor] said that she [the
> queen] did not have many soldiers, and that she retired to a house, very
> sad and angry about what happened, and did not talk to anybody, and for
> that reason sent the *macunzes* to take the *quelumbo*, which is a local or-
> deal, to prove that she had nothing to do with nor ordered what happened
> (Sousa 1985: 299).

The governor summarizes here the apparently "spontaneous" testimony of an anonymous African captured by the Portuguese. Rather curiously, the testimony of the "negro" recalls the arguments Njinga had used to prove her sincerity to the Portuguese. Are we faced, then, with a false testimony, directly "inspired" by the instructions of the queen? The governor's "Extensive report" suggests continuously the charisma and the influence Njinga exercised not only over her own subordinates, but also over broad groups of the African population theoretically controlled by the Portuguese. It must not have been difficult for her to organize and control the circulation of certain 'rumors'. Thus, the "testimony" of the anonymous slave may have been a rumor deliberately spread by the queen to strengthen her credibility among the Portuguese. The following passage of the governor's diary evokes another history of rumors:

> Ginga, knowing that Aire [Aquiloange] had gone to the fort, revealed her mood and convoked all the *sobas* of Coanza to declare war on him. She pretended that the *sobas* had told her that he [Aire] had gone to the fort and, by the same occasion, taken the title of "king", and that, therefore, they wanted to declare war and not obey him, and [that] they had asked her to approve them and to give them a chief capable to lead them to war. She, Ginga, had answered that she did not order the war, but, as they wanted to launch it, she would give them a chief – it was a *macota* ["elder"] of hers (Sousa 1985: 240).

It is clear that in the eyes of the governor, the debate between Njinga and the *sobas* about the opportunity of a war against Aquiloange Aire is pure "fiction", a story invented by the queen in order to delude him into thinking that only under pressure of the *sobas* had she undertaken the war. But how was this "fiction" transmitted to the governor or to his representative in the war zone, the field marshal Bento Banha Cardoso? The most likely answer is that the queen herself spread the rumor of her lack of responsibility in the launching of the war, a rumor that may not have been a complete "fiction" because the attitude Njinga imputes to the *sobas* does not seem to be a mere product of her fantasy. In fact, the governor himself presents many formal testimonies confirming the anti-Portuguese attitude of several African chiefs. In June 1629, for instance, he notes that the *soba* Andala Quionza of the *sobado* of Andala Queçuba refused to receive the "ambassadors" of the Portuguese field marshal. Back from their mission, the *macunzes* declared in the presence of several witnesses that

[...] traveling to the lands of the said Andala Queçuba, they arrived at the *libata* (that is a residence) of a *macota* (that is an adviser) who lives on the border of the lands. [This *macota*] did not let them pass to transmit the *milonga* they brought for his *soba* Andala Queçuba, but he told them to deliver the message they brought from [Aire] Angola, because they did not know the captain [field marshal] neither wanted to have anything to do with him (Sousa 1985: 337).

The unfriendly attitude of this *makota* shows that the traditional chiefs were not necessarily willing to collaborate with the Portuguese. At the same time, they did not always feel strong enough to undertake war against them. The best option was, in that case, "passive resistance". Fernão de Sousa's report is full of stories showing attitudes of this type, but it also offers examples of more radical attitudes of resistance. Particularly hostile was the attitude of *soba* Bujlla or (A)mbuyla. The Portuguese, considering his territory part of the "kingdom of Angola", demanded his submission. Mbuyla, however, always proclaimed to be a vassal of the king of Congo (Sousa 1985: 258-259, 269). The differences between Mbuyla and the Portuguese threatened to develop into an "international" conflict because the king of Congo, who supported the *soba*, was at that time an ally of the Dutch, competitors of the Portuguese in Africa as well as in Brazil. Considering the gravity of the situation, Fernão de Sousa did not hesitate to threaten the king of Congo, reminding him, in good Africanized Portuguese that "*moca-nos*[25] ["problems"] among kings had to be decided by arms" (Sousa 1985: 259). His transcription of Mbuyla's speech deserves our attention:

Bujllas became even more arrogant and said that Bento Banha [the Portuguese field marshal] had to be his *macota* ["elder"] and that he [Mbuyla] had to be appointed governor in Loanda, and he started to upset the *sobas* vassals persuading them that they should revolt, [saying] that he was *mani Puto* ["lord of Portugal"] and his wife *mani Congo* ["queen of Congo"] (Sousa 1985: 340-341).

Where did the governor hear the inflammatory speech he imputes to Mbuyla? As he does not reveal his sources, we must assume that he is drawing upon rumors spread by the *soba* to create confusion in the

---

25  *Mocano.* "Mocanos are judgments realized from person to person without any paperwork involved" (Cadornega [1680] 1972, II: 61). Kk. *mòkána, mòkéné*, to entertain, to speak with each other (Sw.). Kmb. *múkanu* (class *mu-mi*), condemnation.

territory "controlled" by the Portuguese. If we accept the authenticity of Sousa's transcription, Mbuyla was clearly trying to radicalize the struggle against the Portuguese. In contrast to queen Njinga, whose intermittent war against the Portuguese was basically defensive, Mbuyla seems to have formulated the ideological bases for an anti-colonial movement of a messianic type (Queiroz 1977). By declaring himself *mani* of Portugal, he claims (near) divine *status* of the distant European king. In other words, he assumes the right to choose, to his liking, the personalities to whom he will entrust the different local governments. His wife will rule the kingdom of Congo; a mestizo, as he declares later, will govern that of Angola. The Portuguese field marshal will have the privilege of being one of his own "elders". Ironically, there is no place left for the actual governor, Fernão de Sousa. Mbuyla's speech presents an openly messianic utopia. The prophet, thanks to his supernatural power, will invert the actual political situation. As in other similar cases, the power of words substitutes power the speaker is not likely to win. As a matter of fact, the messianic utopia Fernão de Sousa attributes to Mbuyla is only an extreme form of a seemingly widespread "dissidence" among the *soba* "vassals" of the Portuguese.

## 10. The language of flight

Until now, little attention has been paid to the interventions – at least the more or less "autonomous" interventions – of common people in the "dialogue" or "war of discourses" between Africans and Europeans in "Angola". Unfortunately, the Portuguese chronicles and reports do not offer much evidence about the speech and the attitudes anonymous Africans used to adopt under the known circumstances. Apart from occasional testimonies about events witnessed only by them, common African people – free, freed or enslaved – do not speak on the pages of Fernão de Sousa's "Extensive report" nor on those of any of the other documents I have mentioned. Their part is mostly reduced to that of *pieces* in a game played by others, Africans or Portuguese. It is not easy, therefore, to recover their "discourse", but, with some effort, we can retrieve a few allusions to their more "practical" attitudes. In a way, an attitude is also a "language". In the Angola wars, the most common attitude of the African masses is to flee. Besides its

practical purposes, flight is a sort of language used mainly by those
with no voice in the sphere of power. The message that common Africans delivered by their flight was their refusal of Portuguese colonization and its perverse effects on their traditional life. Fernão de Sousa
clearly understands this language. The Africans, he explains, flee to
escape war and to avoid enslavement by the Portuguese or their African allies. Often, he acknowledges, they try to take refuge on the lands
controlled by queen Njinga or to flee to the residence of a still independent *soba*. All these "statements" in the language of flight clearly
underline the common African's aversion to European colonization.
The Portuguese quickly felt the veiled threat contained in such "messages". Sebastião Dias Tissão, the old soldier capable of speaking in
riddles like his Bantu interlocutors, informed the governor that "Ginga
had recruited people and planned to reconquer the land; that our slaves
ran away again taking refuge with her, through which she made herself more powerful and weakened our position" (Sousa 1985: 241).
How to respond to the fugitives? Portuguese opinions on this point
greatly differed. Preoccupied by the constant erosion of their slave
capital, some Portuguese settlers proposed to Fernão de Sousa to "capture people of Quiçama [a still independent territory] in order to exchange them for the slaves of ours they have" (Sousa 1985: 323). The
governor categorically rejected this proposal. He was afraid of "what
could happen if said people were captured, as well as of the assaults
they necessarily would launch on account of the protestations". All
this, he argued,

> might lead to a revolt and block the shipment of provisions to this city
> [Luanda] as well as the navigation of the ships sailing upstream with
> goods, besides other accidents that might happen to the Portuguese trad-
> ers who sail up and down the Coanza river, like the seizing of merchan-
> dises; by defending them, people might be killed, the *quilombo* [military
> headquarters] being to distant [to intervene].

Drawing attention to the catastrophic consequences to which a raid in
Quissama might lead, Fernão de Sousa places the phenomenon of
flight in the wider context of the "dialogue" between Portuguese and
Africans. He understands that such movements must be "read" as
signs of the only language threatened or enslaved Africans have at
their disposal when they wish to be "heard" by the Portuguese: flight.
As a matter of fact, Africans, by fleeing, show a certain disposition to

"dialogue". That is what the governor tries to explain to the slavers: if they want to avoid the outburst of a general revolt that might even threaten the permanence of the Portuguese in the area, the have to decipher correctly the flight movements of the Africans. In contrast to the (common) slavers, the governor was aware of the danger implied by a unilateral breaking off of the "dialogue" with the Africans.

Another event referred to by Fernão de Sousa shows the consequences of the breaking off of the "dialogue". In 1627, the politically-inadequate response given to the massive flight of the slaves of Luiz Mendes de Vasconcellos, former governor of Angola, caused a perilous situation in Ilamba (Souza 1985: 286). Pursued by Portuguese soldiers, the fleeing slaves joined a substantial number of free blacks and some "misguided" whites. With their two thousand bows and the political dynamics their guerrilla-like activities provoked, this uncommon army presented a serious threat to the Portuguese power in that zone. When the governor sent troops to avoid a 'general mutiny'

> [...] the *tendalas*[26] ["representatives"] disappeared and did not obey the messages of Manuel Antunes [the Portuguese commander] and hid in the *mato* with the aim of defending themselves, out of fear of the crimes they had committed and of eating human flesh (Souza 1985: 286).

The breaking off of the "dialogue" is followed by the emergence of a nightmarish phantasm: the return of the Africans to the *mato*. If we recall the connotations of the *mato* as a space of "evil" in the imaginary of the Portuguese, the governor's preoccupation cannot surprise us. Should the Africans return to their *matos*, all efforts of conquest and colonization would have to start all over again, and under much worse conditions. In contrast to the recently "discovered" Africans, the fleeing slaves, the freed slaves, or the whites who felt tempted by the liberty promised by the "bush", had all the time necessary to 'study' their enemies. Moreover, they could oppose them with modern weapons.

## 11. Conclusions

At the beginning of this essay, I suggested that the war that developed in the sixteenth and seventeenth centuries between Portuguese and

---

26  Kmb. *tandála* (plural *ji-*).

Africans in the *matos* of the Congo-Angola region could be read as a sort of "dialogue" – or a "war of discourses" – between the European conquerors and their African adversaries. I hope to have demonstrated the interest of this approach. It allows us to "discover", in documentation written by the European aggressors, the different ways Africans – chiefs, common people, and slaves – "responded" and reacted to the penetration of the slave trade. The complicated histories I have tried to disentangle at least show that the inhabitants of Congo and Angola did not undergo passively the political, social and economical cataclysm caused by the Portuguese invasion. However, their "discourse" does not refer always to an attitude of radical resistance to the European conquest or to slavery. Many, maybe the majority, of the local chiefs seemed rather inclined to renounce a part of their sovereignty if by doing so they could take advantage of the economic possibilities promised by the presence of the European slave traders. Others, like queen Njinga, accepted the "dialogue" with the Portuguese, but without renouncing the defense of her sovereignty. Only few undertook the road of a more radical resistance. As for the African "masses", victims of the struggle between their chiefs and the European intruders, they fought above all for survival and against deportation to America, moving in accordance with the evolution of the military and political situation. Some fugitives managed to organize themselves as guerillas, threatening in this way the Portuguese power.

Throughout the whole story, the ones who dictated the rules of the game were, without any doubt, the Portuguese. How did they succeed in imposing their political hegemony? Their commercial power certainly impressed and attracted many local chiefs and may have persuaded them to fully cooperate with the foreigners. This argument, however, is not sufficient to explain the feeble reaction of many African chiefs to the Portuguese appropriation of the strategic points of their territory. There may be, of course, many reasons to explain the lack of "strategic" reaction of the local chiefs, but the most important, in my opinion, is the "rational" use of indiscriminate violence by the Portuguese. By following the traditional rules of war and negotiation they had learned throughout their local history, the Africans positioned themselves, from the beginning, in a place of strategic inferiority before a handful of truly "macchiavelian" intruders. Most likely, the advantage the Europeans won in the wars of Congo and Angola was not their, uncertain, military superiority, but the terror they managed to inspire in the autochthonous population through acts of unpredictable, unjustified, indiscriminate, and murderous violence. In the first pages of this essay, we had the opportunity to appreciate, and be horrified by, several cases of such "strategic violence". As in other places where, at nearly the same time, Europeans established their hegemony or domination, the inexorable progress of the Portuguese conquest of Central Africa definitely conveys the triumph of a "modernity" that banishes, in the name of colonial efficiency, any consideration based in – European or local – tradition or ethics.

# Bibliography

Afonso, Baltasar ([1577-1584] 1989): "Cartas, 1577-1584". In: Ferronha, António Luís Alves (ed.): *Angola no século XVI*. Lisboa: Alfa, pp. 135-140.

Almeida, José de Lacerda ([1798] 1989): Diário da viagem da vila de Tete, capital dos rios de Sena, para o interior da África. In: Santos, María Emília Madeira (ed.): *Textos para a história da África austral (século XVIII)*. Lisboa: Alfa, pp. 81-131.

Assis Júnior, António de (1947): *Dicionário de Kimbundu-Português*. Luanda: Argente Santos & Cia.

Bakhtine, Mikhael [V. N. Volochinov] (1977): *Le marxisme et la philosophie du langage. Essai d'application de la méthode sociologique en linguistique*. Paris: Minuit.

Balandier, Georges (1965): *La vie quotidienne au royaume de Kongo du XVI^e au XVII^e siècle*. Paris: Hachette.

Cadornega, António de Oliveira ([1680-1681] 1972): *História geral das guerras angolanas, 1680-1681*, 3 vols. Ed. José Matias Delgado. Lisboa: Agencia-Geral do Ultramar.

Capela, José (1978): *Escravatura: A empresa de saque*. Porto: Edições Afrontamento.

Cavazzi de Montecúccolo, João António ([1687] 1965): *Descrição histórico dos três reinos do Congo, Matamba e Angola*. Lisboa: Junta de Investigações do Ultramar.

Chatelain, Héli (1888-1889): *Kimbundu grammar. Gramática elementar do kimbundu ou língua de Angola*. Genebra: Schuchhard.

Costa, Padre Diogo da (1989): "Carta do Provincial de Portugal". In: Ferronha, António Luís Alves (ed.): *Angola no século XVI*. Lisboa: Alfa, pp. 157-167.

Dapper, Olfert ([1688] 1964): *Umständliche und eigentliche Beschreibung von Africa anno 1668*. Ed. Rolf Italiaander. Stuttgart: Steingrüben Verlag.

Ferronha, António Luís Alves (ed.) (1989): *Angola no século XVI*. Lisboa: Alfa.

Glasgow, Roy Arthur (1982): *Nzinga. Resistência Africana à investida do colonialismo português em Angola, 1582-1666*. São Paulo: Perspectiva.

Gomes, Claudio Miralles de Imperial y (1951): *Angola en tiempos de Felipe II y de Felipe III. Los memorials de Diego de Herrera y de Jerónimo Castaño*. Madrid: Instituto de Estudios Africanos.

Gorender, Jacob (1985): *O escravismo colonial*. São Paulo: Ática.

Heintze, Beatrix (ed.) (1985): *Fontes para a história de Angola do século XVII* (colectânea Fernão de Sousa, 1622-1635), vol. 1. Stuttgart: Franz Steiner Verlag Wiesbaden.

— (ed.) (1988): *Fontes para a história de Angola do século XVII* (colectânea Fernão de Sousa, 1622-1635, vol. 2. Stuttgart: Franz Steiner Verlag Wiesbaden.

História ([1594] 1989): "Historia da residência dos padres da Companhia de Jesus em Angola e coisas tocantes ao Reino e conquista". In: Ferronha, António Luís Alves (ed.): *Angola no século XVI*. Lisboa: Alfa, pp. 175-210.

Informação ([1576] 1989): "Informação acerca dos escravos de Angola". In: Ferronha, António Luís Alves (ed.): *Angola no século XVI*. Lisboa: Alfa, pp. 118-123.

Lienhard, Martin (1999): "'Métissage culturel' et communication. Succès et déboires de l'évangelisation en Angola au XVIe siècle". In: Grunberg, Bernard/Lakroum, Monique (eds.): *Histoire des métissages hors d'Europe.Nouveaux mondes? Nouveaux peuples?* Paris: L'Harmattan, pp. 51-63.

— ([4]2003): *La voz y su huella*. México, D.F.: Ediciones Casa Juan Pablos y Universidad de Ciencias/Artes de Chiapas.

Maestri Filho, Mário José (1988a): *Depoimento de escravos brasileiros*. São Paulo: Ícone.

— (1988b): *A servidão negra*. Porto Alegre: Mercado Aberto.

McLuhan, Marshall (1967): *The Medium is the Message*. New York: Bantam Books.

Motolínia, Frei Toribio de ( [1541] 1985): *Historia de los índios de la Nueva España*. Ed. Georges Baudot. Madrid: Castalia.

Oliveira, Mário António Fernandes de (1968): *Angolana. Documentação sobre Angola*, vol. 1. Luanda: Instituto de Investigação Científica de Angola/Lisboa: Centro de Estudos Históricos Ultramarinos.

— (1971): *Angolana. Documentação sobre Angola*, vol. II. Luanda: Instituto de Investigação Científica de Angola/Lisboa: Centro de Estudos Históricos Ultramarinos.

Pigafetta, Filippo/Lopes, Duarte (1951): *Relação do reino do Congo e das terras circunvizinhas*. Capeans, Rosa (transl.). Lisboa: Agência Geral do Ultramar, Div. de Publ. e Biblioteca.

Queiroz, Maria Isaura Pereira de (1977): *O messianismo no Brasil e no mundo*. Preface: Bastide, Roger. São Paulo, Alfa-Omega.

Rodrigues, José Honório ([3]1982): *Brasil e Africa: outro horizonte*. Rio de Janeiro: Nova Fronteira.

Saco, José Antonio (1853): *Obras de J. A. Saco López, compiladas por primera vez por un paisano del autor*. Vingut, Francisco Xavier (ed.). Nova Iorque: Librería Americana y estrangera de Roe Lockwood y Hijo.

Simões, Padre Garcia ([1575] 1989): "Segunda viagem de Paulo Dias de Novais". In: Ferronha, António Luís Alves (ed.): *Angola no século XVI*. Lisboa: Alfa, pp. 93-109.

Sousa, Fernão de ([1625-1630] 1985): "O extenso relatório do governador aos seus filhos". In: Heintze, Beatrix: *Fontes para a história de Angola do século XVII*, vol. 1. Stuttgart: Franz Steiner Verlag Wiesbaden, pp. 217-362.

Swartenbroekx, Pierre (1973): *Dictionnaire kikongo et kituba-francais*. Bandundu (Zaire), Ceeba.

Vansina, Jan (1985): "L'Afrique équatoriale et l'Angola. Les migrations et l'apparitions des premiers États". In: *Histoire générale de l'Afrique*, vol. IV. Paris: UNESCO/ NEA, pp. 601-628.

— (1990): *Paths in the Rainforest. Toward a History of Political Tradition in Equatorial Africa*. London: James Currey.

Wing, Reverend P. van (1921): *Études Bakongo: histoire et sociologie*. Bruxelles: Goemaere.

Ineke Phaf-Rheinberger

# Myths of Early Modernity:
# Historical and Contemporary Narratives
# on Brazil and Angola[1]

In this paper I will argue that for the cultural history of *Slavery and the Rise of the Atlantic System* (Solow 1991), studying *The Lettered City* (Rama 1996), by the Uruguayan critic Ángel Rama, is very useful. Rama's basic idea was to link the colonial period to the process of independence and modern democratization in the republics of Latin America. According to his argument, the lettered city is a main agency and a cultural reference board for illustrating the complexity of this development from a long-term perspective. The colonial "dream of an order" dating back to European expansion overseas designed a spatial mapping that maintains its impact until today. Such an organization delivers a framework for reading social hierarchies and tensions against which the differential philosophies can be laid out. This lettered city includes everything written and otherwise made visual.

For this lot of material evidence of the lettered city and its ideas on the rise of the Atlantic system, the work of the Dutch poet and philosopher Caspar Barlaeus – or Caspar van Baerle, who lived from 1584 to 1648 – might serve as a paradigm. In the context of their work on slavery and the slave trade in the so-called Dutch period, Barlaeus is familiar as Barléu to Brazilian historians. Barlaeus's volume *Rerum per octennium in Brasilia* (1647), regularly consulted in Brazilian research, described the maritime route between Brazil and Africa, and with special emphasis on Angola. In *O trato dos viventes* (Trade in Humans, 2000) about the formation of Brazil in the South Atlantic in the sixteenth and seventeenth centuries, Luiz Felipe de Alencastro resumes Barlaeus's position by pointing to his premonitions concerning the Christian "justice" of trading humans. Barlaeus is thus seen as

---

1 Another version of this article will appear in the forthcoming issue of CR: *The New Centennial Review* (2008).

questioning this trade, and I will analyze Barlaeus's treatise in the first part of this essay. Having thereby provided a background, I will compare his vision with its critical projection in three recent narratives by Angolan and Brazilian authors on this same subject.

## 1. The Dream of an Order laid out by Caspar Barlaeus

Although the slave trade is not a main concern in Rama's *The Lettered City*, it must be noticed that he repeatedly refers to the presence of African languages in America. His point of departure, however, is the insertion of the lettered city into a European network of mercantile relationships, within which the urban settlements overseas functioned as agents of the empire's "dream of an order". Rama's central point emphasizes the effect of long-term continuities and stressing the role of the city founded by Europeans from colonial times. Its three over-lapping hemispheres – the ordered city, the city of letters, and the city of protocols – offered colonizers a center for their administration and defense, which obeys the

> same regulating principles as the checkerboard: unity, planning, and rig-orous order reflecting a social hierarchy [...]. Circular plans perhaps con-veyed even more precisely than square ones the social hierarchy desired by the planners, with governing authority located at the center and the living spaces assigned to respective social strata radiating from the center in concentric circles (Rama 1996: 5).

The principles of this physical mapping and the distribution of space find their echo in writing from the sixteenth century and succeed in creating an autonomous space from the imposed norms:

> While the lettered city operated by preference in a field of signifiers, constituting an autonomous system, the city of social realities operated in a field of people, actions, and objects provisionally isolated from the letrados' chains of logical and grammatical signification [...]. This laby-rinth of signs is the work of the letrados, or collectively, the achievement of the city of letters. Only the letrados could envision an urban ideal be-fore its realization as a city of stone and mortar, then maintain that ideal after the construction of the city, preserving their idealized vision in a constant struggle with the material modifications introduced by the daily life of the city's ordinary inhabitants (Rama 1996: 27-28).

In accordance with Rama's view, the methodical planning of this ide-alized vision was carried out in the New World empires, whose spirit [did not stem] merely from the need to build cities, of course, although cities were its privileged settings, the artificial enclaves in which the autonomous system of symbolic knowledge could function most efficaciously (Rama 1996: 10).

He equally comments that this symbolic knowledge in Latin America was connected through major or minor ties with cities all over Europe:

[...] even though Madrid, Lisbon and Seville were located above the apex of this structure, [...] practically nobody ruminated that, at least in economic terms, other European cities like Genoa or Amsterdam might stand higher still (Rama 1996: 14).

These economic terms are the result of the link between European colonization and the expansion of consumer society throughout the network of urban trade. Gustavo Remedi (1997) even says that Rama inspired a new model of mapping cities, taking their spatial environment as a democratic project, the city as a "myth of modernity" in mercantile and military globalization, into account. Rama does that by connecting the different layers according to a scope that shapes an urban grammar, a ritual that constantly is challenging the colonial dream with reality and is revealed in the letrados' works. For them, when reflecting on the slave trade within the framework of this urban modernity, they concentrated on a port city, of course, which was the doorway to the transatlantic circuit as well as, until far into the twentieth century, provided the link between the global world and the hinterland.

Caspar Barlaeus belongs to this letrado-group for his mapping of the social hierarchies and the tensions in the realm of the South Atlantic trade. He lived in Amsterdam as success waned for the Dutch East and West India Company. His volume *Rerum per octennium in Brasilia* (Barlaeus 1647) was written there and fulfills all the conditions to offer the best vision of the European "dream of an order" in the foundational period of modern Europe. The author describes the development of the Dutch West India Company from 1621, the year of its official start, in reference to the Dutch conquest of parts of northeast Brazil as well as of the West African Coast – São Jorge de Mina, Luanda, São Tomé – from the Portuguese. He pays special attention to the government of Count Johan Maurits van Nassau-Siegen in Brazil from 1637 to 1644 because, after the count's return to the Netherlands, Barlaeus, who had never been in Brazil, was invited to write the report on van Nassau's successes. The book was presented as a real multimedia show because it contained poetry and prose (by Barlaeus), as well as abundant visual material such as maps, city views, sea views, and images of battles and fortress constructions mostly from the hand of the painter Frans Post (1612-1680).

The familiarity of Brazilian historians with Barlaeus's volume does not come as a surprise. Cláudio Brandão, commissioned by the Ministry of Education, translated the Latin text into Portuguese in 1940, and this translation has been reprinted several times in a facsimile edition until, finally, it came out with all the original illustrations in 1980. In *Innocence Abroad. The Dutch Imagination and the New World, 1570-1670* (2001), Benjamin Schmidt remarks that perhaps "no figure lent more prestige to the literary project of America than the esteemed humanist, Caspar Barlaeus, and certainly no work did more to celebrate the tropical feats of Johan Maurits than Barlaeus's *Rerum per octennium in Brasilia*" (1647: 254-255). Schmidt continues calling the book "a monumental work", a "princely volume in every sense", and possibly "the outstanding work overall of seventeenth-century Dutch geography". The *Rerum per octennium* was published at a particularly strategic moment, one year before the Treaty of Münster/Peace of Westphalia finally was confirmed in 1648, and Barlaeus must have been well aware of the terms for the upcoming agreement. It brought not only the end of the Thirty Years War in Germany but also peace with Spain and European-wide diplomatic recognition of the Seven United Provinces. Portugal, meanwhile, was at war with Spain, and the Brazilian case was most difficult to handle. According to the Brazilian historian Evaldo Cabral de Mello, Brazil was seen as a business deal between the various European partners, about which the definitive decision only would be taken in 1669 after long years of hard negotiations. The title of Mello's book, *O negócio do Brasil* (1998), is a quotation taken from a letter of the Portuguese ambassador Francisco de Sousa Coutinho, stationed in The Hague from 1643 to 1650. Mello provides information about the overall interest of the Dutch *grauw* (ordinary people) in the question of Northeast Brazil. The West India Company's investments in those years were open to small stockholders and therefore closely followed at all levels of the population. This explains the publication of anonymous pamphlets such as *De Brasilsche Breede-Byl* (Byl 1647), in which two servants accompanying their masters for business in Brazil discuss the current situation there.

In this context Barlaeus responds to what Rama offers as the adoption of American surroundings to European merchant conditions, whose greatest desire is the perfect "dream of an order" as the condition for proper investments. City life, thus, was important in Barlaeus's vision. Living in Amsterdam since 1631 profoundly influenced his philosophical discourse. During this period of rapid economic expansion, a ring of canals, the *grachtengordel*, was constructed and this experience of urban innovation considerably determines Barlaeus's view of the world. It even makes him, according to historian Johan Huizinga, "in many senses one of the most complete representatives of the civilization" in the Dutch seventeenth century (Huizinga 1998: 79). However, Barlaeus's book on Brazil did not hold Huizinga's attention. (Did he read the 1923 translation into Dutch?) This is different for Brazilian historians, as we have mentioned before, but research in Brazil does not merely copy Barlaeus's opinions; rather, it questions the philosopher's state of mind. Alencastro (2000: 211, 355), for instance, explores various crucial aspects of Barlaeus's philosophy. In his section on the war for slave markets, he quotes from an initial report by Johan Maurits sent to Amsterdam in 1638, in which the count summarizes a few necessities in the following practical format: colonists with European capital + soil and tropical agricultural technology + African workers. As governor he warns the administrators of the West India Company that scruples against this truth are useless. Furthermore, Alencastro recalls Barlaeus's cautious deliberations on the slave trade and on slavery in general. Via his manuscript Barlaeus complains that

> The desire for profit has grown stronger even among us Christians who embraced the pure teachings of the reformed church while we engaged in arms and warfare. In so doing we have returned to the custom of buying and selling human beings created in God's likeness, saved by Christ, the Lord of Creation, who least of all presents an image of slavery due to a lack of natural ingenuity (Barlaeus 1647: 185).[2]

---

2    Note: All the translations from Latin in this essay are done by Blanche Ebeling-Koning, whose translation of Barlaeus's volume into English is in process.
    *Nunc, postquam invaluit etiam inter purioris & in melius mutatae Fidei Christianos lucri cupiditas, aperiente viam bello & armis, rediimus & nos ad morem*

Barlaeus continues enhancing his own argument with rhetorical questions and remarks about the cruelty and inhumanity of abusing them as men, or rather as animals. Alencastro's second reference concerns the epilogue of the *Rerum per octennium*, consisting of the poem "Mauritia è Brasilia redux" ("Maurits back from Brazil"), written in 1644 and included in the Latin volume. In this poem Barlaeus repeats all his main points and deliberates again upon slavery:

> Why is a man deprived of his rightful liberty and why/ is it in the nature of things that he should suffer slavery? For whoever is human/ is made in the divine image. Born innocent, he rejects violence./ We mortals are all created with equal laws/ and rights;/ but soon injustice, the furor of war/ and savage madness made us unequal (Barlaeus 1647: 339).[3]

These admonishments are remarkable when considered against the assumption that protest against slavery and the slave trade gained ground in the Dutch public opinion only one century later (Paasman 2001: 481). Barlaeus lived through the years in which the Dutch "modernized" international trade by relating it to the Stock Exchange in Amsterdam. We learn from his most famous inauguration speech, *Mercator sapiens* (*Wise merchant*, 1967) on 9 January 1632, that Barlaeus is utterly enthusiastic about the changes in this city. He addressed the city's merchant in his daily preparations for international trade by outlining that Amsterdam was a central point in his global networking. One day earlier, Barlaeus's friend Gerardus Vossius had given another inauguration speech about the utility of history. They were the first professors of philosophy and church history, respectively, appointed to the recently founded Atheneum Illustre. Distinguished men, such as the Mayors Andries Bicker and Jacob de Graeff, who had strongly supported the foundation of this illustrious school, were in their audience.

Bicker and de Graeff were Arminians, one of two poles in the religious bias that divided the United Provinces at that time. The problems originated from a profound disagreement between Franciscus

---

emendi vendendique hominem, Dei quantumvis imaginem, à Christo redemptum, imperatorem universi, & nihil minus, quàm naturae ingeniique vitio servum (Barlaeus 1647: 185).

3    *Cur bona libertas homini subduceris? & cur/ Vis servum natura pati? coelestis imago est,/ quisquis homo est, natusque sibi vim respuit insons./ Mortalis aequis generamur legibus omnes,/ Jure pari, mox dissimiles injuria fecit,/ Et belli furor & rabies insana nocendi* (Barlaeus 1647: 339).

Gomarus and Jacobus Arminianus that the eponymous political ide-
ologies resulted (Israel 1998: 420-449). Whereas the Gomarists were
the symbol for rigidity and the hard hand in the war against Spain, the
Arminians were more inclined toward pacifism and negotiation.

Barlaeus belonged to this last category, and for him, the inauguration of the Athenaeum Illustre was a major event. He certainly knew
best how to address the spirit of that moment in history. Van der
Woude, the editor of the bilingual edition of *Mercator sapiens* (Barlaeus 1967), argues that in contrast with Vossius's long-forgotten
words, Barlaeus's speech struck the essence of the Athenaeum by establishing a link between academic education and business life. This
implied that education was not simply reduced to transferring practical
concrete knowledge. Rather, it assumed the task of guiding the moral
qualities of the student's character in view of his (future) mercantile
activities.

Such a noble objective fell into place in a city whose merchants
lived intoxicated by the impact of great economic expectations. Barlaeus perceptively grasped this spirit and made it the central topic of
his speech. After addressing almighty God, the representatives of the
municipal council and the church, the merchants, and the young people in his audience, he explains why he chose his subject: to establish
a relationship with the opulent township and to evoke its splendors:
"No matter how often I look at your city, which is now also my city,
letting my eyes wander over all its beauties and ornaments, I hesitate
what to admire first or last!" (Barlaeus 1647: 27).[4]

To further elucidate this vision Barlaeus praises the temples dedicated to God, buildings harboring the poor, towers and lighthouses
stretching up through the clouds yet grounding themselves on rotten
pine trees, quays constructed along canals, wharfs and hydraulic ele-
vators, the merchant's stock market as well as the curves and arches of
the bridges. He continues exalting the beauty of this harbor city with
its shops full of merchandise, enormous fleet, and incessant coming
and going of people. He cleverly seizes the contrast between the gods
of commerce and wealth, Mercury and Pluto, and those of science and

---

4    *Quoties urbem hanc vestram, jam quoque meam, intueor, et oculos per ejusdem
     decora omnia et ornamenta circumfero, pendeo animi, quid primum in ea, quid
     secundum, quid postremum mirari debeam* (Barlaeus 1647: 27).

art, Athens and Apollo, to draw attention to his argument that the Athenaeum offers an equilibrium between opulence and wisdom. Invoking ideals prevalent in antiquity, and to Aristotle and Cicero in particular, Barlaeus assures the public that the Greeks and the Romans were knowledgeable on this matter. They repeatedly asserted that real wisdom lay with showing the virtues of the merchant's activities. To inhibit the vices most reprehensible to him, corruption and dishonesty, Barlaeus recommends valuing the role of experience, conscience, cunning, innovation, power of judgment, as well as dialogue. These virtues become the standard norms for his moral philosophy (borrowed from antiquity), which he distinguishes from the speculative philosophy (practical, concrete, and modern knowledge) comprising geography, natural sciences, astrology, oceanography, mathematics, cartography, and the knowledge of many languages as well as of different cultural habits in a global mercantile network. It allows success in foreign countries, and Amsterdam offers all these indispensable tools, which privileges her above other European cities: "For this reason, I think of Amsterdam as a blessed city, because here the merchant can also be a philosopher and the philosophers can carry on his trade as a merchant" (Barlaeus 1647: 46).[5]

The eloquence and self-confidence of Barlaeus resulted from his auspicious appointment to the Atheneum after considerable obstacles in his professional life. During the National Synod of Dordtrecht in 1618, when he defended his Armenian point of view, the ideals of pacific tolerance were thrown overboard. The Gomarists won and, as a consequence, Barlaeus was dismissed from his public functions as a subregent of the Ecclesiastic College and lost tenure as professor of logic at the University of Leiden. To support his family he resorted to lodging students and giving private lessons. He introduced himself at the stadtholder's court in The Hague by writing Latin verses about heroic facts in the republic. Barlaeus loved experimenting with an elegant, learned style and equating events from antiquity with contemporary occurrences. He frequented humanist circles through which

---

5   *Quae cum ita sint, beatam hanc Amstelodamensium rempub. puto, in qua jam mercatoribus philosophari, et philosophis mercari concessum* (Barlaeus 1647: 46).

he came into contact with other learned men such as Pieter Cornelis Hooft and Constantijn Huygens (Horst 1978).

This humanist orientation is the crux of Barlaeus's discourse contrasting the vanity of material wealth on the one hand with wisdom, the constant value of divine wealth. He strengthens his argument by pointing to the frequent rise and fall of capital accumulations in contrast with the permanent role of wisdom in human history. Barlaeus is not against the race for profit because this conforms to natural law. But this law needs regulation through wisdom displayed when the merchant practices a moral codex reminding him of virtues such as honesty, loyalty, hospitality, prudence, generosity, and civil service to the community. In Barlaeus's opinion this moral codex would be put in circulation by using coins stamped with the symbols of these virtues, whose instructions are administered by the Athenaeum founded by the Amsterdam municipality. Barlaeus expresses the hope that it will succeed in conducting the ship of destiny with a secure hand to the haven.

Fifteen years later, in his *Rerum per octennium*, Barlaeus recalls his inaugural speech. He obviously perceives a link because he remarks that this time he has to eliminate his main addressee, the almighty God, and speaks about situations and people who actually exist. He notes that this gives him less freedom of expression. In his dedicatory to Johan Maurits, Barlaeus immediately points to the mercantile goals:

> You continued overseas what you had accomplished in this country. There, as here, you devoted your military service to freedom and religion, to your country and the church, to the well being of mankind and the wishes of merchants. On these two occasions you honored the glory of the United Provinces (Barlaeus 1647: Dedication).[6]

The text praises the count's famous success in battle and evokes his ability for building fortresses, castles, and cities that capture the admiration and the astonishment of the "barbarous". The port cities of Luanda and Mauritsstad/Recife are particularly important. Frans Post included two oversized (in comparison to the other engravings) city views of Luanda and Mauritsstad/Recife, respectively, in Barlaeus's

---

6    *Quod dudum feceras domi, factum à te foris. nempe ut arma commodares Libertati & Religioni, Patriae & Ecclesiae, hominum saluti & mercantium cupiditati. utrumque Foederatorum gloriae* (Barlaeus 1647: Dedication).

volume. Meanwhile, Barlaeus briefly describes Luanda, conquered by
the Dutch in 1641, but emphasizes the newly built Mauritsstad as the
symbol of Dutch superiority: "Let the destruction of Olinda be meas-
ured against the building of MAURITSSTAD in your honor" (Barlaeus 1647: Dedication).[7]

To illustrate the impact of Dutch splendor in Brazil, Barlaeus extensively describes the former richness of Olinda, capital of Portu-
guese-held Pernambuco:

> I have heard from a trustworthy source that in one day forty ships loaded
> with sugar sailed from Olinda's harbor, while this same quantity, enough
> to lead forty more ships, remained in the warehouse (Barlaeus 1647:
> 41).[8]

The magnificence of Olinda's past manifests itself in descriptions of
its ecclesiastical buildings, which, in Barlaeus's opinion, should be
rebuilt in the future. Notwithstanding his conciliatory tone, these opinions underscore the contrast of Olinda in ruins, destroyed by the
Dutch, with the present magnificence of Mauritsstad in front of the
harbor Recife, with its bridges, horticulture, palaces, scientific planning, and commercial activities. Barlaeus extols the achievements of
Johan Maurits:

> He annexed the island Antonio Vaz through a dike with fort Frederick
> built in a pentagon form. The swamps and the shrubs of this space caused
> creeping flesh so that it needed a superhuman belief to think that a city
> could be built there. But although it seemed impossible, we believe that
> due to Nassau's industry and courage he succeeded, even when nature
> forbad it, to proceed with skill and art (Barlaeus 1647: 146).[9]

That Barlaeus was fascinated with America is supported by his biog-
rapher Worp (1885-1889), who reports that Barlaeus owned 27 books
about traveling to the West Indies in his personal library in Leiden.

---

7   *Proponatur in conspicuo ruentis Olindae facies & surgentis in laudes tuas MAU-*
    *RITIAE* (Barlaeus 1647: Dedication).
8   *Non vanis autoribus habeo, uno die ex Olindae portu solvisse naves saccharo*
    *onustas quadraginta, relicta adhuc in conditoriis ea sacchari copia, quae ad*
    *totidem navium vecturam satis esset* (Barlaeus 1647: 41).
9   *Insulam Antonii Vazii, Frederici castro quinquangulari, vallo annexuit. quod*
    *spacium omne stagnis interfusis & arbustis horrebat, ut supra humanam fidem*
    *fuerit, urbem illic condi posse. At nunc conditam esse, Nassovii industriâ, oculati*
    *credimos. utpote cui ingenium & audacia erat, etiam quae natura prohibuisset,*
    *per artem & laboris tentare* (Barlaeus 1647: 146).

This interest in America was a general phenomenon in Barlaeus's days, and he contributed by translating the first volume of the general history of the New World by Antonio de Herrera, the official chronicler of the king of Spain, into Latin in 1622. In contrast to Herrera, though, Barlaeus describes the American continent from a humanist point of view stressing its novelty in comparison with antiquity, whose authors could not report on that part of the world. He remarks that Olinda, Pernambuco, Mauritiopolis, or Tamarica replace Cartago, Rom, Latium, or Gallia, and enemies of war are now known as Tapuyas, Nariquites, Petivares, Caribes, Chileans, and Peruvians.

Barlaeus underlines the emergence of this New World that cannot but arouse the restless spirit of the merchant whose

> [...] mind is given to restlessness. No amount of good fortune can come his way or pursue him so completely that it satisfies his wishes. Finding faults for which he can blame his assistants becomes second nature. While chasing his expectations, he wants at the same time to have all his wishes already satisfied (Barlaeus 1647: 199).[10]

The delight of Brazil, for Barlaeus, lies in its sugar, the apotheosis of taste. His poem, "Triumphus super capta Olinda, Pernambuci urbe, Brasiliae Metropoli" (The Triumph of Having Conquered Olinda, the City in Pernambuco, the Metropolis of Brazil) of 1630 ends with the reference to the "yearly obtained sugar from excellent canes" (Barlaeus 1660: 247).[11] And in "Maurits è Brasilia redux", the author finds pleasure in "its very sweet sugar ... secretly touching our hand" (Barlaeus 1647: 335).[12] After a long treatise on sugar production in general, Barlaeus finally reveals his personal predilection for it: "But the sweetness of sugar makes me drool, moistening the pages of this nar-

---

10 *Inquieta res est mercantium animus. nunquam illi tam plenè occurrere & obsequi ulla fortuna potest, quae vota exsatiet. Facilè invenit, quod amplitudinis suae curatoribus imputet. ac dum suas spes anteire parat, vellet confectum, quicquid animus destinavit* (Barlaeus 1647: 199).

11 "[...] annuaque excelsis extundi saccharra cannis (Barlaeus, Triumphus super capta Olinda, Pernambuci urbe, Brasiliae Metropoli". In: *Barlaei Poemata. Pars 1*, 1660: 247).

12 [...] *sua sacchara nostras/ Laetatur tractare manus dulcissima tellus* (Barlaeus 1647: 335).

rative with saliva when I compare the sugar of antiquity with ours"
(1647: 71).[13]

He is quick to add that this delectable sugar is impossible to produce without the toils of Africans.

For Barlaeus, therefore, the delight of Brazil is intrinsically linked
to sugar consumption, underlying the commercial spirit of the Ba-
roque. It corresponds with the citizens who are also consumers in
Rama's so-called "artificial urban enclaves" in America, and Barlaeus
provides their merchants with a moral codex. The scientific advances
that inform his speculative philosophy permit him a feeling of superiority over his counterparts in antiquity as well as over the Iberians.
For example, according to Barlaeus, Georg Markgraf's method of
measuring the solar eclipse in Recife was more advanced in comparison with observations in Spanish America. Or, in his opinion, the as-
sertions of Arias Montanus that the ships of Salomon had crossed the
ocean are false because this king never would have been able to do
that without help of the *magnetica directione*. Loyal to his Zeitgeist,
Barlaeus also documents the plants and animals in Brazil. This part of
his text does not seem to be very convincing, though. More precise
information is available from other sources, which explains why
Whitehead and Boeseman (1989) hardly mention Barlaeus in their
book on Dutch seventeenth-century Brazil.

There is another aspect of this modern speculative philosophy,
pointed out by Alencastro among others, as belonging to the colonial
strategy of *divide et impera*, and that is the attitude toward the African
American and Amerindian populations. The *Rerum per octennium*
contains many pages describing habits of Africans *(nigrita Loanda)*,
Amerindians *(nomadum Tapuya)*, and Chileans *(Araucanos)*. These
ethnographic notations were traditionally included in European early
modern history writing about countries overseas and responded to the
exigency of allying with these native inhabitants if Europeans were to
maintain and strengthen their position on the coasts and the sea routes
to America. Simultaneously, however, these contacts raise the most
precarious question of what remains of Barlaeus's actual stance in the

---

13  *At mota mihi sacchari dulcedine salivâ, non alienum fuerit, eodem succo adsper-
    gere narrationis hujus paginas, & veterum sacchara cum novis conferre* (Bar-
    laeus 1647: 71).

debates surrounding slavery and the slave trade in relationship with the non-European population.

We have seen that Barlaeus's rhetoric was critical of slavery. Through his discussions with the count and daily contact with his students, many of whom were involved in overseas trade and diligently followed financial reports, Barlaeus must have been aware of the increased involvement in the slave trade. In this respect his report on the 1643 expedition to Chile in *Rerum per octennium* acquires a surprising dimension. He first mentions the Company's plan to occupy Buenos Aires and enable overland travel to Peru, thereby accessing Potosi, the rich silver mine. Notwithstanding its clear objectives, this plan did not materialize, and a second plan was established. A secret military expedition was sent from Texel to Recife under the command of Admiral Hendrik Brouwer. The ships departed from there to sail to Valdivia, and the long and detailed description of this expedition at the end of Barlaeus's book documents its relevance.

Barlaeus reproduces the instructions of the administrators of the West India Company. Brouwer's first task was to inform the Chilean chiefs that the Dutch were combating the Spaniards as bravely and successfully as they themselves had done. As a show of good faith, Brouwer also brought them letters from the prince of Orange and the States General with the invitation to come to Holland and study the country's buildings, markets, and government and thus to seal their friendship with mercantile relationships. The chiefs of the Arauco, Tucapel, and Purén were the first to be addressed because they lived closest to Valdivia in the area with the most gold and fertile soil.

After Brouwer's death, his assistant Elias Herckmans was appointed leader of the expedition and continued the negotiations. Barlaeus speaks favorably of Herckmans, the "poet-adventurer" who had written a book about maritime expeditions. He informed the chiefs that the happiness of merchants in Holland would be complete when they extracted minerals. Naturally, this upset the Araucans, who still remembered the cruelty of the Spaniards when they were forced to extract gold for them. According to Barlaeus, the chiefs proposed that the Dutch do this job themselves. Alternatively, the Chileans recommended they attack Lima, Arica, and other Spanish cities. The Peruvians, like the Chileans, craved liberation from the Spaniards and would support Herckmans's claim to the silver of Potosí. Herckmans, however, confronted with the threat of mutiny among his men, decided to return to Recife. Barlaeus reproduces the Chilean chief's propositions to retain Herckmans. In fact, they insisted on supporting the extraction of minerals in their territory "when caved by Africans", and Barlaeus repeats this argument:

> They [the Dutch ] were urged to return with renewed energy and courage, to continue where they had left off. They should bring Africans to work in the mines and they were promised support for this enterprise (Barlaeus 1647: 281).[14]

That Barlaeus does not give any critical comment on this proposal is striking. He seems to disconnect it completely from his philosophical remorse that has been pointed out above. How can this be understood? Does the moral codex only apply to the level of the "dream of an order", whereas reality contradicts its Christian horizon? Even if it is not clear what the Chileans themselves actually might have said, Barlaeus reproduces their proposal without further comment.

Barlaeus's interpretation of the encounter with the Chilean chiefs might express that, for him, moral philosophy means that, as a Christian, slavery and the slave trade must be judged immoral because they are unnatural. Hence, Barlaeus seems to recognize that the work in America cannot be done without the Africans and that the only ones who can say this freely are their "rivals", the Amerindians. To negotiate this deal, knowledge of their customs, language, and habits belongs to the realm of speculative philosophy, to the practical knowledge for mercantile Christian purposes. Apparently, Barlaeus judges that Christians cannot approve such things publicly, although that this logic does not apply to heathens. They are different, as we learn from his observation when speaking of the sweetness of sugar: "And it is really astonishing that the barbarians do not wish to cook their food and continue having wild and rude customs, even when they eat nectar and ambrosia" (Barlaeus 1647: 71).[15]

---

14  *Hortabantur, ut redirent novisque viribus & animis restaurarent coepta, Nigritas secum eruendis fodinis adducerent, ipsos non defore ista agentibus* (Barlaeus 1647: 281).

15  *Et mirum sanè, tam miti alimento non desaevire barbariem, & durare morum asperitatem ferociamque, pastis hoc nectare & ambrosia* (Barlaeus 1647: 71).

## 2. Early modern myths in contemporary narratives of Angola and Brazil

Taking into account the formation of this "double consciousness" in early modern history, the question remains whether the bias in Barlaeus's moral and speculative philosophy continues having its effects in contemporary literature. We have seen that Amsterdam's moral codex was the main addressee in Barlaeus's *Mercator sapiens*, whereas Luanda and especially Mauritsstad/Recife are central in *Rerum per octennium* as Atlantic port cities and main agencies for the Dutch trade overseas. For this purpose, however, the non-Christian "barbarians" were removed to the practical level of speculative philosophy with some "contact zones" (Pratt 1992) concerning the moral philosophy of urbanized Christian merchants. These links are discussed in three recent novels written by authors from Angola and Brazil. These novels relate to this merchant mentality of the seventeenth century in Recife, Luanda, and Rio de Janeiro. Their urban environments are connected to mythological personalities of that time: Queen Nzinga and Zumbi, legendary because of their heroic strategic warfare. How do these authors relate to the slave trade and its practical and ideological needs from a contemporary point of view?

The authors draw their plots around the two national heroes of Angola and Brazil. Queen Nzinga Mbandi lived from 1582 to 1663, constantly at war with the Portuguese. The legends of her cruelty and eccentricity originate from historical Christian interpretations, which branded her behavior as barbarian notwithstanding her conversion to Christianity. One particular episode has vividly survived in oral and written reports. In the name of her brother, King Ngola Mani a Ngola, Nzinga visited Luanda in the early 1620s for peace negotiations and was received with all the honors dictated by the conventions of international diplomacy. Unfortunately, during the conversations with the Portuguese governor João Correia de Sousa in his palace, no seat was offered to her while he was seated in an armchair. Unflustered, Nzinga ordered one of her slaves to cower down and serve her as a stool, thereby preserving her honor and self-esteem. Martin Lienhard (2005) shows how precarious this matter of asymmetrical seating was, which explains even more Nzinga's ability to negotiate a treaty face to face and on equal terms.

Few Brazilians are unfamiliar with Zumbi, whose uncle, Nganga Zumbi, was the king of Palmares at the time of Zumbi's birth there in 1655. Barlaeus also reported on the existence of Palmares and on the plans of attacking this *quilombo* or settlement of escaped slaves, fugitive whites, and indigenous people in the interior, which is said to have had more than 30,000 inhabitants. Soon after his birth Zumbi was kidnapped by the Portuguese and given to a Catholic priest for his education. He escaped and returned to Palmares in 1670. Because of his extraordinary gift for strategy, Zumbi became king in 1680, when the settlement was regularly attacked by Portuguese military expeditions and destroyed after a long siege in 1695. Zumbi escaped that attack but was captured and killed some time later.

These legendary personalities play a crucial role in the three contemporary novels written by Pepetela from Angola, the Brazilian Alberto Mussa, and José Eduardo Agualusa, also from Angola. Pepetela, the name of the first author, means "eyelash" in Umbundu and is the *nom de guerre* of Artur Carlos Maurício Pestana dos Santos, born in Benguela in 1941. He fought against Portuguese colonialism, then occupied positions in the republican government and became professor of sociology at the University Agostinho Neto. *A Gloriosa Família* (*The Glorious Family*, 1997) is his ninth novel and spans the so-called Dutch period in Angola from 1641 to 1648. Pepetela was obviously inspired by historical research from Brazil because the subtitle *O tempo dos flamengos (The Time of the Flemish)* of his novel is copied from José Antônio Gonsalves de Mello's standard work on the Dutch period (1947). Pepetela also quotes from other sources such as the *História geral das guerras angolanas* (*General History of the Wars in Angola*, 1689) written by Antônio de Oliveira Cadornega, a Portuguese chronicler who appears as himself in the novel.

The plot is organized around the lives of the members of the influential van Dum family of Flemish-Angolan origin. They are traders and farmers, or better yet, entrepreneurs. The domestic slave of the patriarch Baltasar van Dum is the main narrative voice. Born mute and without a name of his own, he follows his master everywhere as a shadow and constantly meditates on his own situation. The reader learns that he is the son of an Angolan slave and a Neapolitan missionary at the court of Queen Nzinga in Matamba, located in the interior. Therefore, he knows the situation in the *kimbos* (villages) and the *mato* (forest and savanna) from his own experience. In Luanda the coastal zone is his permanent companion. He visits the island in the bay or overlooks the Atlantic from the height of his master's property. The ocean connects with Brazil, the most important export market for van Dum, and Brazil is a frequent subject of discussion in Baltasar's permanent conversations with family members, friends, colleagues, and functionaries.

This slave (and his master) meet Barlaeus, who in Pepetela's interpretation traveled with Johan Maurits to Recife and is now on his way back to Amsterdam via Luanda in the company of Georg Markgraf, the German astrologist who died in Angola. Pepetela's fictional Barlaeus is a painter of land and city views, as was Frans Post, who illustrated the 1647 book of the real Barlaeus. This fictional Barlaeus explains to the slave and his master the details of modern landscape painting while depicting the view of Luanda on the beach during his stay in Angola. Luanda is so omnipresent in Pepetela's narrative that the reader can possibly draw the map of its streets, buildings, and natural environment from the information given in the text.

The novel ends when the Brazilians recapture Luanda from the Dutch in August 1648. But the slave storyteller does not exactly welcome them as liberators and reports the events in a rather critical tone. It is general knowledge that General Salvador Correia de Sá is the descendant of a prominent family from Rio de Janeiro, including governors and captains among their members. The general is also a bigot who, upon arrival in Luanda, unpacks a portable altar to celebrate Mass. Everybody was obliged to be present, but Salvador de Sá is seemingly uninterested in the well-being of these believers. The afternoon of this day of liberation is even characterized as tragic because another of the general's official acts is to order the burning of every "demonic Calvinist" document in the city. Within the flames of this fire, all the plans for the eventual improvement of the infrastructure of the city are consumed. The domestic slave (presumably voicing Pepetela's views) apparently does not consider colonial warfare synonymous with liberation.

The second author is Alberto Mussa, born in Rio de Janeiro in 1961, who takes his readers even further back in time in *O trono da rainha Jinga* (*The Throne of Queen Nzinga*, 1999). It is Mussa's first novel and received much attention when it was announced as the first of a series of five novels about Rio de Janeiro. In 25 short chapters the writer includes fragments of the life of Mendo Antunes, a Portuguese. Through them the reader learns that Antunes establishes himself first in Goa in 1609, where he trades with the people in the interior, fears the Arab and Spanish competition, and encounters the practices of the Brahman religion. From Goa he leaves for Angola in 1612 and enters the slave business, for which he presents himself at the court of Queen Nzinga. Again, he observes the unusual customs at this court with astonishment. Finally, in 1623 he arrives in the Brazil under General Auditor Gonçalo Unhão Dinis. This part of Antunes's life is told in retrospect because Mussa organizes the chronology around the next three years, during which strange things occur in Rio de Janeiro. The city map as such, however, does not occupy a relevant position in Mussa's book; its environment is indicated only through the action of the characters in various houses and streets in and outside the actual urban nucleus.

For the third author, José Eduardo Agualusa, in contrast, the urban environment of Rio belongs to a realistic as well as imaginative semiotic construction around the whereabouts and the meeting places of his characters: Favela Morro da Barriga, Market of San Christopher, Motel Carinhoso, Rodrigo de Freitas Lagoon, Hotel Glória, Botanical Garden, Galeão Airport, Restaurant Yoruba, and Portuguese Hospital, to name a few. Luanda, with its Beer Bar Biker in particular, also appears as the site of action. Agualusa was born in Huambo in 1960 and lives as a writer and journalist in Lisbon and Angola. He also stayed in Recife and Rio, where the action takes place in *O ano em que Zumbi tomou o Rio* (*The Year that Zumbi Took Rio*, 2002). Two black Angolans identify with armed resistance in the *favela* Morro da Barriga, led by a Black Commando. This Commando consists of a small group of militant black youngsters that rebel against social injustice and discrimination in Brazil. Agualusa, who published his book in April 2002, depicts Lula as president, who renounces his position to protest the intervention of the army. He therefore situates himself on the side of the Black Commando, followers of Zumbi, the legendary hero of Palmares. They all adhere to the message in the text of a popular, provocative rap song, "Preto de Nascença" ("Born Black"), which relates the metamorphosis of the docile black Brazilian into a Zumbi. Not only the title of Agualusa's novel, but these repeated allusions to Palmares and its historical settings indicate the omnipresence of this myth in the plot.

It is evident that all three contemporary authors refer to myths that date back to the seventeenth century. The role of Queen Nzinga in Angola and Brazil even plays a central role in Pepetela's and Mussa's novels. Pepetela also evokes the positive memory of the Dutch period in regard to the necessary improvements to Luanda's infrastructure as well as recognition of the role played by art and science in urban life (Phaf-Rheinberger 2004). However, the author's principal motif is the criticism of slavery. Pepetela's domestic servant, whose descent is intrinsically linked to Queen Nzinga's court, certainly does not live in the shadow of the text: he is the novel's main character. Van Dum received him as a gift from the queen when Baltasar first introduced himself to her. Therefore, this slave knows every detail of van Dum's enterprises from its very beginnings, and though illiterate and mute, he has an adequate interpretation for everything he observes. Furthermore, his centrality to the text is brought to the fore in that he was one of the queen's most precious properties. He was bestowed upon Baltasar as a token of her confidence that a Fleming or, rather, a Dutchman would be a loyal partner in negotiations against the Portuguese. But, as the slave knows, Baltasar deceived the queen as he secretly discusses his affairs with both colonial partners.

Pepetela's slave questions slavery and the unreliability of colonial merchants in the form of a historical novel, which contains substantial actual information on that time. Whereas Queen Nzinga's famous chair scene forms merely one of many memories of his slave storyteller and does not play a special role, Mussa recalls it in the title of his novel and presents it as a crucial episode in the organization of his plot. His main character, Mendo Antunes, personally witnesses it in Luanda. Shortly afterwards he goes to Rio, where a secret brotherhood of African slaves, *irmandade*, has been poisoning white Portuguese, killing them during robberies, or setting their prisoners free. The leader of this brotherhood is a woman, following the example of Queen Nzinga. In his affinity with this queen, and therefore with the *irmandade*, lies the clue to Mussa's work.

The two Angolan characters in Agualusa's plot are the elegantly dressed colonel Francisco Palmares and the dwarfish, homosexual Euclides Matoso da Câmara, a radio and television reporter. In Rio the colonel sells weapons to the Black Commando and joins the struggle against (what he calls) the colonization of black people in Brazil. Agualusa refers to the assassination of eight street children by police on 23 July 1993 near the Church of Nossa Senhora da Candelária in Rio. This massacre, which was known worldwide, lies at the base of Agualusa's narrative protest against such abuses of state power. Moreover, he claims that it is the result of the enslavement of black people that continues to have an impact in Brazil. Agualusa maintains that, first, a Portuguese prince declared independence for a country that was thereafter always governed by whites and in which black Brazilians were assigned to and still generally occupy the lowest level of the social hierarchy. His Black Commando is the personification of the armed resistance against this history of black submission, finding supporters at all levels of Brazilian society.

Criticism, subversion, and armed resistance against (the consequences of) slavery on all levels of daily life are thus the main motifs for the logic of the three narrations. For Pepetela, Luanda, with its European influences and visits from or trade with Brazil, obtains coherence through the bonds of the slave (and his master) with the interior, intertwining with members of the van Dum family, the "contact zone" between black and white. The slave understands that the family's behavior is sometimes imposed from outside (i.e., is white) and sometimes reflects local custom (i.e., is black). His owner, Baltasar, emigrated from Flanders in 1616 and married a woman from an indigenous aristocratic family. This woman speaks mostly Kimbundu at home to her children and servants. Many of them belong to the biological category of mulatto, but the storyteller barely mentions this word and prefers formulating other criteria for describing social allegiances. At the end of the book, Pepetela describes a discussion about mulattos between the ambassador of the king of Congo and the Dutch director Ouman. The latter argues that the Portuguese are creating unnatural monsters by having children with native women, whereas the Mani Congo responds that the Dutch also seem to have a similar custom. Obviously, Pepetela avoids the impression that societal divisions operate along the color line, trying to bring in as many inside views as possible. For this purpose he recounts the drama of one of the van Dum's daughters who felt in love with a slave. This man was killed for this "crime", and nobody did anything to hinder or revenge this assassination.

Pepetela's seventeenth-century Angola shows a more differential environment than a community bluntly divided into black and white camps. It is ironic that the Brazilian author Mussa does not rely on such categories. Instead, he designs his chronology by juxtaposing the chapters of various speaking voices without identifying the speaker or defining the relationship between the voices beforehand. Meanwhile, through them Mussa testifies to the existence of a mysterious manuscript in the Kimbundu language that speaks of slaughter: "Bravo, the devil arrived. He killed father; he killed mother; he killed uncle; he killed nephew; he killed a blind man falling down; a cripple on the road" (Mussa 1999: 9).[16]

In the course of the book, these Kimbundu verses turn out to be a canto for initiation rites and the swearing of eternal loyalty to the *irmandade* in correspondence with the customs in Matamba as well as in Rio. In the first half of Mussa's novel, therefore, the suspense builds around the question of which narrating voice might be involved in this secret organization. The suspense dissolves only after narrating Queen Nzinga's human throne scene, and it becomes clear that everyone in Rio who has been in Angola is initiated. Antunes, the Portuguese ship owner and friend of the highest Portuguese representatives in town, is just as much incorporated in this circle as the Africans or African Brazilians, which erases the ethnic and cultural hierarchy between these sectors of Brazilian society.

Antunes's secretary turns out to be the missing link. He is an unusually educated man of Arab descent who was bought in Salvador da Bahia. He has a Christian name, Inácio, and only at the end of the book it is revealed that he possesses a Kimbundu name as well, Camundele. He is obviously the author of the mysterious manuscript. Through this character the author constructs a complex familiarity – he calls it friendship – between the writing culture of "heathens" and Christians, who are both represented in the secret brotherhood. The question of whose criteria are appropriate is not raised. Mussa is concerned with demonstrating the subversive force of a Kimbundu soci-

---

16  *Múcua njinda / cariapemba uabixe/ uajibe tata uajibe mama/ uajibe dilemba uajibe muebo/ uajibe quitumba bunjila/ ni dicata buquicoca* (Mussa 1999: 9).

ety in Rio in those times of violence, in which the representatives of the *irmandade* achieve equality in Christian society.

Angola in Brazil is also the theme of Agualusa, as we have seen above. He works with paradoxes and hyperbole to emphasize controversial positions. In his descriptions of personal relationships, Agualusa is aware of the impact of various shades of skin color and corporal or sexual differences in personal relationships. In the political arena, however, such sensitive gradations are not reflected in the author's position that the Afro-Brazilians have not yet freed themselves from colonialism. It is the decisive motif for the armed resistance of the Black Commando. The author suggests remuneration for damages inflicted upon the communal black spirit in the form of a symbolic reward for all Brazilians of African origin and a public excuse for centuries of exploitation and oppression. He argues for the introduction of a system of quotas for Afro-Brazilians to prevent insufficient representation (less than 40 percent) in universities, public service, or the army.

Agualusa's story is framed in a circular structure and informs the reader from the very beginning that it will not have a happy ending. The colonel and the journalist have died in Angola at the start anew of the civil war after the elections in November 1992 but are resurrected in Rio in 2002 to assist in the battle there. Just as with the *quilombo* Palmares, military forces intervene here and destroy the powerful Black Commando in the *favela* Morro da Barriga. Its leader is killed and immediately transformed into a legendary hero. The two Angolans have different destinies. Loyal to his last name, Colonel Palmares fights until the end, and although he is the real hero of the story, Agualusa does not tell the story of a hero. Rather, he compares his fate with that of Peter Pan with a twist: the colonel is forever tied to violent scenarios. As a reporter and political journalist, the other Angolan character, Euclides, performs a different role by constantly referring to the traumatic events in Luanda. It is impossible to eliminate those memories, and this truth is apparently as relevant as the recent occurrences in Rio.

The exaggerated fragmentation of the narrative codes increases the feeling of affinity nurtured by the omnipresence of music and literature. Agualusa quotes singers such as Caetano Veloso, Chico Buarque de Holanda, Maria Bethânia, Zeca Baleiro, Martinho da Vila, or rap-per MV Bill. Their contributions are just as important as those of poets Lídia do Camo Ferreira, Aldir Blanc, Ruy Knopfly, António Risério, Olavo Bilac, Noel Rosa, Lya Luft, Ferreira Gullar, and Nuno Júdice. By way of these references Agualusa's novel resembles a hymn to poetry and music in Brazil and Portuguese Africa. They all coincide in a celebration of the word "black" at the end, reproduced in the languages to which Agualusa has access: *fekete, negro, grunho, bumbo, swart, sort, zwart, schwartz, musta, nègre, prieto, burakku* (Agualusa 2000: 273). This verbal apotheosis takes place in Hotel Gellert in post-communist Budapest in an art deco setting, where Euclides finds himself, in expectation of better times, after the destruction of the Black Commando. Obviously, the color black has an outstanding significance.

## 3. Concluding remarks

To sum up, we have shown that Barlaeus, Pepetela, Mussa, and Agualusa provide a comparative perspective on Angola and Brazil. All of them stress the asymmetrical hierarchies that reign in (former) slave societies. These works are part of Rama's model of the lettered cities, as I have argued, shifting its center to the South Atlantic. They concentrate on urban port environments on both sides of the ocean, these doorways of the trade between Africa and America. The authors' rhetorical inquiries take up the "double consciousness" of modernity that Paul Gilroy (1993) wrote about, but now with its roots in the mercantile philosophy. Barlaeus describes its mechanisms in the seventeenth century in his *Rerum per octennium in Brasilia*, whereas the contemporary writers denounce the complex control mechanisms through which they are maintained. For that purpose, they embody them in the characters of the slaves in colonial society or of the inhabitants of a *favela* in present-day Rio de Janeiro. Especially Agualusa's literary techniques of paradoxes, an overflow of stereotypes, ambiguity and hyperbole are reminiscent of a similar pattern in Carlos Fuentes's novel *Christopher Unborn* (1990) or in Luis Rafael Sánchez's fabulation *La importancia de llamarse Daniel Santos* (1988). These Spanish-American writers equally discuss the role of popular music, in their case the bolero, as a unifying force in an increasingly fragmented

urban scenario, as Agualusa does with the rap song "Preto de Nascença".

Pepetela, Mussa, and Agualusa's novels all denounce slavery and
its consequences as a criminal practice. Their moral codex for justice
is conceived within the horizon of "myths", which has its roots in the
seventeenth century, of Queen Nzinga in Angola and Zumbi de Palmares in Brazil. Both these myths are national symbols of resistance
and survival of their respective countries. The materiality of the author's narrative environments of Rio de Janeiro and Luanda is different from Barlaeus's portrait of Luanda and Mauritsstad/Recife. Barlaeus's treatise emphasizes natural sciences, geography, mapping,
linguistics, and anthropology, supporting the function of urban constructions in the service of Dutch overseas expansion. In contemporary fiction the authors display the details of daily life in the port cities
of the former South Atlantic route and question the concept of democracy in their fictional realities. The burdens of the past are still influential and it appears that more literary works addressing this problem
in the lusophone world are forthcoming. The recently published novel
*Um defeito de cor* (*A Defect of Color*, 2007) by Ana Maria Gonçalves,
for example, discusses the transatlantic connections between the kingdom of Dahomey and Salvador de Bahia in the nineteenth century.
She treats gender issues in more depth and once again underscores the
demand for staging slavery conditions in times of post-colonial globalization because, obviously, it is necessary to inquire whether they
are still operative today.

## Bibliography

Agualusa, José Eduardo (2000): *O ano em que Zumbi tomou o Rio. Romance*. Lisboa:
    Publicações Dom Quixote.

Alencastro, Luiz Felipe de (2000): *O trato dos viventes. Formação do Brasil no
    Atlântico Sul. Séculos XVI e XVII*. São Paulo: Editora Schwarz.

Barlaeus, Caspar (1647): *Rerum per octennium in Brasilia*. Illustrations: Post, Frans.
    Amsterdam: Iohannis Blaeu.

— (1660): *Barlaei Poemata. Pars 1. Heroicorum*. Amstelodami: Ioannes Blaeu.

— (1967): *Mercator Sapiens*. Edition and translation: Woude, Sape van der. Ams-
    terdam: Universiteitsbibliotheek.

Barléu, Gaspar ([1940] 1974): *História dos feitos recentemente praticados durante oito anos no Brasil*. Preface: Ferri, Mário G. Translation: Brandão, Mário. São Paulo: Ed. Da Universidade de São Paulo.

Byl. De Brasilsche Breede-Byl; ofte t'samen-spreak (1647): "Tusschen Kees Jansz. Schott, komende uyt Brasil". In: Maet, Jan: *Koopmans-knecht, hebbende voor desen ook in Brasil geweest, over De Verloop in Brasil*. Amsterdam: n.p.

Cadornega, Antônio Oliveira de (1940-42): *História geral das guerras angolanas*, 3 vols. Delgado, José Matias (ed.). Lisboa: Divisão de Publicações e Biblioteca, Agência Geral das Colónias.

Fuentes, Carlos (1990): *Christopher Unborn*. Transl.: MacAdam, Alfred, and the author. New York: Vintage.

Gilroy, Paul (1993): *The Black Atlantic. Modernity and Double Consciousness*. Cambridge, MA: Harvard University Press.

Gonçalves, Ana Maria (2007): *Um defeito de cor*. Belo Horizonte: Editora Record.

Horst, Koert van der (1978): *Inventaire de la correspondance de Caspar Barlauus 1602-1648*. Assen: Van Gorcum.

Huizinga, Johan (1998): *Nederlands beschaving in de zeventiende eeuw. Een schets*. Ed. Anton van der Lem. Amsterdam: Contact.

Israel, Jonathan (1998): *The Dutch Republic. Its Rise, Greatness and Fall*. Oxford: Oxford University Press.

Lienhard, Martin (2005): "O Diálogo entre os Portugueses e Africanos nas guerras do Congo e Angola nos séculos XVI e XVII". In: *O Mar e o Mato: Histórias da Escravidão*. Prefácio: Dongala, Emmanuel. Luanda: Editorial Kilombelombe, pp. 71-108

Mello, Evaldo Cabral de (1998): *O negócio do Brasil: Portugal, os Países Baixos e o nordeste 1641-1669*. Rio de Janeiro: Topbooks.

Mello, José Antônio Gonsalves de ([1947] 2001): *Tempo dos flamengos. Influencia da ocupação holandesa na vida e na cultura do norte do Brasil*. Prefácio: Freyre, Gilberto. Rio de Janeiro: Topbooks.

Mussa, Alberto (1999): *O trono da rainha Jinga*. Rio de Janeiro: Ed. Nova Fronteira.

Paasman, Bert (2001): "West Indian Slavery and Dutch Enlightenment Literature". In: Arnold, A. James (ed. in chief)/Kutzinski, Vera/Phaf-Rheinberger, Ineke (sub-eds.): *A History of Literature in the Caribbean*, vol. 2. Amsterdam/Philadelphia: Benjamins, pp. 481-489.

Pepetela (1997): *A Gloriosa Família. O Tempo dos Flamengos*. Lisboa: Publicações Dom Quixote.

Phaf-Rheinberger, Ineke (2004): "Pepetela's roemrijke familie in Angola. De lotgevallen van een Atlantische cultuur". In: Kempen, Michiel van/Verkruijsse, Piet/Zuiderweg, Adrienne (eds.): *Wandelaar onder de palmen. Opstellen over koloniale en postkoloniale literatuur en cultuur*. Leiden: KITLV Uitgeverij, pp. 379-388.

Pratt, Mary Louise (1992): *Imperial Eyes: Travel Writing and Transculturation*. London: Routledge.

Rama, Ángel (1996): *The Lettered City*. Preface and translation: Chasteen, John. Durham, N.C./London: Duke University Press.

Remedi, Gustavo (1997): "Ciudad letrada: Angel Rama y la espacialización del análisis cultural". In: Moraña, Mabel (ed.): *Ángel Rama y los estudios latino-americanos*. Pittsburg: Instituto Internacional de Literatura Iberoamericana, pp. 97-122.

Sánchez, Luis Rafael (1988): *Importancia de llamarse Daniel Santos. Fabulación*. San Juan: Editorial Universidad Puerto Rico.

Schmidt, Benjamin (2001): *Innocence Abroad. The Dutch Imagination and the New World, 1570-1670*. Cambridge: Cambridge University Press.

Solow, Barbara L. (ed.) (1991): *Slavery and the Rise of the Atlantic System*. Cambridge: Cambridge University Press.

Whitehead, Peter J. P./Boeseman, Martin (1989): *A Portrait of Dutch 17th Century Brazil. Animals, Plants and People by the Artists of John Maurits van Nassau*. Amsterdam/Oxford/New York: North-Holland Publishing Company.

Worp, Jan Adolf (1885-89): "Caspar van Baerle". In: *Oud Holland*, nr. 3-7.

# Sounds

**Gerhard Kubik/Tiago de Oliveira Pinto**

# African Common Denominators
## across the South Atlantic: A Conversation

**T.:** In the series of lecture on *AfricAmericas* in the Fall and Winter of 2004-2005, we dealt with numerous aspects of the history, sociology, literature, visual art of the African heritage in the Americas and its feedback to Africa. What seems to me to be a thrilling issue from a Brazilian point of view is the finding of 'common denominators' between contemporary cultural expressions in Brazil and those in African regions, whose history has become important to our country. Is there any such common denominator and how could we approach this question through our research? For example, if there are a hundred types of samba in existence, where are the common unifying principles to allow us to speak of all these variations as samba? Is there a common denominator? Assuming that there is, than we stumble upon certain African traits, which can be traced unequivocally to central Africa, and notably to Angola. Some of these common principles seem to include: a) three levels of rhythmic interaction; b) *toques* as a space-sound-motion concept; c) the concept of time-line patterns, including the idea of an inherent time-line; d) specific motional behavior and sound production; e) the interface between language and musical patterns, expressed in mnemonic syllables and phrases; f) responsorial form in song phraseology; g) timbre as an important aspect of musical composition besides rhythm, melody, etc. In addition there is the phenomenon of aesthetics and sensibility as a deep-level creating structure, which cannot be traced as such to Africa but are analogous to the African forms due to a similar approach to composition and to comparable mental procedures.

**G.:** Congratulations! You have in part answered your question already and your list of comparable traits and forms of behavior that link samba with certain types of Central African music is impressive, moreover since you do not stop at trait by trait analysis, but quite obviously proceed to a level of analogous thought patterns and forms of

behavior that are not easily explained. I would like to add a few remarks about methodology that might be of use to anyone pursuing this
set of questions. It is important to distinguish between designations
and phenomena, i.e., the forms and behavioral patterns they describe.

In the first place, samba is obviously a designation, as much as
jazz, blues, etc. What these designations mean is variable in time and
space. For example, in Central Africa there are numerous groups that
call themselves jazz bands, even some famous ones, such as the historical "OK Jazz", of the late Franco in Kinshasa, but no jazz student
would call what those musicians play jazz. In Malawi there is the
"Fumbi Jaz Band". They play a kind of music derived from the *chi-
murenga* music of Zimbabwe. There is not a trace of jazz in their performances. And yet, they call themselves a jazz band. In Mozambique,
my colleague Moya A. Malamusi discovered a group of Lomwe-
speaking musicians with a drum chime playing a new kind of music.
They called their music "Samba Ng'oma Eight". I am sure that, if they
ever claimed that their music was samba in the Brazilian sense of the
word, Brazilian observers would not agree. Luckily the leader of this
group, Mário Sabuneti, explained this concept to Malamusi. He said
that that the term samba, as he uses it, comes from the verb *kusamba*,
which means 'to bathe' in his language. He found that his hand movements playing all those eight drums were comparable to the movements of a person bathing in the river, even swimming. The example
is quite instructive. It demonstrates how across different cultures an
apparently identical word can have very different implications.

For this reason, I think we have to be methodologically careful
and perhaps avoid taking terminology as a starting point in the search
for common denominators by first categorizing as samba various
types of Brazilian musical forms that may be historically connected or
not and then trying to construct a common denominator. In that sense,
samba would merely be a phantom concept. I would opt to start the
other way around and begin with the phenomenon, begin with one or
two or three specific groups in a selected region and find out what the
performers themselves call their music, including their audiences, and
then through trait-by-trait analysis check whether designation and
salient traits can be matched. Finding out common denominators is
possible, but it is not always possible by starting from a mass of wild
data and proceeding down to the individual groups. It is advisable to

start from a small set of data, perhaps just one group, and gradually build up your potential for comparison to a level of similarities on which we can be sure that the groups are still stylistically comparable.

Therefore, a question such as the one posed: "If there are a hundred types of samba in existence, where are the common unifying principles?" actually translates this way: "If there are a hundred different forms of music in many different areas that different people all call samba, what common basis justifies calling these phenomena by one name?" I am concerned with the observers' thoughts without taking their behavior of categorizing for granted. I'm asking the question why is such and such a person calling this animal a cow and not a buffalo? Are they really similar or do they appear to be similar only from the angle of the person's narrow experience?

So, in other words, I recommend that we should also go into the cognitive aspects of the question, before we decide about common denominators that might be scientifically valid. I suspect that all these so-called forms of samba are, in fact, very many different traditions and they have only been given one name, a popular name, because there is no other category to stimulate people's imagination. Could it be that the term samba is becoming more and more generic?

**T.:** Not necessarily. On the one hand, there is indeed the necessity of having a general popular term for a national genre, which is samba, no doubt. But what I mean goes far beyond the stage of just identifying genres that are called samba. For this kind of misleading approach we have a good example with the *batuque*, the designation of a musical genre that already came up in sixteenth-century Angola and also in Brazil, keeping its designation to our days. Across the centuries, *batuque* just meant "music and dance performed by Africans", a characterization used by the Portuguese colonizers without reference to any other trait that could define the phenomenon in some way. If there are single genres nowadays called *batuque* – like the one at Capivari, São Paulo that you also have studied – these are more recent developments. My hypothesis regarding samba takes only those forms into consideration that are conceptualized by musicians and amateurs as having common elements, which are considered as identifying samba, or that at least are obviously samba-like. Not even the designation of these genres must necessarily contain the term. Take for instance bossa nova, or *partido alto*, which are two clear samba forms. In the Recôncavo region of Bahia, it is apparent that the different ways of designating and practicing samba in *samba-de-roda*, *samba chula*, or *samba-de-viola* share common ideas, which at the same time are related to a broader concept of samba.

**K.:** It is legitimate to analyze historically certain present-day expressions, such as *samba-de-roda* as performed by Nicinha do Samba from Santo Amaro in the Recôncavo. We can apply two methods: one is trait-by-trait analysis, for example, we determine which of the so-called asymmetric time-lines are used by the group, what kind of multipart patterns occur, what kind of organization between lead singers and group response can be found, and so on.

The other method is conceptual analysis. We find out what kind of terminology these people use when they communicate within their musical group, and we also find out what kind of aesthetics is the basis of their value system, i.e., what is good from their viewpoint and what is considered to be bad in sound or combination; in other words, what is agreeable, what is acceptable. We observe how they correct what they call mistakes within the group. Such a methodology gives us intimate ideas about group specifics and at a later stage we can compare the data-base obtained by this method with a similar data-base obtained from another group and thereby – you understand – build up a larger sample. At the last stage of this research, if the aim is to trace certain characteristics to their ultimate historical background in the music history of another continent, we can continue the process of inquiry on that other continent and analyze relevant materials here.

**T.:** Your suggestive viewpoint reminds me that in our research we bring up interesting new insights by adopting some sort of elaborated empirical methods. Since we are dealing with expressive culture, e.g. with performance in a broad sense – musical structures, dramatic aspects, dance, linguistic particularities, or ritual contexts, just to mention a few elements that attract our attention in the field – we must be aware that gathering this huge amount of data is just a first, though indispensable stage in our cultural research on transatlantic connections. It never ends here (otherwise we could easily be considered folklorists collecting materials for a museum of folk arts and crafts). Interpreting our data is, therefore, the other important task in order to shed light upon this significant chapter of a history of mentalities on both sides of the Atlantic Ocean.

Getting back to the previously mentioned subject, I could say that my hypothesis regarding different, but pertinent samba genres, is that by selecting their traits in order to isolate those particular elements that are shared by all *sambistas*, *sambadores*, *sambaristas*, and *sambadeiras* as being relevant to identify samba as such, we will get to the ultimate level of African concepts and of African aesthetic feeling. It is of utmost importance to stress that this African aesthetic feeling has its source in Central Africa, among Bantu-speaking people. I am afraid that this idea can be upsetting, causing discomfort to many intellectuals dealing with local and popular culture in Brazil (and with national and world cultural expressions as well). There is hardly any other musical genre that expresses more convincingly a broad Brazilian sense and common feelings, independent of what its signification may be, than samba. Therefore, you can imagine what it means to some of my compatriots if it turns out that the essence, something like a 'common denominator' of samba, is African, more precisely Bantu, and that it has remained as such for centuries. In such a case the notion of Brazil as a melting pot determining the completely different social environment of people of African descent in the country is a shambles. What about the alleged originality of Brazilian culture? These and similar concerns might possible be brought up by those startled by our findings.

I can give you an example of the ambiguous status of samba, something with an African flavor that has been covered up by a national identity. In the 1960s, Vinícius de Moraes and the guitar virtuoso and composer Baden Powell created their *afro-sambas* to make clear that they were digging deeper into African cultural elements in Brazil and suggesting at the same time that samba alone is not "Afro". The most curious fact is that most of Vinícius's and Baden Powell's *afro-sambas* are not sambas in a strict sense at all! They have been inspired by and adopted from Candomblé religious music from Bahia, and do not constitute any special form of samba, regardless of their designation.

I'm trying to argue that, in the framework of transatlantic expressive cultural principles, research on samba stands for an illustrative paradigm of a common meaningful state of mind that has remained and becomes the foundation of a manifold cultural output on both sides of the Atlantic Ocean, an output of creativity that has never ended, despite all adverse impositions by history.

Regarding the term "black music", this had gained importance in the United States but has never been really en vogue in Brazil. Instead, *música afro* is more popular, especially in the Bahian musical scene, than *música negra*. In the case of the *afro-sambas* mentioned above by Vinícius and Baden Powell the term "black" simply does not exist. During my field research in the Recôncavo in Bahia in the 1980s, I did hear neither the term *música negra* nor *música afro* among the local population. But, as soon as the popular *blocos afro* from Salvador invaded the small cities in the Recôncavo at the end of the 1980s and were adopted mainly by teenagers, the term *música afro* came into sight designating new, modern, and young local genres.

There is another color symbolism in music, not referring to the skin of the performers but to the sound spectrum (timbre) of a sound sequence, for example the specific sound of an instrument like *berimbau*, with its unique *squitim* etc. The way Brazilian musicians deal with these specific colors can also refer to African concepts. When I participated at the meeting at the Ministry of Culture in Brasilia to discuss among experts the implementation of a Museum of Afro-Brazilian Culture in Salvador, Bahia, in 2002, I used the term in this double sense, arguing, that the constitution of Brazilian culture up until our days can show, that the color of sound ("a cor do som") has not to do a priori with the skin color of the people who play this music. I think, this is a very instructive and rather Brazilian feature of Afro-American culture across the South Atlantic Ocean. Meanwhile, a Museum of Afro-Brazilian Culture has been inaugurated in São Paulo in 2005 as the result of the efforts of Emanuel Araújo, whose private collection comprises the biggest part of the museums' exhibition space.

One of the outstanding pioneers of Afro-American studies is W. E. B. Du Bois, who wrote down his remarkable observations concerning the "soul" of African-American people more than a hundred years ago. *The Souls of Black Folk* as formulated by Du Bois might bear the essence of the idea of Afro-American cultures expressed by performance models of different kinds. *The Souls of Black Folk* is the first original theoretical tool for understanding Afro-American culture and reality. Could Du Bois's concept of "soul" – as a metaphor for concept, idea, African community feeling – also embody a common designation of African and Afro-American cultures?

**K.:** I read W. E. B. Du Bois many years ago and I'm particularly grateful that Henry Louis Gates Jr. has written a very informative introduction to a new edition of his work first published in 1903, now available as a pocket book in several editions. When re-reading Du Bois it was fascinating for me to learn how the first impressions I had gathered from *The Souls of Black Folk* have not changed over decades. This is a book that has stood the test of time and it is a fountain of information that never runs dry. This includes his description of late nineteenth-century musical developments among people of African descent in the United States. In a restricted social environment such as on the plantations, it was virtually impossible for the African population to carry on with expressive traditions handed down by their ancestors if not in the context of Christian religion or working conditions. Of course, these had to be modified according to the new social circumstances. It is fascinating to learn that sentences such as the following could have been written in 1903:

> Little of beauty has America given the world save the rude grandeur God himself stamped on her bosom; the human spirit in this new world has expressed itself in vigor and ingenuity rather than in beauty. And so by fateful chance the Negro folksong – the rhythmic cry of the slave – stands to-day not simply as the sole American music, but as the most beautiful expression of human experience born this side the seas. It has been neglected, it has been, and is, half despised, and above all it has been persistently mistaken and misunderstood; but notwithstanding, it still remains as the singular spiritual heritage of the nation and the greatest gift of the Negro people (Du Bois 2005: 186).

**T.:** Yours and recent studies of several of our colleagues stress again and again that the analysis of African music in general, and including Afro-American music, cannot be based on concepts such as 'indigenous' versus 'foreign', or 'traditional' versus 'modern'. Furthermore, it seems to me completely misleading to describe musical sounds as either 'genuine' or 'hybrid'. No culture, and here specifically no music, can be described as 'hybrid', for everything that exists does so genuinely, and every culture is ultimately a mixture of the most diverse elements that came together in history. This term has been borrowed from genetics to describe phenomena, which often are non-genetical, that is to say, they are learned in specific ways.

**K.:** I don't think it is necessary that we bother Gregor Mendel to explain how the history of cultures develops. Genetics and cultural studies were two different areas of research until recently. One was considered to belong to the so-called hard sciences using the standard scientific methods for research. The concept hybridization, for example, refers to the reproduction of species through the extended network of transplantations that connects them (Müller-Wille/Rheinberger 2007). The attempt to transfer this concept from the natural sciences to philosophy and history of cultures does not always work. The first question that comes to mind would be: if there are any so-called hybrid cultures, what is the opposite? The problem is that no opposite can exist in this case unless we assume that there are cultures that have existed in a stable state for thousands of years. For such an assumption, however, there is no evidence, neither archaeological nor based on other kind of sources. On the contrary, we can proceed from the assumption that cultures have constantly changed in history through the forces of borrowing, adaptation, and innovation. In other words, all cultures are by nature hybrid. From that perspective the concept of hybrid cultures has lost its diagnostic significance.

What we can do in cultural studies in reference to a certain region, for example, Minas Gerais or Bahia in Brazil, is to work with the data material provided by our written, pictorial, musical, and other sources in order to reconstruct the processes activated during certain time-periods changing human life and human interaction. This enables us to learn a great deal about what really happened in the past. We can confidently dispense with models or even labels (such as hybridization, cultural memory, roots etc.) that pretend to explain facts even before we have put them on the record.

**T.:** Gerhard, you seem to like deconstructing most of the terminological tools used in cultural studies. Those you mentioned may be more or less outdated, but then, what remains from an established terminology for our 'cross-cultural and transatlantic' and recent research?

**G.:** By far not outdated are Melville J. Herskovits's tools he has given us long ago for this kind of research. His concepts of selection, retention, survival, reinterpretation, and cultural focus are still useful tools for the study of cultural contacts. I am not the only one who has had the courage to declare this, but many other colleagues, including blues researcher David Evans, share my opinion. It is important to understand that Herskovits did not want to create models to determine or describe the outcome of cultural contacts, but most of his descriptive vocabulary has aimed at unraveling the behavioral patterns human beings develop in a situation of cultural contact. Confronted with another culture the following basic mechanisms in the human brain are activated: 1) Cognitive reactions; and 2) affective-emotional reactions. Herskovits was particularly concerned with the cognitive realm and he discovered that in contact with another culture we always select what we wish to incorporate into our conceptual world, what we want to adopt, while many other things are rejected. That is what Herskovits used to call selection. Simultaneously we tenaciously retain certain forms of behavior, certain modes of thought, and certain habits, which we have brought along. That is Herskovits's retention. But the most important concept, which Herskovits developed, is the concept of reinterpretation. It describes the fact that, when we human beings are confronted with something unusual or unknown, we tend to reinterpret it in terms of the categories familiar to our own conceptual world. We translate, so-to-speak, the new experience into a comprehensible framework of previous experiences. All these reactions are highly important and they have determined the behavioral patterns of people from all over the world who came together in America. Herskovits's ideas allow us to reconstruct case by case how the participants in this 'encounter' have reacted towards each other, attempting to understand in their own ways the meanings of the other groups' actions. Such an encounter is very complex and can only be researched with a vast data base. It cannot be described with simplistic notions such as "New World", the "melting pot", or "hybrid cultures", "cultural identity" etc.

I described a very nice example of reinterpretation in the sense of Herskovits in my book *Extensionen Afrikanischer Kulturen in Brazilien* (Kubik 1990) for the Brazilian *umbanda* religion. *Umbanda* comes from Angola. In Angola the term means "traditional medicine", "traditional healing practice". The person who is in charge of this medical practice is called *Kimbanda*. In Brazil these Angolan concepts were reinterpreted. Umbanda has become something like a religion promoting contact with the transcendental world through an initiated medium. It is also sometimes used synonymously with the Brazilian concept of *magia branca* (good, healing magic, considered to be white). *Kimbanda* appears in Brazil under the spelling *quimbanda*, but it has totally changed its original meaning. It no longer refers to a person, but the term addresses the force opposite to healing magic, called *magia negra* (black magic).

What has happened? Reinterpretations have a psychological purpose. They satisfy the needs in the people concerned that may be unconscious. We are witnessing here what an essentially racist society is doing to African terminology. While *umbanda* as a healing practice with a religious background was accepted in Brazil, the African practitioner of this healing practice was apparently not acceptable. So, the notion *kimbanda* was depersonalized. It became a symbol of evil forces, of witchcraft. All these Angolan concepts had the fate of being reinterpreted in terms of a basically racist black/white dichotomy, black being synonymous with evil, white synonymous with good.

**T.:** I am sure, that due to recent research and to the systematic collection of data in the near future, the dissemination of knowledge about African cultural history in Brazil can increase constantly, and people will become aware of cultural reinterpretations like this you just mentioned. At least you feel at the moment a real general interest in that field. This may also be due to a Federal Law from 2003 that foresees the implementation of courses in African history in elementary schools across the country. Even if there are not enough teachers, who can integrate these courses in the school curriculum yet, it is encouraging to see that many institutions have reacted positively to the law. The Center of African Studies at the Department of Anthropology of our university in São Paulo (USP) has implemented a one-term extensive course in African Studies for schoolteachers and interested students since 2004. And we have experienced serious attempts to do the same at the Federal University of Pernambuco in Recife, during our Summer School in March of this same year.

A few examples of text books for teachers on African and Afro-Brazilian history have been published meanwhile, with the purpose of introducing the subject to an educational system which until now has neglected it almost completely. Even if still far from having at our disposal a comprehensive bibliography published for a wide public on Africa and its history in Brazil, never before we experienced such an effort in informing on the African presence in the country, especially for teenagers and the younger generation.

## Bibliography

Du Bois, W. E. B. (2005): *The Souls of Black Folk*. Intr.: Gates Jr., Henry Louis. New York: Bantam Dell.

Kubik, Gerhard (1990): *Extensionen Afrikanischer Kulturen in Brazilien*. Aachen: Alano Verlag.

Müller-Wille, Staffan/Rheinberger, Hans-Jörg (eds.) (2007): *Heredity Produced. At the Crossroads of Biology, Politics and Culture, 1500-1870*. Cambridge/London: The MIT Press.

Tiago de Oliveira Pinto

# "Crossed Rhythms":
# African Structures, Brazilian Practices,
# and Afro-Brazilian Meanings

## 1. Cross Atlantic cultures

Music belongs to the cultural domain that has been defined as intangible. In fact, immateriality is present from the very beginning of Afro-Brazilian history, since the "material" that African slaves could take with them across the Atlantic on their forced way to the Americas, was just their own body. When they succeeded in surviving the transatlantic passage, the only belongings Africans carried with them were ideas, religions, concepts, among which also their musicality. Any cultural goods introduced so far into the New World by Africans were intangible. This fact, which is absolutely singular if compared with the cultures of other diaspora – which always brought along some sort of resources – gains special importance when we accept the prominent position of body-based cultural expressions in Afro-American societies in general. Throughout history, the strong notion of a particular individual body of African slaves and their descendants also shaped the existence of a social body in the New World that is responsible for an immense amount of expressive forms, among them a rich and varied musical culture. Therefore, intangible cultural heritage regarding Afro-American music must be connected to a particular and strong "material" component, if we agree that once in the Americas, Africans could produce culture primarily through their own body. This body would express their ideas, beliefs, concepts, and a specific musicality, which, in its way, contained all of the previous.[1]

---

1    The recent broad discussion on cultural heritage has placed the human body as a central vehicle of intangible expressions. Ethnomusicological research, performance studies, and the experience with African culture in the Diaspora, strongly influenced this viewpoint (Gilroy 2001; Wulf 2004, among others).

When discussing Afro-Brazilian music, I refer rather to musicality, in connection with specific sound concepts, since music conceived as an audible product in and of itself, only would be valid in Western, but not in African, musical aesthetics. From a wider African perspective, it will therefore be easy to recognize that expressions like samba, *maracatu*, *capoeira*, etc. represent true Brazilian *music*, whereas their implied *musicality* can always bear an additional strong African character. Even if we are able to detect specific musical structures of African shape, the way they are used compose their "Africanity", sometimes more ubiquitously than the "African type". A similar process happens also the other way around, when Brazilian musicians use an instrument of apparent Portuguese or European origin, bringing it to sound in an "African" manner, although performing Brazilian music.

It took decades before musicology and ethnomusicology began to comprehend these multifaceted phenomena. The paradoxes between material and intangible expressions, between the apparent lack of logic evidences concerning concepts of African nature and the traditions of strong Catholic expression they are part of, or the contradiction, that African manifestations no longer remain attached exclusively to Afro-descendant Brazilians–all these and many other paradoxes become superficial in the moment in that one particular aspect emerge: there is a dynamic in the whole of the America's African culture that seems incommensurable, a source plenty of possibilities for local manifestations to become national and, above all, for national musical expressions to obtain world wide recognition.

## 2.  Ethnomusicology

In its previous form as comparative musicology in Europe and North America and as musical folklore studies in Brazil, ethnomusicology paid attention to African Brazilian music only relatively late. Especially for European scholars, the presence of African cultural elements in South America was not considered an authentic cultural expression of the country, nor as an African output since, in their opinion, Africa only embraced the area at the other side of the Atlantic. Similarly, cultural anthropology of the nineteenth and early twentieth centuries in the New World was mainly interested in indigenous populations. United States and Brazilian cultural anthropology turned their focus on Afro-American traditions later. In Europe it took even longer for a factual anthropological interest in Afro-Americans to arise. This can be recognized in the large collection of Edison wax cylinders in the Phonogram Archive of the Ethnological Museum in Berlin, brought together from all parts of the world until the late 1930s. Almost no recording of Afro-American expression will be found among these early recordings, collected and archived for ethnological research (Simon 2000).

Brazilian musicologist Mário de Andrade (1887-1945) first understood the importance of African cultural history in Brazil and in the America's through its musical expressions.[2] For him musicological study could be understood properly only in connection with other cultural domains, like language, literature, games and dramatic plays, visual art and the ever-changing socio-cultural context in the New World. To believe in indigenous music as the only "authentic" one in Brazil never made sense to Andrade. It is true that one of his uncompleted book projects, *A Música dos Brasis*, was devoted mainly to the music of Brazilian Indians, but this was merely one among other projects on traditional music in the country.

Mário de Andrade believed in the interaction between expressive arts; therefore, the interdisciplinary approach was unquestionable for the study and documentation of musical traditions in his country (Pinto 2006). As head of the Cultural Department of the city of São Paulo for a short period of time, Andrade was able to organize a musical research mission to the Northeast of Brazil *(Missão das Pesquisas Folclóricas)* in 1933. With Mário de Andrade, Brazilian ethnomusicology soon recognized the importance of a dialogue between the humanities.

Andrade's approach was typical for Brazil. Whereas after the Second World War European and North American universities developed ethnomusicological theoretical approaches, research in Brazil could not rely on a specific methodology. Musicological study was still part of a larger repertoire of the humanities without a proper, delimited place. This would change only by the late 1970s.

---

2   Bahian physician Raimundo da Nina Rodrigues and particularly ethnologist Arthur Ramos, who pioneered Afro-Brazilian studies in Brazil, although without having a musicological basis for their research.

An important aspect of the history of ethnomusicology is the experience with sound recordings, which became part of anthropological research since 1907, when German ethnologists Theodor Koch-Grünberg (from 1911 to 1913) and Wilhelm Kissenberth (from 1907 to 1909) travelled through the Amazon region making the first sound recordings in the field, which later were analysed by comparative musicologist Erich Moritz von Hornbostel and others in Berlin. The impact of the Edison Phonograph's recorded exotic sound from all over the world on Western research was rather impressing The possibility of transporting sounds and extending them outside their original contexts through phonographic recording gave European scholars the opportunity to substantially renew their knowledge of the "other". It is, in a certain way, thanks to the phonograph that the Western academic world became aware of the relativity of concepts of what is music and what is not. This development consolidated ethnomusicology as a discipline.

Systematic sound recordings in the 1950s and 1960s in Africa (Hugh Tracey, Gilbert Rouget, André Didier, Gerhard Kubik) helped to fill the gaps in the musical land chart of the continent. The constitution of new musical forms in Africa under the impact of Afro-American music from the 1940s on – *highlife* in Ghana, *kwela* in South Africa or the Congo *rumba* in Zaïre/Congo (Rycroft 1961/62, Kubik 1965; 1966) – led to a new awareness of musical parallels or similarities and their historical connections with cultural areas on both sides of the Atlantic Ocean. Ethnomusicological research contributed to the rise of consciousness on cultural diversity through music.

In describing and trying to understand African or Afro-American musical culture, however, one was still indebted to Western musicological terminology. To find new terminology and to adapt those of musicological common sense has always been a challenge for ethnomusicological research. Significantly, early terminology for African music came from jazz research (Waterman 1952). In addition, cultural and social sciences contributed enormously not only with methods, but with terminology as well.

New Brazilian ethnomusicology finally has been preoccupied with cultural areas on both sides of the Southern Atlantic, addressing questions arising in the last two decades. Without having achieved any definite conclusion, some of these topics came up in cultural studies as well as in African, Caribbean, and Latin American literary theory.

**A Selection of Studies in Afro-Brazilian Music**

| | |
|---|---|
| Music, dance and movement | Mário de Andrade, 1937 |
| Old slave work songs *(vissungos)* | Ayres da Mata Machado Filho, 1948 |
| Sound structures; the musician | César Guerra-Peixe, 1950 |
| The popular song | Oneyda Alvarenga, 1959 |
| Historical links, comparative research, musical structures, Angolan traits and its functions | Gerhard Kubik, 1979 |
| Bantu musical contribution to Brazil | Kazadi wa Mukuna, 1979 |
| Anthropology of music, music making and musical concepts | Tiago de Oliveira Pinto, 1986 |
| Historical sambas in Rio de Janeiro | Carlos Sandroni, 2001 |
| Ethnography of musical rites and applied ethnomusicology, community-based research projects | Francisca Marques, 2004 |
| Discourse and musical sociability in urban peripheral contexts, community-based research projects | Samuel Araújo & group, 2006 |

## 3. Sources and structures

In historical terms, the diversity of African cultures in Brazil is intimately linked to the geographical origins of the African slaves brought to the country. Regarding the transatlantic connections, a continuous "flux and reflux" of Africans of Brazilian birth and sundry goods contributed to this diversity.

Musicological studies of sound structures across the Atlantic gain special importance in the context of reconstructing the history of the Atlantic of the past five centuries. This is possible because, apart from miscegenation, syncretism, or hypotheses of cultural hybridity, the African musical heritage in the New World shows us that there is never a total blending of its different elements in sound and performance structures. Vestiges of its origins remain intact as in few other areas of culture; no amount of mixing is able to completely eliminate the marks and structures of these musical styles. Therefore music manages to manifest the present while simultaneously evincing its past.

How can we address the history of African structures in musical practices and their meanings in Brazil? Few written sources directed specifically to this musical phenomenon are available until the beginning of the twentieth century. Even less, and only occasionally, we find some documentation in musical scores. Therefore, we assume basically two sources for the research of this music, one essentially historical and the other of a systematic character:

(1) The documentation and evaluation of historical sources: written and iconographic sources, and objects such as musical instruments;
(2) The documentation and systematic evaluation of contemporary field material (audio recordings, film, video, photos, empiric facts, oral culture).

Depending on the focus of the research, African and Afro-American sources are consulted comparatively. It is already impossible to speak generally of "traditional music", rather of translations of a certain period in a specific cultural space. Any comparison, however, has to be done with utmost care.

Important examples of historical sources are iconographies in travel accounts or in archives of artists. Many of them are already known, while others are still awaiting analysis. Or, in the specific case of musical practices, the material aspect becomes most important, in the first place the musical instruments. We have examples of old instruments in museums and private collections, whose moment of fabrication might demonstrate significant historical links with specific regions of the African continent (Kubik 1979; 1986). Musical iconographies as well as the study of musical instruments are central for ethnomusicology.

When we are attentive to reading historical sources, we can find surprising facts. Jean-Baptiste Debret, the famous French artist and chronicler, who was in Brazil from 1816 to 1831, makes a key observation in his *Voyage pittoresque et historique au Brésil* (1834). He refers to the various African nations of the slaves in the streets of Rio de Janeiro, recognizable through their dances and songs. Debret argues that when the African is overwhelmed by nostalgia for his country, he intones a song, and then the others back him and contribute with a strange refrain based on only two or three notes. They stand in a circle and mark the rhythm by clapping in their hands.

Debret observes here a rhythmical pattern in the Afro-Brazilian cultural context that today has extended to almost everywhere in Brazil. We can transcribe its pattern in the following way:

(8)    x . . x . x . .

      (x = struck pulsation; . = mute pulsation or pause)

We have here the proof of a "time-line", an essential element in African music, the rhythmical formula that orientates the other musicians involved.

To exemplify some basic elements of the sonorous structure and its relationship with movement sequences, we take the example of the samba taught in samba schools, the most famous ones in Rio de Janeiro. In these schools, sound and movement know different levels of configuration, partly represented by the instrumental groups of the orchestra. Let's take a closer look at six of these levels of configuration, which contain elements to be found in several musical cultures in Africa, independently of the specifics of their performance:

*Elementary pulses*: these are shorter units, which serve as a base to the musical sequence. The samba is always based on a cycle of sixteen pulsations, which according to the degree of strengthening "neutralizes" the pulsations of shorter duration without a pre-established accentuation. The beats introduced by the musicians and the musical accents ultimately play on the base of one of these elementary pulsations. These short units leave as little distance between two tones as possible. During a musical succession, the elementary pulsations can become audible or visible through dance and movement.

*Beat & off-beat*: the beat as resounded by large *surdo* drums marks the rhythmical rise and fall of the samba. The marking consists of the *beat* and the *off-beat*, whereas samba players speak about "questioning" and "answering." They perform this marking on their percussion instruments of a different size. In relationship to the elementary pulsation this marking can be represented in the following way:

(16)  . . . . . . . . . . . . . . . . .
(16)  x . . . x . . . x . . . x . . .

*Time-line-pattern*: the rhythmical line of samba. It is an asymmetri-
cally structured and cyclical sequence of strokes that generally is performed on a high or sharp tone, especially on the small frame drum
*(tamborim)*. Called "time-line", such formulas are in reality composed
of elementary pulsations, heard or silent. So it is possible to perceive
in the "time-line" the basic rhythm of the piece concerning its cycle
of elementary pulsations, for instance, eight, twelve, or sixteen. The
rhythmical line in the samba consists of sixteen elementary pulsations
that figure as a cyclical line:

(16)  x . x . x x . x . x . x . x x .

The "time-line patterns" are responsible for a variety of repertoires of
Brazilian music and function as orientation for the further parts of the
musical performance. Moreover, historical links become manifest,
confirming, for instance, the Bantu origin of the *samba-de-roda* or the
Yoruba and/or Fon of the Gege-Nago Candomblé. Therefore, and
similar to ethnolinguistic research, the profound study of music, such
as that realized in the research of Gerhard Kubik, contributes as scientific support to reconstruct the history of the African cultures in Brazil,
namely the *kachacha* rhythm from Angola:

(16)  x . x . x . x . x x . x . x . x

Due to the stability of this musical element, the time-line formulas
survived in the Brazilian diaspora and in the migrations within Africa
so that in the analysis of African and African-American music, it is
possible to attribute "diagnostic" qualities to them. We see this, for
instance, in the formula of twelve in the Candomblé:

(12)  x . x x . x . x . x x .

*Fluctuation of rhythmical patterns:* this concerns the difficulty of reg-
istering certain rhythmical evolutions of the samba in the score of the
Western system of transcription. This system is not related to poly-
rhythmic structures or apparently irrational values of the samba, which
come from a continuous fluctuation inherent to the musical flood almost imperceptible at its conception.

*Tonal melodies:* the samba and many other musical genres do not know the temporal organization of rhythms. Many musicians call the "melodic sounds" they are playing *melodies*. The sound of an instrument can be creatively transfigured through different performance techniques.

*Movement as a component of music*: this is valid for many musical cultures from Africa. Music is rarely understood as a purely acoustic phenomenon; it is expressed through the music on the one hand and, on the other, through the listener who "listens" with his whole body. The duration of the tones of different extensions – a half note, a charter note, a quaver, etc. – seems a bit strange for the musical sensibility of the samba players. On the contrary, the technique of the samba is based on a large number of "action units" of beats, pauses, and up and down movements, which are simultaneous or consecutive. They all fit in the scheme previously established by the elementary pulsation. Consequently, when a movement produces a sound or is "silently" performed, it participates in the whole of the musical performance.

The above-outlined levels of configuration are linked in a relatively stable continuity, thus establishing a strict order of sounds and movements. To decipher the internal organization of these interdependent facts means recognizing the broadest musical structure in its multiple details. In an analysis of a *berimbau* (a musical arch instrument) played by a "mestre de capoeira" (teacher of *capoeira*) in Santo Amaro da Purificação in Bahia State, I departed from short units, those that identify the *toque*, to observe how the larger units were going to be constructed. My intention was to observe the construction of the music in a predetermined and organized form regarding the disposition and combination of the shorter parts. I concluded that what the musicians call *improviso* has nothing unforeseen in reality because it obeys the rules of combination and among the shorter parts. Unexpected developments are certainly possible can happen but always within what is foreseeable, which is determined by the musical culture of the *berimbau* in the Recôncavo Baiano. To understand this music, therefore, requires knowledge of the local musical setting. A recognized teacher of the instruments and composer imposes his individual version without ignoring the existing musical rules.

The definition of the musical pattern – an important structural element of music called *toque* in Brazil – also surfaces when we see that the African concept of "pattern" is hardly linear but multi-directional. Let's go back to the musical repertoire of the *berimbau*. When trying to define what the local term *toque* means, we see two basic components for its definition:

(1)    the horizontal component – the rhythmical-metrical sequence that extends itself over a cycle of at least eight half-note pulsations;

(2)    the vertical component – the variability in the reach of the tones, or a successive disposition of two distinct tones in the cycle of pulsations.

One of the definitions of the pattern in African music as being "a longer sequence repeated consecutively" is also applicable to rhythmical formulas in the most varied Afro-Brazilian orchestra, as well as for playing the *berimbau*. For this last instrument I found that the production of its sound is anchored in the regular succession of two different basic tones, which are repeated cyclically, constantly announcing the beginning of a new one (Pinto 1991: 71-78).

The performance is much more illustrative than the sounds fixed in an annotation system, the comparison of diverse repertoires and techniques for musical performances, or when pieces of music played on the xylophone, drums, and the *berimbau* are transcribed. Much more than the pure acoustic experience, it is important to see with which movements the musician is generating his sounds. In African or Afro-Brazilian music, some movements produce a variety of sounds according to the quality of the movement. Other types of movements, which leave out sound, give sequence to a continuity of an organized performance.

## 4.  Meaning in Afro-Brazilian musical performance

After presenting briefly a few of the structural elements in African and Afro-Brazilian music performance practices, the question arises, whether the meaning of these musical languages gain new semantically relevant contents when they cross the Southern Atlantic Ocean.

"Musical meaning" is a topic that has been questioned almost as long as the existence of a theoretical explanation about music. Also, much has been written about whether music has meaning, how it functions, and how it can be described. In any case, meaning in music is to be treated differently than meaning in literary works, although, especially in Africa, musical sound structures and spoken language are intimately linked. More generally, I propose an initial explanation of musical meaning in Afro-Brazilian culture based on the function of a specific piece of music, its role within a broader performance framework, as well as on the effect and impact the entire piece evokes (Tomlinson 1991).

In the context of samba, *maracatu, capoeira,* etc., musical performance comprises the process from structures of sound and movement to patterns of meaning. This process from the morphology of sound to the framing of events is particularly instructive in order to understand African presence in the history and culture of the Americas, since functional meanings transcend and are independent of musical structures only. The logic found in the relations of various factors that work together and constitute the performance practice, links it with a wider dimension, understood as a worldview, intrinsic to such manifestations as *capoeira* or samba. It is important to say, anyhow, that those musical structures we are dealing with represent cultural features without bearing any preconceived intention per se. This suggests that in its purest acceptation as an expressive form, music is absolutely devoid of pre-conceived imagination, including discrimination or racism. When they appear, meanings of this sort are injected into musical structures *a posteriori.* As non-verbal communication, which conveys its specific messages, even if they cannot be deciphered in the mode a verbal text is translated, music always remains a system open for semantic input. This property may explain why music has been used so widely to express feelings, to formulate social contest, or to reaffirm cultural identity, especially in Latin America.

In fact, the quest for translating meaning out of the musical process cannot be compared with the decoding of verbal meaning. An example from the *capoeira* repertory illustrates this: *Apanha laranja do chão Tico-tico* ("Take up the orange from the ground, Tico-tico") is a verbalized phrase used to memorize and characterize a musical pattern, especially in melo-rhythmic terms. At the same time, the pattern contains a specific code for dance movements. In this case, the semantics of the verbal phrase are less important, if at all. Memorizing musical patterns with syllables or short phrases is an orally-based procedure for transmitting musical culture in Africa, which has been kept in Brazil, as this specific musical bow *(berimbau)* pattern demonstrates.

Translating meaning from one language is a complex procedure, which in anthropological linguistics involves more than simply going from one native language to another:

> It implies a long series of interpretations and decisions that are rarely made apparent in the final product ... As Malinowski maintained ... translation assumes an ability to match words with the context in which they were uttered (Duranti 1997: 154).

In our case, searching for meaning in a non-verbal communication system like music and finding it concretized in words with clear semantics is only possible within the communication system of the manifestation as a whole. Anthropologists document the spoken language; they transcribe myths and oral literature with their own linguistic methods. Music is different. Even if it represents a semiotic unit, its semantic content cannot be translated or unequivocally understood by anyone who listens to it (Eco 1976). But, as argued, an explanation of particular meaning laid down in musical structures can function if analyzed within its cultural system. Thus, the idea that the basis of meaning rests in the manners of relations that signs like words, gestures, dance movements, sounds, colours, or mimicry have with one another in a specific cultural system, remains valid for the exploration of musical culture on both sides of the Southern Atlantic Ocean. Regarding this transatlantic cultural transfer, music has functioned always as a medium for knowledge and cultural behavior.

To give an example from Africa and a final one from Brazil on the study of multipart aspects of music and its verbal concepts, the outlining of precise native theories can contribute to domains of scholarly interest much ahead of supposed ethnomusicological concerns. Although terms like polyphony, polyrhythm, or hocked are Western-based terms, there are some basic ideas which are broader and regard the concept of "multipart" in music. Music as sound always belongs to a larger unit of expressive culture and its correlated forms of expression. Speaking of Shona music, the Ghanaian musicologist K. Nketia mentioned "multipartness" as the understanding that the Shona people of Zimbabwe bring in their performances when they use the word *kutengezana* to mean the sum of all the parts in a performance. Among these people the wholeness and unity of all of life is kept in mind (Nketia 1974). The musical contribution to this phenomenon comes out through the successive parts of a performance, the simultaneousness of musical lines, as well as by the involvement of the different human actors and their understanding of the semantically-relevant underlying sound structures.

Meaning through musical performance also surfaces also in connection with verbalized concepts, when the diaspora forces the contact between African and European performance traditions and thoughts. In the Recôncavo Baiano in Bahia, the tradition of the *viola-da-samba* or the *machete* (small guitar) reflects one of these conceptions, truly local theories, which make use of a completely re-signified Western terminology. This local modality of the Bahian samba, which has no relationship whatsoever with the samba of the samba-schools in Rio de Janeiro, has been included in the list of masterpieces of the immaterial Patrimony of Human Culture of UNESCO in November 2005. In a certain way it is one of the direct precursors of the samba of Rio because it arrived with the migrants from the Northeastern region of Bahia State to Rio, when this city was still the capital of Brazil.

The characteristic instrument of this samba of the Recôncavo is the small *viola*, also called *machete*, of Portuguese origin, more precisely of the Island of Madeira. However, the Bahian version of the instrument shows that it would be an error to insist on this origin for understanding this musical tradition because the provenance of the instrument is in no way responsible for the music played on it. Similarly, the use of determined musical terminology does not reflect a priori the concepts it comprises. We know that African concepts, or their derivatives, crystallize independently of whether the instrument genuinely belongs to the African traditions or not. The evidence is the innumerous regional styles of music for the guitar in Africa, the US (in the blues, for example), and in the Recôncavo, with its *samba-de-viola*. In such a way, "crossed rhythms" produced on the strings of this instrument sound as an allegory of different cultural elements, which meet and produce new configurations, recreating symbolic values and historical knowledge in virtue of new social significations.

In the case of the *machete,* the responsible conception for the sonorous production is based in a "spatio-motor-thinking" (Bailey 1995), in which is found

- defined patterns of sequences of movements;
- specific techniques of interlinking of two rhythmical configurations, produced by the forefinger and the thumb of the right hand; and
- in relationship with the accentuation and harmony of the whole.

All these elements manifest a musical mentality of their own, clearly African. Besides, this theoretical reference board of the music of the *machete* of Bahia State is based on the notion of five distinct "tones": *ré-maior, dó-maior, lá-maior, sol-maior,* and *mi-maior.* Meanwhile, the semantics of this terminology are much more far-reaching than those of the musical theories taught in European conservatoriums, since this knowledge is bound to terms as *ré-maior, dó-maior,* etc. without taking the concept of the repertoire of the *samba-de-viola* into account. Although the absolute tonal relationship between the five *tons de machete* coincide with the Western tonality concept, the local native theory goes into another direction. It values the "*machete* tone", i.e. the sonorous realization of patterns of a defined movement, as we have seen above. Each one of the five "tones" has its formulas of movement and its own acoustic experience as well as implies the degree of highness of each one of the tones on an imaginary scale.

The acoustic-motional patterns of each "*machete* tone" contain an aesthetic character that will have its repercussions in the music and in the choice of the "tone" at the moment of its performance in the band. The "tone" that is most suited for the accompaniment of a samba *puxado* (led by the drums) for singing the *chula* verses in a "free" and "excited" way is *ré-maior,* whereas *mi-maior* is considered the "heaviest" and "hardest" tone. The *ré-maior* is played preferably to bring a good mood to a party and the feet of the dancers into a steady swinging rhythm as well as to offer a favorable basis for singing the improvised *chula* verses answered by the singers. In order to test a drummer who has just arrived, the players introduce the *mi-maior* tone, already difficult by nature, but even more so for the dancers. The precise differentiation between the five "*machete* tones" in the musical practices and conversations and comments among the musicians re-

reveals important aspects of the musical theory of the Recôncavo Baiano.

There are certainly many other aspects of Africa-influenced sonorous structures and musical performances, which have an audible and visible continuity in Brazil and in other parts of the American continent – for instance, different melodic rules, laws of polyphony, a combination of letters and music, the polymeters, or the study of dance – each of them representing a universe of its own. All of them certainly have in common the "Africanist" characteristics of sensibility in thinking and doing expressed in music and in its movements, as well as in dancing and in the instrumental performance, or even in the listening or active body-based participation of the audience. More than all this, however, this brief recapitulation attests that the categories presented above may contribute to a detailed vision for a profound revaluation of the cultural and social studies in Brazil and Latin America. At the same time our knowledge of the African influences in Brazilian cultures is growing. This is what I mean when speaking of "rhythms that cross" everywhere. They respond to time lines that teach, guide, and accompany Brazilians today. They report the similarities in historical past and present and make us understand the presence of rhythms and distant lines in the New World, exactly because they are familiar to so many of the people living on both sides of the Southern Atlantic Ocean.

## Bibliography

Alvarenga, Oneyda (1959): *Música popular brasileira*. São Paulo: Duas Cidades.

Andrade, Mário de (1937): "O samba rural paulista". In: *Revista do Arquivo Municipal*, 41, 4, pp. 37-116.

Araújo, Samuel et al. (2006): "Conflict and Violence as Theoretical Tools in Present-Day Ethnomusicology: Notes on a Dialogic Ethnography of Sound Practices in Rio de Janeiro". In: *Ethnomusicology*, 50, 2, pp. 287-313.

Bailey, John (1995): "Music and the Body". In: *The World of Music*, 37, 2, pp. 11-30.

Debret, Jean-Baptiste (1972): *Viagem pitoresca e histórica ao Brasil*, vols. 1-3. Translation and notes: Millet, Sérgio. São Paulo: Martins.

Duranti, Alessandro (1997): *Linguistic Anthropology*. Cambridge: Cambridge University Press.

Eco, Umberto (1976): *A Theory of Semiotics*. Bloomington: Indiana University Press.

Filho, Ayres da Mata Machado (1948): *O negro e o garimpo em Minas Gerais*. Rio de Janeiro: José Olympio.

Gilroy, Paul (2001): *O Atlântico Negro. Modernidade e dupla consciência*. São Paulo: 34 Letras.

Guerra-Peixe, César (1950): *Maracatus do Recife*. São Paulo: Ricordi.

Kubik, Gerhard (1965): "Neue Musikformen in Schwarzafrika. Psychologische und musikethnologische Grundlagen". In: *Afrika Heute*, 4, pp. 1-16.

— (1966): "Die Popularität von Musikarten im Afrika südlich der Sahara". In: *Afrika Heute*, 15, pp. 370-375.

— (1979): *Angolan Traits in Black Music. Games and Dances of Brazil. A Study of African Cultural Extensions Overseas*. Lisboa: Junta de Investigações Científicas do Ultramar.

— (1986): "Afrikanische Musikkulturen in Brasilien". In: Pinto, Tiago de Oliveira (ed.): *Einführung in Musiktraditionen Brasiliens*. Mainz: Schott, pp. 121-147.

Marques, Francisca (2004): O samba de roda na Festa da Boa Morte: Entre o ritual e o divertimento das mulheres negras baianas (*Sinais Diacríticos* 2). São Paulo: SOMA-USP.

Mukuna, Kazadi wa (1979): *Contribuição Bantu na Música Popular Brasileira*. São Paulo: Global.

Nketia, J. H. Kwabena (1974): *The Music of Africa*. New York: WW Norton & Co.

Pinto, Tiago de Oliveira (1986): *Brasilien. Einführung in die Musiktraditionen Brasiliens*. Mainz: Schott.

— (1991): *Capoeira, Samba, Candomblé. Afro-Brasilianische Musik im Recôncavo, Bahia*. Berlin: Reimer.

— (2006): "The Invention of Brazil: The Ethnography, Folklore and Musicology of Mário de Andrade". In: Oliveira Pinto, Tiago de/Ribeiro M., Izabel (eds.): *The Idea of Brazilian Modernismo*. Berlin/New York/London: LIT, pp. 128-151.

Rycroft, David (1961): "The Guitar Improvisations of Mwenda Jean Bosco". In: *African Music*, Part 1: 2, 4, pp. 81-98.

— (1962): "The Guitar Improvisations of Mwenda Jean Bosco". In: *African Music*, Part 2: 3, 1, pp. 86-101.

Sandroni, Carlos (2001): *Feitiço decente. Transformações do samba no Rio de Janeiro (1917-1933)*. Rio de Janeiro: Zahar.

Simon, Artur (ed.) (2000): *Das Berliner Phonogramm-Archiv 1900-2000 / The Berlin Phonogramm-Archiv, 1900-2000*. Berlin: wvb.

Tomlinson, John (1991): *Cultural Imperialism. A Critical Introduction*. Baltimore: Johns Hopkins University Press.

Waterman, Richard (1952): "African Influences on the Music of the Americas". In: Tax, Sol (ed.): *Acculturation in the Americas*. Chicago: University of Chicago Press.

Wulf, Christoph (2004): *Anthropologie. Geschichte – Kultur – Philosophie*. Reinbek: rororo.

**Donald Kachamba in Berlin (1993)**

Photo: Jürgen Dietrich, courtesy private archive Gerhard Kubik.

Gerhard Kubik[*]

# Transformations and Reinterpretations of American *Jazz*. An Inside Account of Jazz Performances in Chileka, Malawi, Home Area of *kwela* Flutist, Guitarist, and Composer Donald Kachamba

Jazz has had a profound impact on the rise of new musical forms in southern Africa. It began in the 1930s with ballroom dance music and intensified in the late 1940s in South African cities and townships when kids took up swing jazz with toy instruments and developed *kwela* "flute jive". From the early 1960s, South African jazz clubs were ablaze with Bebop and other forms of modern jazz played by groups such as the Soul Jazzmen from Port Elizabeth, the Jazz Faces Quintet, the Lionel Pillay Trio, the Malombo Jazzmen, and many others. Meanwhile street-band *kwela* had spread to the neighboring countries, notably the Federation of Rhodesia and Nyasaland (now Zimbabwe, Zambia and Malawi). At the same time Brazilian popular music spread to Mozambique and Angola, and somewhat earlier Cuban rumba to the Congo and Kenya.

My personal account traces the transformations American jazz, rumba and other forms of New World music have undergone in our own musical group in Chileka, near Blantyre, southern Malawi, focusing on a particular period of crisis and renaissance between July 2000 and September 2002.

---

[*]   Acknowledgements:Research leading to the preparation of this paper was carried out in the context of project P 17751-G06 "Musical Cultures of East and Southeast Africa: Historical Perspectives", a three-year ethno musicological research project financed by the *Wissenschaftsfonds*, Vienna. In the name of our research team and myself I would like to express my gratitude for this support.
      Donald Kachamba's life work and the compositions by his successor band have been copyright-protected by AKM *(Staatlich genehmigte Gesellschaft der Autoren, Komponisten und Musikverleger)*, Vienna. His estate is stored at the facilities of the "Oral Literature Research Programme", Chileka.

The paper takes a look at intimate processes of composition by the band members involved and discusses how African and Blues harmonic ideas have been integrated and reconciled, leading to the reinstatement of *kwela* in the broader stylistic framework of modern jazz. It also analyzes how a younger generation is gradually taking over the leadership from the founders of this music.

## I.

The developments described in this paper began in July 2000 when Donald Kachamba (1953-2001), leader of our musical group for 26 years, was still active. A few months earlier, in December 1999, Donald had returned from his stay as Artist in Residence at the University of California, Los Angeles, equipped with a long video of his teachings and his final, public performance with the U.C.L.A students on December 4. In his air baggage he also had several Stan Laurel and Oliver Hardy motion pictures in their original, uncut versions, which he had obtained with the help of one of his student friends. From boyhood on, Donald had been an enthusiastic Laurel and Hardy fan, and he also loved other 1920s and 1930s comedians like Buster Keaton, Charlie Chaplin, and the Marx Brothers. But especially the culture of Laurel and Hardy had been part of his artistic life and even his personal behavior, for instance, after seeing this duo singing "Honolulu Baby":

> When he was nineteen he used to laugh with such vigor and so incessantly in public cinemas across Europe that audiences were turning their heads! Some elderly women complained. Later, he used to do a good deal of acting during concert shows, and even in private, some of which is recorded on video (Kubik/Malamusi, Video Nr. 31).

Donald Kachamba had been at U.C.L.A. for three months, from September to December 1999, giving courses at the Department of Ethnomusicology on invitation by Professor Jacqueline Cogdell DjeDje. From there he returned to Malawi. When I too flew back to Malawi from Europe, arriving in Chileka on June 28, 2000, to spend some months in our home village, Singano near Chileka, Donald was waiting for me at the airport together with many other relatives of our family. I found that he looked somewhat slim, but he gave me the impression of being vigorous.

As in the years before, we began to get together regularly in his house for rehearsals with our "Donald Kachamba's Kwela Band" (see Discographic and Cinematographic references). With Donald on guitar, Moya Aliya Malamusi on one-string bass, a youngster on rattle and myself on E-flat clarinet, we set out to revive much of the music he had composed beginning in 1985, with titles such as "Namaseko", "Ife timakonda kuyimba", "Talekani miseche", "Pang'ono pang'ono tatopa nchito", "Pafibe zikomo" etc., beautiful music that was no longer *kwela* in the strict sense. It had become something else. The best way to describe it would be to say that it was Donald's music and the music of his unique band. There was no other music like that in Malawi. Most other groups were imitating the current international pop music disseminated by the mass media. Our recent tours to Europe had included Germany, Belgium and France, with recordings made at Radio France, Paris, on January 23, 1995, and then in 1997 we participated in a festival at the German Film Museum in Frankfurt am Main and also gave a concert in the *Gewandhaus* Leipzig.

In July 2000, in Donald's house we were embarking on something slightly different with Donald's student Sinosi Mlendo on guitar. We were trying out new compositions such as "Sinjonjo Blues" and "Sena Twist" (in an AABA chorus form). Donald volunteered to play second clarinet, as in the old days when Moya's young brother Fulaye, aged 16, had played guitar. That was in January 1982 (CD Pamap 103, LC 07203, Günther Gretz, Frankfurt am Main). Now we played again "Chikumbutso Lumba", in memory of Fulaye who had died at that young age of Pneumococcal meningitis. But this time – in the year 2000 – Donald found it hard to play clarinet. He complained of short breath and general weakness. Even playing the flute was becoming difficult.

We were aware, of course, that he had been a diabetic since 1994, on daily insulin injections; and our last concert tours in Europe had been somewhat difficult, because with Diabetes Mellitus, Donald always had to disappear before an evening concert in a bathroom to give himself an injection. Some people in the audience noticed it and began to construct their own theories.

But in Chileka in July 2000, diabetes was not the actual complaint. His insulin levels seemed to be stable. He simply was not feeling well, he said. He was coughing and had breathing difficulties. He was always feeling tired.

Two years earlier Donald had started to train several young men and boys in the vicinity, mostly relatives, to play various instruments. I once video-taped a delightful session that took place in his garden under the mango tree (Kubik/Malamusi, Video Nr. 54). That was shortly before he left for the United States. The most talented and devoted young man among those trainees was Sinosi Mlendo, whose maternal uncle *(malume)* incidentally is Moya A. Malamusi. First Sinosi had learned from Donald all the standard cyclic patterns on the five-string guitar used for dance-band performances and he internalized Donald's feel for swing and prominent accentuations. At this "junior" stage, Sinosi can be seen with Donald, Moya, and another boy, Khilizibe, in a delightful - though somewhat falsely synchronized – production by Television Malawi under Producer Waliko Makhala in 1999, before Donald's trip to the United States. The five-string guitar is an invention by Donald's elder brother, the late Daniel J. Kachamba (1947-1987). Daniel can be seen playing it in a cinematographic documentation *Kachamba Brothers*, that I made in 1967, now also on DVD (production Wolfgang Bachschwell, Vienna). There are various tunings; Daniel had used one he called "Key G high six", while in Donald's band the so-called LG tuning is used (Kubik 1974: 36-37). It is an adaptation for plectrum guitar in band performances. Six-string African finger guitar playing would not be suitable for this style. But five-string guitar played "vamping" – to use an expression coined by John Low (1982: 44) – allows for unusual chord progressions and fingerings.

Other trainees of Donald included Stuwadi Mpotalinga, painter, on rattle and bass. He had already been with us on tours to Europe in 1991 and in 1995. Christopher Gerald alias "Khilizibe" was another of Donald's trainees. He had started music on a home-made banjo in 1994 as a teenager with his own band that he called "Tingoyesa Band" (We-are-just-trying Band) (Kubik/Malamusi, Video Nr. 32). And there was Dayina, Moya's second daughter, then about twelve years old, a very lively girl, fond of games. When Donald, in July 2000, became increasingly hesitant about attending rehearsals, his sparkling nature only occasionally returning to its former energy levels, the group of youngsters simply went on by themselves. And I played the clarinet with them. No one was yet seriously worried about Donald. We believed that he would soon get better.

Since Donald could no longer blow the flute without pains in his chest, let alone play a second clarinet, I always felt somewhat relieved when he came to play lead guitar with us. I was worried and began to discuss with Moya how we might persuade him to have a thorough medical examination.

Sinosi Mlendo found himself increasingly taking over Donald's role on the guitar. He also became interested in trying out new ways, such as experimenting with chords beyond those, which are basic to southern African popular music. Looking for ways to depart from the cyclic forms of *kwela* and *mbaqanga* – South African genres of popular music (Coplan 1985) – he got attracted to the 12-bar blues and AABA chorus forms while retaining Donald's rhythmic structures unchanged: *sinjonjo*, double-step (also called *simanje-manje* by elderly musicians in southern Malawi), twist, or *lumba* (rumba) (for Kachimba Brother's terminology see Kubik 1974).

I said to Sinosi: "If these are the directions you want to take, let us develop the theme of 'Sena Twist' to include a clarinet melodic phrase repeated *across* your changing chords in the AABA form". Sinosi had written down the chords in a little book in the standard notation for jazz chords. I then played the theme and several variations on the E-flat clarinet in Sena style. The "bridge" or B part was also suggestive of Sena progressions (Sena is an ethnic group in Southern Malawi and Central Mozambique, known for specific chord sequences in their xylophone and other music, Tracey 1991). Played in twist rhythm, as it is called in Kachamba terminology, but all chord changes on the guitar are off-beat; they come one elementary pulse-unit earlier, before the inception of a measure, and they occur on an up-stroke of the guitarist's right hand. This is why in our transcription of the theme the chord symbols are written ahead of the bar lines. Next we began to work on the twelve-bar blues, "Sinjonjo Blues", we had played the other day in Donald's house. *Sinjonjo* is a dance-pattern in a 12-pulse cycle. It originated in southern Africa in the 1950s. For *sinjonjo* it is very important to understand that we musicians internalize an elementary pulsation, i.e., a continuous reference grid of very fast units without any pre-conceived accentuation. On top of it there is the second reference level: the beat shared with the dancers' steps. But the guitarist has to play evenly; he will not watch the dancers. While the beat in *sinjonjo* combines three pulse-units, creating the impression of a music in fast triplets, the guitarist in his hand movements, up and down, executes duplets. The result is a duple/triple interface. In addition – also in "jive and twist" – all chord changes are anticipated in relation to the dancers' and the rattle player's beat by the value of one elementary pulse-unit. That gives this structure a kind of "kick", i.e., there are strong offbeat accents on pulse-units six and eleven of a measure.

### Fig. 1 (*sinjonjo* movement pattern)

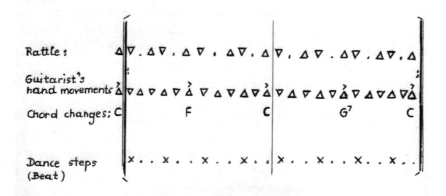

To the best of my knowledge such a structural scheme does not underlie the rhythm of blues accompaniment in American jazz, Rhythm & Blues, or rural blues. It is something specifically southern African, a rhythmic reinterpretation of jazz. So in this breeding place of jazz transformations at Singano village, Chileka, something peculiar has come up. A few years later we would call it "Sinjonjo Blues".

In standard *sinjonjo* – we have to remember – all chord changes occur one elementary pulse-unit before the reference beat of musicians and dancers. This is a small but consequential deviation from - American blues in our blues renderings. Anticipatory chord changes were, of course, the hallmark of most South African popular music from the 1950s to the 1970s. Paul Simon did not understand that in his "Graceland" when he played with West Nkosi and other *mbaqanga* musicians. He also got the beat wrong.

Meanwhile the concept of anticipatory chord changes has largely disappeared from contemporary styles in southern Africa. Teenagers in our village are now conditioned by the "gumba-gumba" in the bar next door to a simple, broad ground-beat: "di – di di", etc. Therefore, some of them are as disoriented by the accentuations in our music, notably in *simanje-manje* pieces, as did European teenagers *and* West Africans in the 1970s during our world-wide concert tours with Donald Kachamba. Audio-psychologically, these listeners react to Donald's music with *metric inversion*, i.e., disoriented by the offbeat accentuations and the change of chords on the off-beat, they do not recognize the ground-beat in the places where insiders feel it. Most amusingly, these people then take the offbeat for the beat and dance on it (see Musical Examples 1 and 2).

In terms of Donald's musical concepts, the directions Sinosi wanted to take were both conservative and novel. In Donald's band we had often played pieces in a twelve-bar blues form, more often in the 10-bar shortened form introduced by the late Daniel Kachamba. But Sinosi's versions had something radically different from *kwela* and related styles, not least in the chords. The chorus form had also been used in *kwela*, for example in the Kachamba Brothers' "Mai Lumba", which was modeled on a performance by the Sithole Brothers in Cape Town as seen in Kenneth Law's 1960 film "Pennywhistle Boys". But most of the themes like those by southern African musician-composers were based on cyclic forms whose harmonic basis can be described as (a) $F - C \; (^{6/4}) - G^7 - C$, and (b) $C - C \; (^7) - F \; (^6) - G^7$. Sinosi wanted to change that and explore different harmonic dimensions. It soon turned out that he would play with great ease any traditional 1920s to 1930s jazz tune in the chorus form and rarely get "lost", in contrast to what happens regularly to jazz beginners (see Paul Berliner's comments on the matter, Berliner 1993: 71-82). While retaining Donald's *motional* patterns, *sinjonjo, simanje-manje* etc., he would fall in love with, for example, the theme and chord sequence of

## Musical Example 1

## Musical Example 1a

## Musical Example 2

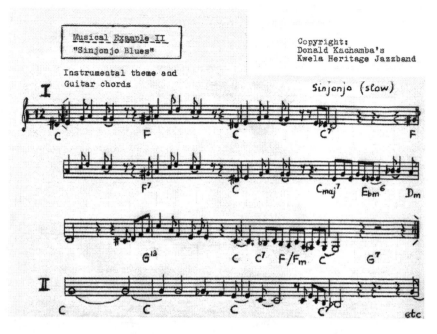

New Orleans's jazz tune "Make me a pallet on the floor". George Gershwin's tune "I Got Rhythm" with its numerous derivatives turned out to be child's play for him, though he was probably not aware that the theme's chord sequence, minus the bridge (which Sinosi mastered easily) had been used from the late 1950s into the 1960s by pre-Kachamba guitarists in Chileka like White Chinyama and Piasoni Chinkhango, whose pictures can be seen in Kubik/Malamusi (1994: 30). The song to which I am referring and which is based on "I Got Rhythm" is called "Ndinalemba kalata". (I wrote a letter). Knowledge of jazz themes based on "I Got Rhythm" spread through southern Africa during the 1940s and 1950s with radio broadcasts and gramophone records. The countries that were combined from 1953-1963 under the name Federation of Rhodesia and Nyasaland – today the independent states of Zimbabwe, Zambia, and Malawi – were a principal market for the South African music business heavily based on jazz.

Within a month, our small band, now held together by Sinosi Mlendo, was developing a jazz repertoire of a dozen items. Donald was watching these developments, and occasionally he came to "sit in" with the wonderful ebony-black guitar he had bought a few years ago in Portugal, before giving a first concert with it at the *Gewandhaus*, in Leipzig in 1997. Unfortunately none of these last sessions in Chileka with Donald playing lead guitar was recorded.

By the end of July, Moya and I were becoming increasingly alarmed about Donald's health. He did not at all get better, and so Moya drove him to one of the more expensive hospitals in the country, where doctors then diagnosed all sorts of "infections", especially of the chest, while giving the impression that they were all curable with antibiotics! We were lulled into a false sense of optimism and misjudgment of the situation.

Although it was on the tip of our tongues to suggest that Donald take a HIV test, we did not dare to speak out what we thought. There is a culture of secrecy about HIV in southern Africa. People who die due to AIDS die "officially" of TB or dehydration, and on the village level AIDS is called the "government's disease" *(matencia aboma)* and is perceived as an unlikely, remote image, a shadowy existence. Why some die prematurely must then be due to witchcraft *(ufiti)*, and that solves all problems of further investigation or prevention. In Donald's case it is even possible, however, that a test was made at some stage; but then we were never informed about the result. Eventually Donald was admitted to a somewhat cheaper hospital, one in Lunzu, not far from Chileka. But since we soon found him walking in the hospital garden whenever we visited him, reading books and talking in his usual humorous way, and since he seemed to look much better than he had shortly before, we gathered the impression that the treatment of his pulmonary infection was adequate. As for the possible immune deficiency, we would see to that later, we thought, once he was out of the clinic.

In the meantime, the band in the village was playing almost every day. We were practicing the new songs and composing more of them. Sinosi used to come to my house even late in the evening to try out new chord sequences, discovering various finger positions on the five-string guitar (tuned to one of the non-standard tunings introduced by the late Daniel Kachamba) for minor, diminished, sixth, and major seventh chords.

The new hit was a *lumba* (rumba) item in the name of Dayina, Moya's twelve-year old daughter, who was sometimes sitting in with us to sing.

### "Dayina Lumba" (see Musical Example 3)

| Text sung in Chinyanja: | Translation: |
|---|---|
| Dayina! | Diana! |
| Tidzipita ku Chaina! | Let us go to China! |
| Tikagule mapaina | So that we buy some pine trees, |
| kwadzala kuno ku phiri! | to plant them here on the mountain! |
| | |
| Dayina! | Diana! |
| Tidzipita ku Chaina! | Let us go to China! |
| Tikagule mapaina | So that we buy some pine trees |
| ku midzi! | there in the villages! |
| | |
| Tikalephera titani? | If we fail to do so, what then? |
| Tidziyimba nyimbo zonsezi! | Then let us just sing all (our) songs! |
| | |
| Dayina! | Diana! |
| Tidzipita ku Chaina! | Let us go to China! |
| Tikagule mapaina | So that we buy some pine trees |
| ku midzi! | there in the villages! |

"Dayina Lumba" was one of the earliest pieces composed in this rapidly transforming band. By Monday, July 10 we had a text outline for discussion. "Composed" is perhaps an overstatement in this particular case, because there were a few problems; one I remember was how to space out the long /a/ in the word *kwadzala*. I think Moya was the one who found the solution (see Musical Example 3, second line). This song simply "happened" to us. Everyone can recognize the 1920s American hit that is behind it. However, with Sinosi on the guitar, this song – first played instrumentally with improvised solo clarinet variations – seemed to reconfigure itself, as if it wanted to return to its "roots" in Africa. We soon discovered that it fit a *lumba* rhythm pattern to the time-line (sticks) (Recordings in Djenda/Kubik Collection) [. . xx . xx . ], i.e., in Donald's conception of rumba, which was a little more Kenyan than Congolese. And it fit our guitar rhythm so naturally that we even suspected that ours might have been the original rhythm to go with it, before it was adapted to the Foxtrot and

Charleston dance culture of the "Roaring Twenties". It must be mentioned here, that in Donald's rumba adaptations all the chord changes coincide with the inception of a measure, they are *not* anticipated. So local kids were dancing enthusiastically to our version of "Dinah", originally published in New York City in 1925.

### Musical Example 3

Fig. 2: Cover page of the original "Dinah"
published in New York City in 1925

The songwriters Sam M. Lewis and Joe Young invented the famous line: "Dinah – if she wandered to China, I would hop an ocean liner, just to be with Dinah Lee!" The lyrics of the song are nonsense lyrics; the words are combined simply because they rhyme: "Dinah, is there anyone finer in the state of Carolina?" Our text of "Dayina Lumba" is also all "nonsense". It is condensed from little images strung together. One inspiration, of course, was the lively Dayina who used to play with great fervor what is called *misumisu* in Singano village, jumping over a string held up by two girls. We needed a personal song for her to sing with us in this band to which we had given a name in her honor: "Dayina Swing Jazz Band". Another image that worked itself into the song text was our fond memories of walks in the Michiru Mountains with the children, not far from our village. During the last few years, most of this Forest Reserve has been depleted mercilessly by charcoal burners, with no authority ever bothering to stop the destruction of one of the last original areas of biodiversity in southern Malawi.

This is, of course, serious. Once all the original trees are gone, including my favorites such as *mulombwe* (bot. *Pterocarpus angolensis*), the forest might be "privatized", with timber companies or whoever planting pine trees and fast growing Australian specimens. The new proprietors will then erect a fence around the reserve. It happens that the name of the girl, Dayina (Chinyanja pronunciation of Diana, no connection with the Princess) rhymes with "China" and also with *mapaina* (pl.), the Chinyanja borrowing of (Engl.) "pine-trees". That is how the song took shape: we would soon have to go to China to beg for pine-trees for our beloved mountains, depleted by the charcoal burners. And if we failed, what then? Sure, in that case we wouldn't blow up anybody in revenge, but simply go on with our music.

The song became quite successful in the village. When Wolfgang Bender, head of the African Music Archive, University of Mainz, visited us from 20 to 25 August, studying the collections in Moya's Oral Literature Research Program, and seeing his Ethnographic Museum, we gave a musical party on the veranda. Many children were flocking to our compound and Malawi TV came with a non-working camera. Waliko Makhala, producer, and a good friend of the house, interviewed us, and he asked me specifically about what kind of message our songs conveyed. In all honesty, I should have replied that they do not convey any messages, but that would have been contrary to what the world expects music to be. Was there nothing to denounce, to criticize, to deplore, perhaps the "power structure", "the system", "globalization", "corporate culture", or some other entity? Was there no moral or educational benefit in those songs? The "unlikely event" of a song by free association of words and images, without any explicit purpose to improve human society, was probably difficult to be accepted by the mass media. Oxygen masks may then be needed to compensate for the loss of pressure: So I declared our "Dayina Lumba" to be an "ecological song" and that we were furiously fighting ecological destruction! In a sense that was even true. We *are* concerned with the destruction of the original landscape of our Michiru Mountains. Even teenage boys in the family, such as Romeo, deplore the fact that they can no longer spot any trees in the mountains to be tapped for rubber glue *(kugoma ulimbo)* to be used for bird trapping. But the song text is merely a game with names, rhymes, and the surprise effect of unusual images. It was not composed to express any social outrage. The same applies to another song with a text in English, in AABA form, composed July 27, 2000. It starts with this chord sequence: $C - E_{bm}^6 - D_m - G^7$, etc., on the five-string guitar, all in a fast *sinjonjo* rhythm, i.e. triplets, with chord changes one pulse-unit before beat 1 of each measure. The words are: "I love you, I love you until tomorrow only!" (Musical Example 4). There are allusions, but no commitments. In spite of the apparent logic, it is a form of textual surrealism marked by an absence of the usual emotional engagement with topics human beings are slavishly attached to: love, social concerns, etc. So when a text appears in our music that seems to be concerned with any of these, it does not mean that it is our concern. For us it is important how the syllables of those words and their tonality conform to the melodic-rhythmic phrases of the musical theme.

By mid-August Sinosi Mlendo's repertoire of jazz-like pieces and *lumba* had increased to a dozen. It included "Break the Blues" (Aug. 1), in which Donald still played lead guitar with us, "Simanje-manje minor" played instrumentally (it would receive a Chinyanja text two years later), "Soul Blues" (Aug. 2), and even the chord basis (Aug. 6) of what in Fall 2006 would crystallize into Theme 2 of "A Walk with John Coltrane". On Friday, August 18, the chord sequence of a new blues, "I walk up the mountain" (Musical Example 5) would be set, a day later the instrumental part of "Chérie m'a refusé", and on August 22, two days before our first public concert, there came "Sunshine walk", instrumentally, with no words yet. We also added an old East African rumba to our repertoire, in an arrangement for clarinet, guitar, rattle, and one-string bass. We called it "Rhino Boys' Lumba". This piece is based on one of the first rumba records appearing in Kenya after World War II, when soldiers had returned from Burma: "Rumba zetu" by The Rhino Boys (His Master's Voice, Rumba N. 17102, OMC. 20227). However, we only adapted theme A of the original piece, not theme B in a minor key. We have no aversion to minor keys, but in this case theme A turned out to be central to us, with a new chord basis, that we did not want to depart from it. There were also some other songs in the making, on the "waiting list" we would say, using airport language. For example, it will interest researchers of the history of this music that the chord sequence of what would be "Ngola e" in the Luchazi language (see our 2004 CD) occurred to us on July 24, 2000, four years before Sinosi would take it up again for the words to be composed.

Donald Kachamba was hospitalized on August 9. In his absence we would have regular rehearsals with Sinosi on guitar, Stuwadi Mpotalinga on bass, Khilizibe on rattle, and myself on E-flat clarinet. There was no flute player. We were waiting for Donald's return, and for this reason no *kwela* flute pieces were played. Dayina would sometimes join us singing.

### Musical Example 4

Text:
I love you, I love you, until tomorrow, only!
I love you, I love you, until tomorrow oh!
Bye, good bye, don't ask me why!
If you need me, don't be so shy!
I love you, I love you, until tomorrow, only!
Bye, good bye, don't ask me why!
Because I think I'll never see you again!
I love you, I love you, bye bye!

## Musical Example 5

Text:
I walk up the mountain and I'm walking all night.
I walk up the mountain and I'm walking all night.
'Cause I'm a stranger-walker, and I'm walking all night.

Moonshine is my pillow and the stones are my bed.
Moonshine is my pillow and the stones are my bed.
'Cause I'm a stranger-walker, and the stones are my bed.

Blues! Don't let me down! Blues! Don't let me down!
'Cause I'm a stranger-walker, Blues don't let me down!

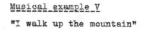

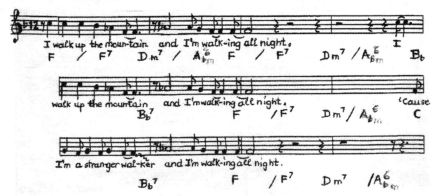

"I walk up the mountain" was Sinosi's most audacious venture into blues composition so far. Like Blind Lemon Jefferson (Evans 2000: 94-95) he would experiment with unusual chords, without, however, abandoning progressions to the subdominant in the second line and to the dominant chord in the third, within the 12-bar blues form. The novelty in Sinosi's song is the riff-like harmonic pattern over the tonic mode, two measures long and functioning like a responsorial phrase to the singer's statements. Its structure $F - F^7 - D_m{}^7 - A_b{}^6$ incorporating blue notes is based on the second *kwela* harmonic cycle obscured by two substitute chords. The effect is startling and gives Sinosi's blues rendering and the backing of his voice line with the guitar riff a strange originality. Incidentally, the text motif of the "stranger-walker" is in a sense symbolic of the singer's identity. Mlendo was his father's name and means "stranger". So this song has indeed some meaning.

On Saturday, August 19, Moya video-taped one of our sessions (Kubik/Malamusi, Video Nr. 36), first on the veranda of my house, where we played "Make me a pallet", then in an opposite line-up of the band within the compound. We played "I love you until tomorrow", "Rhino Boys' Lumba", and "Dayina ku China". Preparations were now starting for our appearance at the launching ceremony of Moya's CD *From Lake Malawi to the Zambezi*, scheduled for August 24.

During the long period of Donald's hospitalization we had more visitors. Dr. Mitchell Strumpf arrived just for a day on Sunday, August 27. At that time he was based at Africa University, Mutare, in Zimbabwe. He is an old friend who has lived through much of the history of the Kachamba Brothers and our family in Chileka. For many years he was teaching at the University of Malawi, Zomba, and at present he is professor at the University of Dar Es Salaam, Department of Fine and Performing Arts. He is also the editor of a book I wrote jointly with Moya A. Malamusi, my wife Lidiya Malamusi and Donald Kachamba: *Malawian Music. A Framework for Analysis*, published in 1987. During the 1980s he made a representative video documentation of lecture performances we gave with Donald in his department. He was sad to hear about Donald's hospitalization, but delighted to listen to some of the new compositions with our band, which we played for him, especially the "bridge" in "Sena Twist".

The last time I saw Donald Kachamba was on Tuesday, August 29. I was already in "packing fever", because my departure to Europe for various urgent assignments was scheduled for the next day. I went on foot from Singano Village, Chileka, all the way to Lunzu, where Donald was staying in Mlambe Hospital. There is no diary note about this last encounter, except that I was tired after the very long walk. But I remember that Donald gave us the impression that he would recover. He was walking, reading and spending most of his time in the hospital garden, not in the ward. When he escorted us to the gate and we shook hands, I did not think that it would be for the last time.

Through September I was on an assignment in Portugal at the *Museu Nacional de Etnologia* in Lisbon to work on a book about their collections of lamellophones from Angola and Mozambique. In the evenings I used to sit in the magnificent park opposite the monastery in Belém, whistling endless variations to "Soul Blues", "I walk up the mountain", "Sena Twist", and other pieces we had composed that year. There was telephone contact, right from the street in Lisbon to Malawi, something unthinkable only a decade earlier. I was surprised to learn, by October, that Donald had still not been discharged from hospital. From a distance, with soothing reports from the village, I concluded that he had "overstayed" only because he was now being subjected to some radical, break-through treatment of the antibiotics-resistant TB. Information was not very detailed, however, and it sounded palliating, as if nobody wanted to be accused later of having been the first to divulge some unpleasant truth.

But it is so sweet to deny reality. After a few weeks I eventually heard that he had been sent home to the village. Again, I did not want to understand the symbolism. Donald's condition seemed to deteriorate increasingly. I had several telephone conversations with him from Vienna, but at the beginning of December we realized, also from his letters, how serious the situation was. Eventually, Moya and I made a rescue attempt with the help of friends in Europe and in America. Domingos Morais in Lisbon, one of Donald's close friends, had an idea. He would arrange for him to be flown on a TAP flight to Lisbon by mid-January 2001, even if he had to be put in a wheel chair. In Lisbon, the world famous hospital of tropical medicine would have a look at this case. In Malawi, his principal student and relative, Sinosi, was taking care of Donald. Sinosi was a witness to the last few days of Donald's life. Apparently, Donald felt such despair that he also stopped injecting himself insulin, and he began to drink sugar-containing "Fanta"! It looks as if he was giving himself up. On January 9, 2001, he fell unconscious; that was just a week before the planned departure to Lisbon. Sinosi drove him immediately to Queen Elizabeth Hospital in Blantyre. There, Donald J. Kachamba, my oldest friend in Malawi and the leader of our musical group for 27 years died on January 12, 2001, without regaining consciousness.

## II.

By mid-July 2002, after an awful year of indecision – with many different professional obligations – I eventually decided to go back to Malawi to have a look at the wreckage of our jazz band. I was surprised when I arrived in Chileka from Johannesburg on Saturday, July 27, to find that Sinosi, Stuwadi, and Khilizibe had been waiting for me all the time. Moya had given Sinosi a somewhat better guitar than the one he used to play in the year 2000. The miracle occurred. From the minute I was back in Malawi, we played again almost immediately. I have diary notes that testify to the miracle. In addition, some reinforcement had arrived from Zambia: Mose Yotamu, a guitarist (see the DVD *African Guitar*, Kubik 1995) who had been on tour with us to Germany and to Finland in 1988 in "Donald Kachamba's Kwela Band", was here to work on our research project *East African Traditions of Chiefdom, Kinship, and Ritual*, financed by the Scientific Foundation, Vienna (Project Nr. P 15007; 2002-2004). At the moment he was working in Makanjila on initiation, but it was good to know that he was around.

What at first looked like a psychological landscape bombed flat, turned out to be sounds waiting for reconstruction; Sinosi's little book contained all the chords for our songs composed in the year 2000 and Khilizibe started a thick book of his own with song texts waiting to be set in music. We then made an inventory of the titles and the dance movements:

| | |
|---|---|
| "Sinjonjo Blues" | Sinjonjo |
| "Dayina tidzipita ku Chaina" | Lumba |
| "Sena Twist" | Twist |
| "I love you until tomorrow only" | Sinjonjo (fast) |
| "Simanje-manje minor" | Simanje-manje |

| | |
|---|---|
| "Chérie m'a refuse" | Lumba |
| "Soul Blues" | (a) Sinjonjo and (b) Simanje-manje |
| "Sunshine Walk" | Sinjonjo |
| "Break the Blues" | Sinjonjo (fast) |
| "I walk up the mountain" | Sinjonjo |
| "Rhino Boys' Lumba" | Lumba |

In addition there was Donald Kachamba's legacy, a hundred-some-thing musical pieces. So we started to work, first on improving the lyrics of some of our own songs, in Chinyanja or English, one even in French. Some other pieces had no song texts, such as "Sunshine Walk", "Rhino Boys' Lumba" and "Soul Blues".

It is perhaps characteristic of the way we compose in our band that it is a group process. We inherited this from the experiences in "Donald Kachamba's Kwela Band" and ultimately the "Kachamba Brothers". In Donald's Band the leader, Donald, would often come up with a melodic idea, suggesting that I play that on the clarinet, developing my own variations. Then he would discuss with Moya the vocal part, how their voices should go together, backing it up with guitar chords, and so on. In our band it is similar. One of us gets an idea, perhaps a melodic phrase for flute or clarinet, then a suitable guitar backing is found. The rattle beat is easily identified. Then we work together on the combination and on variations. It can be that a vocal part with a suitable text is composed years after an instrumental version of the piece has been developed. Vocal lines are sometimes sung solo, in other pieces there is a call-and-response form. When we shape up a chorus phrase, we usually sing in parallel, following African harmonic ideas, in some songs blues tonality. In a few songs the combination of vocal lines can be polyphonic, in which case two people sing, each a different text-line, as in some Sena music of the Lower Shire Valley. It is like a motet.

One can also start with a text-line and then set it out melodically. That was Khilizibe's original approach. But nowadays we follow much more Donald's compositional techniques. Donald normally had a guitar part and a basic voice-line together. But what has come up with Khilizibe recently is most interesting. From about 2005 it has often happened that one of us starts developing a guitar part, then calls Khilizibe who records it on his cell-phone (!) and takes it to his house. The next day he comes back with the words and melody of a perfect song! This is the history of several recent songs we have composed for two guitars and rattle: "Iwe nkazi wanga", "Timtamande" and "Ku-yimba kuposa mbalame" (in the years 2004-2005) and "Mfumu ya bwino" (in 2006), romantic stuff sung by Khilizibe with much feeling. But in 2002 Khilizibe, born 1981, was just a quiet performer on the rattle, with a stable beat and an acute ear for taking part in second- or third-voice lining.

*Diary note*, July 29, 2002:

> Sinosi has just come and we should play... Sinosi brought his guitar to my house because Donald's house is no longer available for practice. It has been rent out by self-appointed relatives to some strangers who are working at the airport. I unpack my clarinet, and we begin our session, as if the interruption of two years had only been twenty-four hours. In the next few days we will rehearse the existing repertoire and embark on some new pieces.

One of these was "Do remember" (Musical Example 6):

### Musical Example 6

"Do remember" is a song composed in little bits. While I was in Vienna, Sinosi and I used to communicate by satellite telephone. In winter 2001, I once faxed my version of a certain chord sequence to him. He then played it back to me on his guitar from Chileka through the phone (!), while I was whistling the main theme, as I would play it on the clarinet.

Thus, our Chileka number +265/1/692-357 is indeed very musical. In addition it has its own secret mathematical structure. For example, if you take one specific permutation of the country code, 256 instead of 265, then (with some luck) you might find Moya and me in Uganda! That was the case from December 31, 2001 to February 4, 2002 when we were working on the totemic clan system of the Kingdom of Buganda. And the number 1 for the area code is ubiquitous and goes with Blantyre as it goes with Vienna and other cities. The next ciphers, 6 and 9, are identical shapes, only inverted (whatever that means) and the sequence 2, 3, 5, 7 is the start of the prime numbers into infinity about whose mysteries one may consult the so-called Riemann hypothesis. There is a 1 million US$ reward for whoever can solve one of these mathematical puzzles, i.e., the law of the order of prime numbers. Perhaps I have now made readers receptive to the idea that there is quite a bit of mathematics in African music and in jazz (most apparently in Thelonius Monk). An instructive example is the asymmetric time-line patterns. Sinosi uses the Angolan 16-pulse time-line in his composition "Timangoyimba kusangalala", and the common 8-pulse stick pattern is the background to "Dayina tidzipita ku Chaina", although nobody strikes it.

*Diary note* of Friday, August 2, 2002:

> This is a joyous day, as far as I can see ahead. It is as if our jazz band had returned to life. Sinosi has unearthed a few pieces by Donald and learned them on the guitar. Not bad indeed, how he plays "Talekani miseche". And when he played "Bop Blues" this morning, a piece which we hadn't managed in the old band, Moya – all of a sudden – appeared at the door during our rehearsal to play it with us on the bass. We have rehearsed three pieces together. In "Talekani miseche" Moya and Sinosi were singing in two-part harmony very nicely. Finally we played "Dayina". It was so funny; the bass-playing Moya imitated his daughter's voice-line! She wasn't around today. It was as if Donald had come to see us, happy with what's going on here. Perhaps he *was* here with us that moment! I believe he thinks positively about us that we continue his and our music.

One of the highlights of 2002 was the development of a piece we had listed in 2000 under the title "Simanje-manje minor". This piece is in a double-step or *simanje-manje* rhythm. Foreign audiences should be careful with their reactions when listening to this kind of rhythm. Almost invariably they get the beat references wrong. Disoriented by strong accentuations on the guitar, in the instrumental and voice parts, listeners tend to invert the entire structure metrically, i.e., they hear the beat on the offbeat. Besides strong offbeat accentuations, this is, of course, stimulated by the fact that invariably chord changes do not coincide with the start of a measure in this music, but are anticipated by the value of two elementary pulse-units. In other words, in a metrical sequence of 1 – 2 – 3 – 4 steps, harmonic changes already occur on 4 and not on 1. Many listeners then take beat unit 4 for beat unit 1 and invert the structure. If they try to dance, they dance on the offbeat. This looks funny to us. *Simanje-manje* pieces in "Donald Kachamba's Band", and indeed in our successor band, require a distinctive bass pattern to be added. Within a simple cyclic chord sequence the base pattern is as shown in Figure 3.

**Fig. 3: Basic pattern of the one-string bass in *simanje-manje***

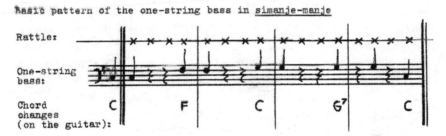

"Simanje-manje minor" – when Sinosi first played it on the guitar in 2000 – was different from all the standard *simanje-manje* items we had played in Donald's band, not in rhythm, but in form because of its AABB arrangement, and in the chords. Once, on July 19, 2000, when Donald was still with us in the village, Sinosi was playing the guitar part casually. Donald heard it and seemed to be somewhat bewildered. He asked Sinosi: "Is that supposed to be *simanje-manje*?" It was as if he wanted to say that Sinosi had not understood the basics of this music.

We have both given thoughts to Donald's comment. But it is obvious what Donald had found unusual: it was the chords. In rhythm it is pure *simanje-manje* or "double step" (as Daniel Kachamba used to call it), but the chord sequence is nowhere to be found in South African popular music, where *simanje-manje* originated. We are sure, however, that after some time, Donald would have come round and accepted this probe into new territory.

Long after we had played it instrumentally, the text in Chinyanja to our "Simanje-manje minor" occurred to me on a long walk to a far crossing of the Likhubula River on August 15 with Ananjeza, Moya's wife, and Nansi, Sinosi's mother. I was unusually quiet on the way, while Ananjeza and Nansi were talking. It is a two hours' walk from our village. My mind was somehow focused on rivers and people searching a ford. In addition, all along our way, the instrumental version of this piece did not get out of my mind; it seemed to repeat itself continuously, as if I had a CD-player somewhere in my head, playing just this one item. Some people need a "Walkman" or some other cassette device (nowadays the iPod) for listening to music while walking. With me it is easier and cheaper. The songs are sounding from inside my brain without any electronic pacemaker.

When we were walking over a bridge, it suddenly "clicked" and I had the first line of the song on my lips! Ananjeza, I suppose, did not notice anything; we had some conversations about different matters – but there was this parallel strand of musical thought. In Malawi, when you approach a watercourse you shout from afar to the people who might be bathing there: "Ku madzi! Ku madzi!" (To the water! To the water!). Then the people reply: "Aime!" (You should stop) if they are undressed. But if they are dressed, they reply: "Apite!" (You may pass!).

This is exactly how our song starts, with words spoken.

Leader (shouting):       Ku madzi! Ku madzi!
Chorus (answering):    Apite!

Song in Chinyanja with English translation:

L. Ku mulatho!                         There at the bridge!
Ch. Musasochere!                    Don't get lost!
L. Tidzipita propanda mavuto!   Let us pass without any problems!
Ch. Inu atsikana mudzatigulire    You girls, you should buy for us
dzikondamoyo!                          *dzikondamoyo* cakes!


Leader (shouting):       Ku madzi! Ku madzi!
Chorus (answering):    Aime!

When I told Sinosi the words, coming home, he burst out in laughter, especially after hearing the last line. He found the text most amusing, and so do many youngsters in our village to this day. But as so often, the words had merely "happened".

Sinosi found the second, upper voice for the vocal part almost immediately.

**Musical Example 7**

I cannot suggest how to interpret the text, except as a sequence of dreamlike images. Some might think it is symbolic. It may be, but it all depends on what one projects into it. A group of boys goes to the river. They want to cross. Yes, they can, but there is a warning: "Don't get lost!" Now, those boys don't want any problems ... On the other side, then, they meet a group of girls, and they demand that those girls buy them some cakes known as *dzikondamoyo* (= those things that love life). Perhaps it is symbolic, but anyone can give our song the meaning they like, and it is always true.

A few months later, Moya would hand over to Sinosi Donald's last flute for practice; so in 2003 we would all be surprised to find Sinosi playing flute. But for now we were determined to arrange one of Donald's last compositions "Chemwali muli kuti?" (Sister, where are you?) for flute, rattle, guitar, and voices. He had composed this piece shortly before 1995. It is a mourning song, but not in relation to his own sister who died much later. Donald recorded a solo version for guitar, rattle and voices in Ghent, Belgium, in 1995, for Herman C. Vuylsteke of the Belgium Radio en Television, Brussel. Vuylsteke had also recorded our band the year before in a bar in Belgium and published the recordings on a CD in the series *La Chant du Monde* (see reference). With Sinosi we were now practicing Donald's "Chemwali", setting the voice lines to the traditional "Lake Malawi" harmony (see also Kubik et al. 1987 for comments on the "skipping process").

**Musical Example 8**

Text in Chinyanja:                    Translation:
Chemwali muli kuti?                   Sister, where are you?
Mwasiya mavuto.                       You have only left misery.
Tichite bwanji?                       What should we do?
Mwasiya mavuto.                       You have only left misery.

Che-mwa-li mu-li ku-ti? Mwa-si-ya ma-vu-to.

Ti-chi-te bwa- nji? Mwa-si-ya ma-vu-to.

Returning from Makanjila, Mose Yotamu would join us on the bass. For Moya's Museum of Ethnographic Objects in Jacaranda House, Chileka, he would also construct a friction drum of the type found in northwestern Zambia and Angola. He even joined us with the friction drum in some items that had a *kachecha* time-line, such as the second part of our song "Ndumba Mangwangwa".

Many new pieces, which would be published two years later on a CD featuring our concert on December 10, 2004 in Vienna's *Sargfabrik* (Coffin Factory), were already with us in 2002, sometimes without words, sometimes in an embryonic state. In a diary note of August 20, 2002, there is a first mention of our composition "New York 9/11" and that it is based on a descending chromatic sequence through major seventh and diminished chords (Musical Example 9). This was the instrumental version. The song text and vocal line on top of the chords was not yet found. We would find it while staying in the Highlands of Upangwa, southwestern Tanzania in 2004!

On Wednesday, 28 August 2002, I wrote into my diary:

> It is unbelievable, but new compositions are somehow dropping into our lap. Right now, this evening, I have been sitting down with the guitar, and as I was somewhat casually changing fingers from a $C^{maj7}$ to a $C^6$ chord, the song outlined above emerged like a mathematical equation!

I was referring to an outline of our "Marabenta Lumba". *Marabenta* today is something like the national popular music in Mozambique. What present-day groups are playing with electrically amplified guitars, however, is only a shadow of original *marrabenta* played with acoustic guitars and other instruments in the townships of Maputo during the 1950s. Apparently, the music was inspired by Brazilian records on 78 rpm. shellac discs. In our conversation in November 2006, Tiago de Oliveira Pinto observed that the term *marrabenta* might be a corruption of *barravento* as one of the three basic *toques* in the Candomblé de Angola, or as a particular type of *samba-de-roda* in the Recôncavo de Bahia called *samba-de-barravento*. The term then appeared on popular records by Custódio Mesquita and Evaldo Rui in 1944, and another popular song was performed by Nassara Frazão in 1940. This roughly conforms to the period in which *marrabenta* began to develop in Lourenço Marques, now known as Maputo.

I remember that I called Sinosi immediately, so that we would work on it and on Friday, August 30, 2002, Mike Kamwendo of *Quest Magazine*, Blantyre, came to see us; he made an interview, photographed the band in action and wrote an assessment of our work. It was obvious that we would soon go on tour overseas with this band and we were beginning to think about a name. Eventually we agreed upon "Donald Kachamba's Kwela Heritage Jazzband". It is a bit long for a band name, but necessarily descriptive (see Musical Example 9).

Mike Kamwendo was the first person outside Singano village to whom we played "New York 9/11". He liked it very much and said that there was no other place in Malawi where one could hear such music. Then he asked Sinosi to tell him where he had learned to play guitar. Kamwendo noted that even the sound of his guitar with the five-string tuning was unusual. It was neither banjo nor guitar, but something else. Sinosi explained that the idea of the five strings and their tuning came from the late Daniel Kachamba. Mike Kamwendo commented that apparently Sinosi had internalized Donald's music from birth (Sinosi was born in 1980). He added, however, that what we were playing had changed since the days of Donald, because we were using other chords. Mike Kamwendo, himself a musician, later wrote a lucid article about us (Kamwendo 2002). It even attracted the attention of American colleagues.

It seems that "Kumalatho" which came out of "Simanje-manje mirror", was becoming a local hit in Singano village, along with "Dayina". People liked it, most certainly because of the words. Musical appreciation in Malawi is text-focused. A song is considered to be a failure if the words do not impress people's imagination. But seeing that we were successful with this song, I began to cogitate about those

## Musical Example 9

Note: Chord changes throughout this piece occur on the last quaver before each measure, i.e. before the bar-line.

words, trying to reconstruct how they had come to my mind in the first place, on that long walk with Nansi and Ananjeza to the river crossing. And why did those keywords "kumulatho" (at the bridge) occur to me at all? Suddenly I remembered that the same day in the morning we had been playing a theme by George Shearing. And Sinosi had made a mistake on the guitar at the "bridge" of this piece!

Time was running out, because I would have to leave for Europe in early September, and even if there was no international tour right away, we would continue with our music in Chileka next year. These were the hassles, I said, of having a band whose members have different passports!

With Donald Kachamba, we had toured on combined lecture and concert trips no fewer than thirty-three countries of the world between 1972 and 1997. His last visit to Europe brought us concerts at the German Film Museum in Frankfurt and in the *Gewandhaus*, Leipzig, Germany. 1999 he was granted a five-year J-1 visa for the United States, on invitation by the University of California, Los Angeles, where he spent a marvelous teaching period. Sadly he was only able to use it for a single entry. Had he lived he would perhaps have built a brilliant future on the U.S. circuit as a musician and composer.

That was the world before September 11, 2001. With visa restrictions everywhere now due to fear of terrorism, combined with reasonable fears of international criminal organizations, Donald would have to operate in a very different world. When we were traveling with him, a Malawi citizen and Mose Yotamu, a Zambian citizen, to Finland and to East Berlin in 1988, complications were negligible: Mose did require a visa for Germany, but could cross over into East Berlin on a day's pass. Donald and Moya had been walking in and out of Germany since the 1970s on their Malawi passports without any requirements for a visa. Now, arranging a visit to Europe for Malawi musician friends could entail the walk to a lawyer signing a guarantee of support. On the other hand, on an EU passport, even after paying 130.00 Euro for a multiple entry visa to Malawi, I myself would regularly get a stamp for a visitor's pass of just 30 days upon arrival. Luckily, it is possible to line up later in Blantyre and get a prolongation, while such facilities do not exist for the Malawian members of our jazz band traveling to Europe on a so-called Schengen visa.

It makes things complicated. We in science and art do not feel many positive aspects of the so-called globalization that in theory should benefit our musical group. On the contrary, boundaries are going up everywhere. Literally, whenever we want to do rehearsals with our musical group, we first have to ask permission from various nation states to do so! For us, this confirms that in our world of the early twenty-first century, artificially imposed "cultural identities" only promote segregation, if not outright racism. There is little space for an unusual artistic group like ours.

Donald did not live to see September 11, 2001, and the sort of psychological trauma left behind. Terror – once state-sponsored with the annihilation of millions of Jews in Central Europe, the wanton destruction of towns and cities like Coventry, Hamburg, Dresden, Hiroshima, and Nagasaki in World War II, but now privatized and within reach of every individual feeling a "mission" – has become a permanent institution. Satellite TV ("Independence Day"), Internet and video games provide models and advice; cell phones have become strategically important tools.

The last song we composed in 2002 was perhaps one of our most unusual: "I feel so lonely". This one *has* a message. Sinosi sings it in English to the accompaniment of guitar clarinet, bass, and rattle. It is plain blues, but not in a 12-bar blues form. The form is AAB, adding up to something like a 24-bar blues. I do not know whether something comparable to our song exists anywhere in jazz. In our remote world at Singano village, Malawi, we would not think of searching in libraries for parallels, let alone the Internet. It would be an undertaking with little benefit.

A first note on "I feel so lonely" is found in my diary on September 5, 2002. This was two days before my departure. The next day we were still practicing the new song. "Shining path" is a hidden reference to the Maoist guerrilla movement *Sendero Luminoso* in Peru. No other comments can be found, except the complete text, which Sinosi Mlendo would sing. Years later we would create a second, interlocking text-line and make it our jazz motet:

### Musical Example 10

"I feel so lonely! (text in English sung by Sinosi Mlendo)
(sung twice)
I feel so lonely,
I feel so lonely,

Without a shining path,[1]
Because you never know,
And you will never know
What I can see!

Oh, my sorrow
Won't go away,
Because you never know
And you will never know
What I can see!

Musical Example XI
"I feel so lonely"

Copyright:
Donald Kachamba's
Kwela Heritage Jazzband

Instrumental theme and
Guitar chords

Sinjonjo (slow)

Vocal part

I feel so lone-ly, I feel so lone-ly, with-out a shi-ning path.

be-cause you ne-ver know, and you will ne-ver know what I   can see ...   Etc.

---

1    "Shining Path" *(Sendero Luminoso)* is a hidden reference to a Maoist guerrilla
     movement in Peru.

# Bibliography

Berliner, Paul (1993): *Thinking in Jazz. The Infinite Art of Improvisation*. Chicago Studies in Ethnomusicology. Chicago: University of Chicago Press.

Coplan, David B. (1985): *In Township Tonight! South Africa's Black City Music and Theatre*. Johannesburg: Ravan Press.

Evans, David (2000): "Musical Innovation in the Blues of Blind Lemon Jefferson". In: *Black Music Research Journal*, 20, 1. Evans, David (guest ed.), pp. 83-116.

Evans, David/Monge, Luigi (2000): *Blind Lemon Jefferson. The Golden Age of Gospel*. Urbana: University of Illinois Press.

Floyd, Samuel A. (ed.) (1999): *International Dictionary of Black Composers*, 2 vols. (see under "Daniel Kachamba" and "Donald Kachamba"). Chicago: Fitzroy Dearborn Publ., pp. 678-683; 684-688.

Herskovits, Melville J. (1941): *The Myth of the Negro Past*. Boston: Harper and Brothers.

Kamwendo, Mike (2002): "Citizens of the World". In: *Quest Magazine*, Second Quarter, pp. 8-9.

Kubik, Gerhard (1974): *The Kachamba Brothers' Band. A Study of Neo-Traditional Music in Malawi*. Lusaka: University of Zambia, Institut for African Studies (Zambia papers Nr. 9).

— (1995): *African Guitar*. Video/DVD. Audio-Visual Field Recordings 1966-1993. Sparta (N.J.): Stefan Grossman.

— (1999): *Africa and the Blues*. Jackson: Mississippi University Press. Accompanying CD separately published by Network Records (Riki Parth), Wien.

Kubik, Gerhard /Malamusi, Moya Aliya (private archive) (1994): Video Nr. 31, *Donald Acting* at Singano village, Chileka, in December.

— (1995): Video Nr. 32, *Tingoyesa Band*, February 7.

— (1999): Video Nr. 54, *Donald Session*, August 8.

— (2000): Video Nr. 66, *Band Session*, August 19.

Kubik, Gerhard/Malamusi, Moya Aliya/Malamusi, Lidiya/Kachamba, Donald (1987): *Malawian Music. A Framework for Analysis*. Zomba: University of Malawi Center for Research.

Low, John (1982): *Shaba Diary: A Trip to Rediscover the "Katanga" Guitar Styles and Songs of the 1950s and 1960s*. Wien: Stiglmayr.

Malamusi, Moya Aliya (1994): "Rise and Development of a Chileka Guitar Style in the 1950s". In: Schmidhofer, August/Schüller, Dietrich (eds.): *For Gerhard Kubik. Festschrift*. Preface: Rycroft, David. Frankfurt am Main: Peter Lang, pp. 7-72.

Tracey, Andrew (1991): "Kambazithe Makolekole and his *valimba* Group. A Glimpse of the Technique of the Sena Xylophone". In: *African Music*, 7, 1, pp. 82-104.

## Discographic and Cinematographic References

Djenda/Kubik Collection: Recordings "Dayina Lumba" by Piasoni and Chinyama in Malawi. Archived in Berlin: Ethnologisches Museum, Musikethnologische Abteilung, 1967.

*The Kachamba Brothers' Band.* DVD. Wien: Wolfgang Bachschwell, Film and Video-Production, 1967.

*The Kachamba Brothers' Band.* AEL Series Phonographica. LP record. Föhrenau/ Wien: Verlag E. Stiglmayr, 1972.

*Daniel Kachamba's solo guitar songs.* 16-mm films E2136 and E 2137. Encyclopaedia Cinematographica. Göttingen: Institut für den Wissenschaftlichen Film, 1977.

*Donald Kachamba's Kwela Band 1978.* Stereo LP record, published by Jazz Club Wiesen. Sauerbrunn (Austria), 1978.

*Donald Kachamba's Band. Simanje-manje and Kwela from Malawi.* GKA Nr. 1, A.I.T. Records, Nairobi 1979.

*Opeka Nyimbo – Musican-composers from Southern Malawi.* 2 LP stereo records with pamphlet English and German. MC 15, Museum Collection Berlin, Artur Simon (ed.). Berlin: Musikethnologische Abteilung, Museum für Völkerkunde, 1989.

*Daniel Kachamba Memorial Cassette – Kaseti ya Nyimbo za Chikumbutso cha Malemu Daniel Kachamba.* Audio cassette and booklet. Strumpf, Mitchel (ed.). Zomba: Department of Fine and Performing Arts, University of Malawi, 1992.

*Donald Kachamba et son ensemble. Concert Kwela.* Le Chant du Monde, LDX 274972 CD, 1994.

"Sadya mbewa" ("They don't eat rats"). Playback composition by Donald Kachamba. *Os Herdeiros da Noite. Fragmentos do Imaginário Negro.* Documentos Sonoros. Pinto, Tiago de Oliveira (ed.). São Paulo: Pinacoteca do Estado, 1994.

*Donald Kachamba's Kwela Band Live and in Donald Kachamba's Studio.* CD Parnap 103, LC 07203, Gema. Frankfurt am Main: Popular African Music, 1999.

*Music! 100 Recordings 100 Years of the Berlin Phonogramm-Archiv 1900-2000.* Simon, Artur/Wegner, Ulrich (eds.). 4 CDs, Museum Collection Berlin, SM 17012. Mainz: Wergo, 2000.

*Donald Kachamba's Kwela Heritage Jazzband. The Sargfabrik Concert, Vienna December 10, 2004.* With Sinosi Mlendo, Moya A. Malamusi, Gerhard Kubik and Christopher Gerald. Vienna Series in Ethnomusicology, Department of Musicology at the University of Vienna. TOL 60011, Tolima, 2005.

*The Kachamba Brothers 1967.* DVD edition of an original 16-mm film, color, shot by Gerhard Kubik in Singano Village, Chileka in 1967. Bachschwell, Wolfgang/Kubik, Gerhard (eds.). Copy in the UCLA Ethnomusicology Archive, Los Angeles.

*Video Documentation of Donald Kachamba's Last Concert*, with UCLA students, on 4 December, 1999. Department of Ethnomusicology, UCLA, Los Angeles. Intr. Jacqueline DjeDje. Los Angeles: UCLA.

*Donald Kachamba teaching his students Sinosi Mlendo, Aliki Mlendo, Stuwadi Mpotalinga and others.* Sunday, August 8, 1999, at Singabo Villega, Chileka. – Video Nr. 54, in Private Archive Kubik/Malamusi, Wien.

*Dayina Swing Jazzband*, with Sinosi Mlendo, guitar; Gerhard Kubik, clarinet; Stuwadi Mpotalinga, one-stringed bass; and Kilizibe, rattle. August 2000, at Singano Village, Chileka, Malawi. – Video Nrs. 66 and 67, in Private Archive Kubik/Malamusi, Wien.

*Rehearsals of Donald Kachamba's Kwela Heritage Jazzband*, with Sinosi Mlendo (guitar), Moses Yotamu (friction drum, string bass, etc.), Stuwadi Mpotalinga, Kilizibe etc., in various combinations. Videotaped August-September 2002. – Video nos. 74-75, and 79, in Private Archive Kubik/Malamusi, Wien.

Other recordings, cinematographic shots and video recordings of Donald Kachamba, his band members and trainees, are scattered in various parts of the world, at radio stations, cultural institutions (e.g. Goethe Institutes), universities and in private possession. – Larger documentations are found, for examples, in the Ethnographic Museum, Berlin (Abteilung Musikethnologie), in Arthur Benseler's Afrika-Archiv, Freiberg am Neckar, in the Phonogram archive Vienna, including the recording of a complete concert at Jazzland, Vienna, given by "Donald Kachamba's Kwela Band" in 1985, and in the African Music Archive, Institute for Ethnology and African Studies, University of Mainz. – In the United States materials can be found at the UCLA Ethnomusicology Archive and at the Center for Black Music Research (Library), Chicago.

# Authors

**Paul Bräuer** received his Master's degree in Musicology, Sinology, and Periodism at the Humboldt University and the Free University in Berlin in 2007. He has traveled to China, and elsewhere in Asia, and South America. Contributions to *Der Tagesspiegel*, the *neue musik zeitung* and *klassik.com*.

**Gerhard Kubik** is a musician and professor of ethnomusicology at the University of Vienna, Austria. He compiled a collection of more than 25,000 recordings of traditional African music and has traveled throughout Africa and Latin America playing music, teaching, and collecting his recordings. Among his numerous publications are: *The Kachamba Brothers' Band. A Study of Neo-Traditional Music in Malawi* (1974); *Angolan Traits in Black Music. Games and Dances of Brazil A Study of African Cultural Extensions Overseas* (1979); *Theory of African Music* (1994); *Zum Verstehen Afrikanischer Musik* (2004).

**Philip Küppers** studies music and media at the Humboldt University in Berlin. He has his own sound studio and conducts research in North and South America. He contributes regularly to Radio Berlin Brandenburg (rbb) and *Der Tagesspiegel* and is preparing two documentaries on the contemporary elaboration of traditional musical heritage in Brazil as well as on the Casa do Samba in Santo Amaro, Brazil.

**Martin Lienhard** is a professor of Spanish and Portuguese literature at the Institute for Romance Languages at the University of Zürich, Switzerland with special emphasis on Latin America and lusophone Africa. He studied in Bazel, Geneva, Coimbra, and Salamanca and has published widely. His books include *Cultura popular andina y forma novelesca. Zorros y danzantes en la última novela de Arguedas* (1998, 3a. edición); *La voz y su huella. Escritura y conflicto étnico-social en América Latina 1492-1988*. Premio Casa de las Américas 1989 (2003, 4th edición); *Testimonios, cartas y manifiestos indígenas (desde la* *conquista hasta comienzosdel siglo XX)* (1992); *O mar e o mato. Histórias da escravidão* (Congo-Angola, Brasil, Caribe) (1998); *Ritualidades latinoamericanas: un acercamiento interdisciplinario – Ritualidades latinoamericanas: uma aproximação interdisciplinaria*, ed. M. Lienhard, colaboración de Gabriela Stöckli, Maria Conti, Annina Clerici y Marília Mendes (2003).

**Christine Meisner** is a German visual artist residing in Berlin. She focuses on drawings, video, and texts covering colonial and post-colonial problems in African countries. Meisner is interested in the on-going impact of cultural processes released by occupation, appropriation, incorporation, or destruction. Her projects are the result of long-term research and traveling (Lagos, Côte d'Ivoire, Brazil, Poland, Belgium, Congo), in cooperation with the Goethe Institutes, the embassies of the countries mentioned above, and international museums. *Recovery of an Image* (a video tale) and *what became* (drawings and texts) were presented in the Musée des Beaux Arts in Nantes, France, the Pinacoteca in São Paulo, the Museum of Modern Art in Recife, and the Victoria and Albert Museum in London.

**Yeda Pessoa de Castro**, born in Salvador da Bahia, is an ethnolinguist. She earned her PhD in African Languages at the National University of Zaire, and was the African Language technical consultant for the Museu da Língua Portuguesa in São Paulo. Professor Pessoa de Castro is a member of the Academia de Letras of Bahia, was director of the Center for Afro-Eastern Studies, founded the Museu Afro-Brasileiro, and is visiting professor of post-graduate studies at the State University of Bahia State, where she teaches languages and cultures of Africa in Brazil. Among her publications are *Falares africanos na Bahia: um vocabulário afro-brasileiro* (2th edition 2005) and *A língua mina-jeje no Brasil: um falar africano em Ouro Preto do séc. XVIII* (2002).

**Ineke Phaf-Rheinberger** is a Dutch independent scholar, based in Berlin. She teaches courses at the Humboldt University and is a research affiliate of the Latin America Studies Center (LASC) at the University of Maryland, College Park. Among her books: *Novelando La Habana* (1990); subeditor of the Dutch-speaking section of *A His-*

*tory of Caribbean Literature*, volume 2 (editor in chief: A. James Arnold, 2001); *Memorias de la fragmentación: Tierra de libertad y fragmentos del Caribe*, ed. (2005); and the forthcoming book, *The 'Air of Liberty'. Narratives of the South Atlantic Past* (2008).

**Tiago de Oliveira Pinto** received his Ph D in ethnomusicology from the Free University of Berlin (1989) and is professor at the Post-Graduate Program of the department of Anthropology at the University of São Paulo, Brazil. He has published widely on Brazilian music and has conducted fieldwork throughout his country as well as in eastern Africa and Europe. From 2004 to 2006 he was president of the Brazilian Society for Ethnomusicology (ABET). He is currently guest-professor at the Institute for Musicology/University of Hamburg. Among his book publications are *Samba, Capoeira, Candomblé. Afro Brasilianische Musik im Recôncavo, Bahia* (Berlin 1990), *Samba und Sambistas in Brasilien* (Wilhelmshaven 1992, together with Dudu Tucci), *The Idea of Brazilian Modernismo* (New York/London 2006, together with Maria Izabel Ribeiro). In preparation: *Natureza da Música. Samba de Roda, Capoeira e outros sons do Brasil* (São Paulo 2008).

**Anja Schwarz** studied geography and African sciences at the Humboldt University Berlin and the Istituto Universitario Orientale in Napels, Italy. Her Master's thesis is about the reception of African literatures in Germany. Currently, she is funded by the Fritz Thyssen Foundation in a three-year project on the Janheinz Jahn reception in Germany in the Janheinz Jahn archive in the Library of African and Asian Studies at the Humboldt University.

**Silke Strickrodt** is assistant professor at the Chair of African History at the Institute of Asian and African Studies at the Humboldt-Universität zu Berlin. She holds a PhD from the University of Stirling (UK). Her PhD thesis deals with Afro-European trade relations on the Western Slave Coast (in present-day Togo and Benin) in the pre-colonial period. In her current research project, she examines African reactions to missionary attempts to Christianize and Europeanize African women in nineteenth-century Sierra Leone. She is author of *'Those Wild Scenes': Africa in the Travel Writing of Sarah Lee (1791-1856)*

(1998), co-editor (with Robin Law) of *Ports of the Slave Trade (Bights of Benin and Biafra)* (1999) and editor of a volume of letters from Africa in the 6-volume series *Women Writing Home, 1700-1920: Female Correspondences across the British Empire* (general editor: Klaus Stierstorfer, 2006).

**Flora Veit-Wild** is professor of African Literatures and Cultures at the Humboldt University, Berlin. Her research interests include the Anglophone writing of southern Africa, francophone writing in central Africa, surrealism, body concepts, and urban literature. A selection of her major publications include *Teacher, Preachers, Non-Believers: A Social History of Zimbabwean Literature* (1992); *Dambudzo Marechera: A Source Book on His Life and Work* (1992); *Body, Sexuality, and Gender. Versions and Subversions in African Literatures*, vol. 1, ed. with Dirk Naguschewski (2005); *Interfaces Between the Oral and the Written / Interfaces entre l'écrit et l'oral. Versions and Subversions in African Literatures*, vol. 2, ed. with Alain Ricard (2005); *Writing Madness. Borderlines of the Body in African Literature* (2006).